Overcoming
Underachieving

Overcoming Underachieving

An Action Guide to Helping Your Child Succeed in School

SAM GOLDSTEIN, PhD

NANCY MATHER, PhD

JOHN WILEY & SONS, INC.

New York • Chichester • Weinheim • Brisbane • Singapore • Toronto

Copyright © 1998 by Sam Goldstein and Nancy Mather. All rights reserved.

Published by John Wiley & Sons, Inc.

This publication is designed to provide accurate and authoritative information in regard to the subject matter covered. It is sold with the understanding that the publisher is not engaged in rendering professional services. If professional advice or other expert assistance is required, the services of a competent professional person should be sought.

Library of Congress Cataloging-in-Publication Data:

Goldstein, Sam, 1952–
    Overcoming underachieving : an action guide to helping your child
  succeed in school / Sam Goldstein and Nancy Mather.
      p.   cm.
  Includes bibliographical references (p.) and index.
  ISBN 0-471-17032-1 (pbk. : alk. paper)
    1. Underachievers—Education—United States.   2. Learning
  strategies—United States.   3. Student adjustment—United States.
  4. Academic achievement—United States.   I. Mather, Nancy.
  II. Title.
  LC4691.G65   1998
  371.92′6—dc21   97-38519

To my wife Janet for her great patience with my writing endeavors and to my wonderful children, Allyson and Ryan.

S.G.

To my parents and the memory of my dear Aunt Gene, whose love and support have helped me to achieve. To my two spirited children, Benjamin and Daniel, who continue to enrich my life as well as educate me.

N.M.

Acknowledgments

Our appreciation is expressed to our friend and colleague Dr. Robert Brooks for his contribution to the Self-Esteem chapter and to Janice Sammons and Mary Black for reading and commenting on the initial draft of this manuscript from a parent's perspective. Cindy McAndrews and Sally Richman shared descriptions of their children and their school experiences. We also wish to thank Kathy Gardner for invaluable clerical and management support and Sarah Cheminant for preparing the index. Alexia Dorszynski's editorial assistance, suggestions, clarifications, and careful reworking of this manuscript are most appreciated. Finally, we wish to acknowledge and thank the many families, teachers, and children we have had the opportunity to get to know. We have seen how effective parents can be in managing their children's social, emotional, and academic development. These rich, rewarding experiences provided the impetus for writing this book.

S.G.
N.M.

Contents

◀ PART III ▶
THE BUILDING BLOCKS OF LEARNING

Introduction

All parents have great hopes for their children—that they will enjoy learning, perform well at school, behave appropriately, and grow up feeling confident and self-assured. And most parents believe these hopes will be fulfilled if they are good parents: nurturing, available, and loving; patient, consistent, supportive, and encouraging; fair in their treatment of their children, and democratic as they discipline them. Unfortunately, the outcomes parents so earnestly desire are not always realized. Nearly 20 percent of America's children—approximately 15 million children and adolescents—struggle in school because of behavioral and/or learning difficulties.

Life experiences play a certain role in the learning problems of children, but the learning problems themselves are blind to a child's sex, ethnicity, and family financial resources. They cut across all social and cultural boundaries. At least 20 million American parents are trying hard, as you are, to do what's right for their child under difficult and often confusing circumstances.

The Puzzle of Underachievement

Good parents strive to understand and help their children, but the problems that interfere with children's being able to learn often make this effort difficult. Contradictions abound. What can be said about a child who will play quietly and contentedly in a sandbox for an hour but cannot sit still long enough to look at a book? Does it make sense that a child is able to remember the batting averages of twenty-five baseball players but not the spelling words for a weekly test; or is an excellent reader but has trouble adding and subtracting? What about the child who scores in the superior range on an intelligence test but can barely produce a simple written sentence; or the one who loves to draw but cannot remember how to form the letters of the alphabet?

When parents confront a child's puzzling school performance and try to identify the reasons for the difficulties, their thoughts typically evolve along certain lines. At first, they decide that there has been a lack of effort. Perhaps they consider the child lazy, immature, unmotivated, or just plain unwilling to learn. But children seek to please their parents and are biologically programmed to learn. Gradually, the parents come to realize the truth: the child does want to learn, and assigning blame does not solve the problem.

Next, parents doubt themselves. How have they contributed to the problem? Teachers' and counselors' pointed questions may add to their uneasiness: "Have you been helping your child study the spelling words?" "Do you go over homework with your child?" "Is something troubling going on at home?" Relatives, friends, and even total strangers may express opinions about the causes of a child's problems and then offer well-meant solutions: "Have you tried a change of diet?" "Do you allow unlimited TV?" More often than not, the advice they offer either introduces further burdens or suggests that the parents have overlooked a quick and "miraculous" solution.

In the vast majority of cases, inadequate parenting is a dead end as an explanation for children's school problems. We frequently remind parents who consult us: "It's easy to be a good parent when you have good children. It's a lot harder when you don't. But that doesn't mean that you aren't a good parent or that your child isn't a good child."

At some point, parents may set out to link the problem to the child's teachers or school. As educational and mental health consultants, we have heard true stories, from parents around the country, about bungled learning diagnoses and indifferent classroom instruction. And, despite their best efforts, many caring teachers simply do not have sufficient expertise or available time to help children who struggle. In addition, as schools cope with educational fads and endure budget cuts, the genuine needs of children may be ignored. But it's also important to realize that *any* child from *any* type of environment may have difficulty learning.

So where *does* the problem lie? The answer is that there are many possible reasons for a particular child's underachieving. Multiple factors affect academic performance. In some cases, poor performance can be attributed to a combination of heredity, temperament, learning disabilities, family stress, and a poor match of child and teacher. In other cases, the causes may be less clear. Having an array of possible causes doesn't mean, however, that there is nothing to be done.

When a child underachieves, berating the child, the teacher and school, or oneself is not the solution. Nor should a parent give in to cynicism or despair. Education should be recognized as a journey with many guides. These include a child's teachers, counselors, and doctors; mental health and educational specialists; members of the broader community; and, above all, the parent.

Your Role as a Parent

As a parent, you are in a uniquely powerful position to guide your child's educational journey. Today, more than ever before, you must assume the role of a navigator, a guide on a safe and productive educational journey. No longer can you rely solely on a teacher or a school to save your child from learning difficulties or even to serve all of his or her educational needs. Instead, your child's education must become a collaborative effort between you and the teachers. This new partnership requires that you pay close attention to your child's progress in school, and work closely and actively with teachers, principals, pediatricians, and learning specialists. Make sure that your child gets the help that is needed—even if you have to provide it yourself. If you are home schooling your child and have assumed the dual role of parent and teacher, find current information on the best ways to instruct your child, particularly if learning seems to be a struggle.

Unfortunately, even when you recognize that your child has a learning problem, you may not know how to get it resolved. It's not uncommon for parents to spend months, or even years, spinning their wheels—trying new programs, asking for special testing for their child, engaging home tutors, consulting educational or mental health specialists—while the child becomes ever more unhappy, angry, or depressed, and falls further and further behind in school.

Why We Wrote This Book

Our purpose in writing this book is to help you and your child avoid this kind of frustration. We bring to this project more than 40 years' combined professional experience with children—one of us in the area of diagnosis, evaluation, and remediation of learning disabilities, the other in the area of children's emotional, educational, and behavioral development and neuropsychology. Our research and hands-on work with thousands of children—and their families—have taught us that it's not enough to sympathize with a child's emotional difficulties, get an accurate diagnosis of any learning deficits, or provide advice on negotiating with the school system. All of these are important steps, but they will not solve the whole problem. Instead, our clinical and practical experience has shown us that the key to helping children who underachieve in school is to provide their parents (and teachers) with a logical, consistent framework that will help them understand and appreciate each child's unique abilities and learning style, and then to offer specific interventions that address individual needs.

Over many years of teaching and counseling, we have developed a framework that we call the "Building Blocks of Learning." Using our building blocks approach, you will be able to evaluate your child's pattern of learning and pinpoint strengths as well as weaknesses. When you are able to understand the ways your child succeeds and the reasons for the learning struggles—and to explain them clearly to school personnel and other educational experts—you will be more effective in getting appropriate professional evaluations and setting realistic educational goals. You will also have a better idea of the educational and behavioral interventions, whether at home or at school , that will be most helpful. And because our system is based on the principle of recognizing and using children's strengths to bolster their weaknesses, you will be safe guarding against continuing damage to your child's self-esteem, thus laying the foundation for future success.

In each chapter of *Overcoming Underachievement,* along with highlighted strategies, you will find dozens of suggestions that you can put into practice at home and share with your child's teacher. We have used all of these interventions with our students and their families, and we have consistently found that they are practical, easy to use, and effective. Although many of the strategies were designed primarily for use by parents of children who struggle to learn because of developmental, behavioral, or academic problems, anyone who works with children will find them beneficial.

We recognize that underachievement represents neither a small problem nor one faced by only a few children. However, the size of the problem is no reason for despair. We are encouraged by the growing amount of research devoted to helping children succeed and by the ways in which educators in our schools are addressing these problems. We are also well aware of the enormous responsibilities of parenting. Helping children achieve requires a great investment of time, effort, caring, and commitment. You are a parent who provides this kind of support, or you would not be reading this book. We offer this text with deep appreciation and admiration for your dedication to helping your child become the best he or she can be.

Quick Solution Finder

Problem	Solutions
Keeping track of due dates	Ch. 6, p. 133
Taking notes	Ch. 9, pp. 231–232
Planning ahead	Ch. 9, p. 223

Physical Behavior

Developing finger control to write	Ch. 7, pp. 154–155
Telling one hand from the other	Ch. 7, pp. 155–156
Reversing letters	Ch. 7, pp. 160–164
Printing legibly	Ch. 7, p. 152
Holding pencils comfortably	Ch. 7, p. 155
Writing legibly	Ch. 7, pp. 158–159
Monitoring neatness of papers	Ch. 7, p. 164

Reading and Spelling

Recognizing letters or words	Ch. 8, p. 187
Recognizing letters' sounds	Ch. 8, pp. 176–179
Remembering letters by sight	Ch. 8, pp. 189–191
Spelling words	Ch. 8, pp. 180–181, 188
Increasing reading rate	Ch. 8, pp. 193–197
Adjusting reading rate	Ch. 8, p. 193
Checking own spelling	Ch. 8, p. 188

Reading Comprehension

Reading attentively	Ch. 9, pp. 204–205
Paraphrasing	Ch. 9, p. 205
Creating ideas and organizing to write	Ch. 9, pp. 209–211
Remembering a story	Ch. 9 pp. 224–226
Building vocabulary	Ch. 9, pp. 213, 214
Understanding long sentences	Ch. 9, p. 217
Checking for errors in final drafts	Ch. 9 pp. 219–220
Organizing essays	Ch. 9, pp. 228–229

Math Calculation and Problem Solving

Counting up or down	Ch. 10, pp. 237, 241–242
Memorizing math facts	Ch. 10, p. 243

◀ Part I ▶

LEARNING PROBLEMS
AND YOUR CHILD

In the two chapters that follow, we present a new way of understanding how your child learns and what can interfere with the abilities to learn and achieve. We also provide an easy way for your to assess your child's learning skills and abilities by looking at past and present behavior and performance. Once you have finished the assessment, you will have a clear understanding of what learning strengths and weaknesses are present, and you will be able to start identifying the most effective strategies for helping your child to learn.

The Building Blocks of Learning

A New Framework for Understanding How Children Learn

It is the end of the school year at Dillworth Elementary School—a time for celebration. Let's follow the parents who have gathered in their children's classrooms for short "graduation" programs. All of them are filled with hopes and dreams for their children's future.

Our first stop is the kindergarten, where the parents have been invited to walk through a display of the students' drawings. As they look at the children's self-portraits on the wall, Chase's parents can't help noticing the difference between their son's work and that of his classmates. The difference alarms them. Chase's self-portrait is at the top of page 4.

Beneath the drawing, Chase has written his name (see the box at the bottom of page 4).

The drawings by the other children contain color and detail. They've written their names legibly. Chase has drawn himself using only crude black, with very little detail, and his name is incomplete. His parents worry that the demands of the first-grade classroom will overwhelm their son, and they wonder what they can do to help him.

In the first-grade classroom, the children have prepared two songs for their parents. As the program begins, the teacher calls the children together to stand in a line. During the first song, it quickly becomes apparent that Julie is out of step. While the others are singing about a dog on

a farm, Julie is singing "The Itsy Bitsy Spider" in her loudest voice. Her parents are embarrassed. Julie had tried hard to learn the songs for the program, and they had hoped that her many rehearsals at home would make a difference. They have not. Julie's parents have noticed that she has trouble with all tasks that involve memorization.

In the third-grade classroom, Mike's parents are also concerned. Mike has not joined the other members of his class in the group's choral reading of several poems. Instead, he looks down at his shoes, fidgeting

nervously. When the teacher leans over and touches him, trying to get his attention, Mike pulls away and continues to look down. This behavior is not new. Though Mike seems to learn, his parents have been told that he spends most of his day at school alone, and seems to be anxious or unhappy.

The children in the fourth-grade class have prepared a skit for their parents. Each child has a few lines to deliver. When Ryan reads his lines from his cue card, his parents once again are confronted by his limited reading skill. Twice the teacher has to help Ryan pronounce a word. His parents wonder why he is having so much trouble learning to read when other things—sports and drawing, for instance—come so easily to him. Though they've hired tutors and sent him to a summer reading program, and he apparently is quite bright, Ryan does not seem to be catching up. They're especially concerned because neither of Ryan's sisters, one older and one younger, has had any difficulty learning to read. His parents have begun to feel that perhaps Ryan just isn't trying hard enough.

Finally, in the sixth-grade classroom, the students are recounting their favorite activities of the concluding school year. Sarah's parents note at once that she seems distracted and has moved away from the group. This is not a new behavior for her; since kindergarten, Sarah has had difficulty sitting in one place and completing assigned tasks. Six years later, Sarah still can't seem to stay focused and complete school tasks.

As they leave the graduation ceremonies, each child's parents wonder what they can do to help their children succeed in the coming years. In one way, these children are unfortunate because they are all at risk for school difficulties. In another way, however, they are all very fortunate indeed, because they have caring, loving, attentive parents.

Education and Underachievement: Yesterday, Today, and Tomorrow

Unless you are a teacher, you're probably reading this book because, as a parent, you share some of the concerns of the parents we've just described—you see that your child is on the road to underachievement. You may be frustrated because tests show that your son is bright but doesn't seem to be working up to his potential, or because your daughter's school performance is so uneven—terrific in some subjects, significantly worse in others—that you suspect she's just not trying hard enough. At the same time, you wonder whether your worries about your child's learning problems are justified or overblown. Are fears about future economic competition exacerbating all parents' natural anxieties about their children and school? Just how important is getting a good education these days? And how much of a threat to a successful future are a young child's learning problems?

A quick review of the history of American education is in order. The original purpose of education in America was to promote religious observance; the first law establishing public education, passed in the Massachusetts Bay Colony in 1647, was known as the "Old Deluder Law" because its purpose was to thwart Satan, the "Old Deluder," in his attempts to keep people from learning about the Scriptures.

By the beginning of the twentieth century, however, the great waves of immigrants coming to the United States had changed the role of education: its key purpose was now to help newcomers learn American ways and blend more easily into society. Though mastery of academic subjects was important, children who struggled in school at the beginning of the century had a respectable option: they could drop out of school and enter the labor force, secure in the knowledge that hard work and a good strong back could compensate for low scholastic skills.

As we prepare to enter the twenty-first century, rapid changes in technology, the economy, and the American lifestyle have begun to reshape the purposes of education anew. Education, at one time considered one of several available paths to success in life, has increasingly become the *only* path to success. To succeed—both in school and, later, in the job market—children must develop skills in reading, writing, and mathematics. When some children do poorly in any one of these three academic areas, or their performance drops substantially below the average of their classmates, alarms go off and parents begin to worry.

As we face a new century, the "global village" that Marshall McLuhan predicted has become a reality. The school problems children experience have thus become a growing liability. The rates of poverty, victimization, and psychiatric disorders, including depression, appear to be on the rise among all children and are even more pronounced in children who underachieve in school. Too many of our children are growing up alienated and angry, without adequate intellectual skills, unprepared to perform even the lowest-paying jobs.

Children with school problems cannot afford to drop out of school before they are scheduled to graduate, because the market for workers whose only skills are a strong back and a willingness to work is limited. Even earning a high-school diploma no longer ensures vocational success. Increasingly, we are a society of "specialists." Nearly all vocations and vocational subspecialties require fairly intensive training and experience. Thus, a good foundation in basic academic skills is not only important, it is essential for all of our children. Furthermore, though it's true that no child loves school all the time, it's equally true that no child likes to fail. Children want to please their parents and teachers by learning, and they become unhappy, anxious, and frustrated when the learning process does not go well.

Understanding Learning and Learning Problems

The learning problems of children usually cannot be resolved quickly or cured with a "magic potion." Instead, they are often chronic and require regular management. It's a parent's job to be the manager and, eventually, to help the child learn to self-manage the problem. To be effective at this job, however, parents must first understand how children learn. What skills are required for school success? How do strengths or weaknesses in particular skills affect a child's mastery of particular subjects?

Children differ in their abilities to perform various tasks. Each has distinct strengths and weaknesses, likes and dislikes. Let's consider two children. The first is a second-grade student who loves physical activities and sports, and excels in soccer, baseball, tennis, and basketball. In school, he enjoys challenging math, science, and computer activities. He also loves to draw intricate sketches of animals and spaceships. He enjoys interacting with people of all ages.

He does not, however, enjoy activities involving reading and writing. He loves to listen to stories, but shows little interest in trying to read or write independently. In first grade, he could not remember the simple sight words he was asked to learn. He had trouble learning how to form letters. In spite of getting extra help with reading, he struggled. When he listened to a story, however, he had no difficulty understanding and discussing the story's ideas. By the end of the school year, this child showed signs of school stress. He complained of stomachaches and began to say that he was "dumb." His parents cannot understand how he can be so successful in math and science, but have such difficulty learning to read.

The second child is a fourth-grade girl. Her parents expected that school would be easy for her because by the age of three years she had already learned to recite the alphabet, recognize shapes and colors, and identify letters and numbers. Her kindergarten and first-grade report cards were outstanding. By the middle of second grade, however, her teacher began to express concerns about her. Although she could recognize and pronounce words, she did not seem to understand what she was reading. By third grade, she had become increasingly less interested in completing tasks that required her to read on her own. However, she continued to succeed in mathematics. Then, in fourth grade, when more complex concepts were introduced, she began having trouble with mathematics as well. Her parents are extremely perplexed. They cannot understand what went wrong between second and fourth grades.

These two children have different learning styles and abilities. The reasons for the first child's struggles differ from the reasons for the second child's. Think a moment about your child. What types of activities are enjoyed? What activities are disliked? What types of academic tasks are easy? What types of academic tasks are difficult?

The Building Blocks of Learning

When your child struggles in school, it's natural to want to help. The first step is to understand your child's individual style of learning. Over many years of working with children, we have developed a framework for understanding why children experience problems in learning. We call this framework the "building blocks of learning."

There are ten building blocks of learning, each of which contains a set of related learning skills. The blocks can be divided into three distinct groups, which then stack together to form a pyramid. At the ground level of the pyramid are the four *foundational* blocks: attention/impulse control, emotions and behavior, self-esteem, and the learning environment. The middle level contains the three *processing* blocks: visual, auditory, and motor. The top level contains the three *thinking* blocks: language and images, and, completing the pyramid, strategies. As you will see, some of these blocks are more important than others for certain types of learning (see figure on page 9).

The Foundational Blocks

We call the building blocks of attention/impulse control, emotions and behavior, self-esteem, and the learning environment the foundational blocks because they provide the support system for all learning. Just as the foundation of a building must be strong enough to support the whole structure erected upon it, these four blocks must be strong enough to provide support for further learning to occur.

The ability to pay attention is basic to all learning. Skills in the block of attention/impulse control allow children to focus on the relevant

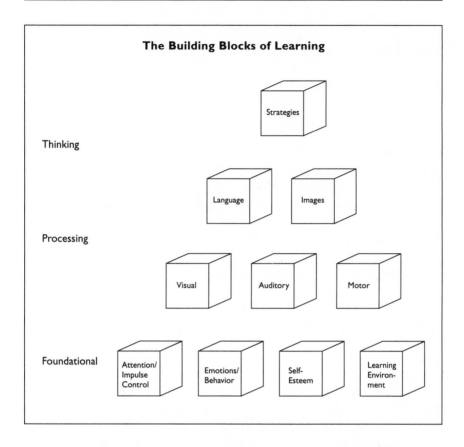

requirements of a learning task. The blocks of emotions and self-esteem contribute to how a child feels about himself or herself, as well as to a willingness to stick to tasks until their performance is complete. The environmental block concerns providing the child with a safe, supportive, appropriate climate for learning, both at home and in school. To succeed at learning, a child requires efficient attention and impulse control, healthy emotions, a positive attitude toward self and learning, and a loving, consistent, supportive environment.

Children who are impulsive or inattentive, or come from disadvantaged environments, or dislike school can and often do learn—but their school performance is affected by these adverse factors. Fortunately, you as a parent can influence many of the components of the foundational blocks. You can help your child develop solid skills in the foundational blocks and a positive outlook toward self and school.

Strengths in the foundational blocks will help your child learn to compensate for lesser abilities and to persist in the face of difficulties. Strong foundational blocks skills do not, however, guarantee that your child will avoid all school difficulties. Weaknesses within the processing or thinking blocks may also affect school performance.

The Processing Blocks

On the second level of the building blocks of learning are those that involve the processing of information through sight, hearing, and touch, or what educators and psychologists call the visual, auditory, and motor skills. These skills make learning easier and enable children to perform tasks that tend to be secretarial in nature, such as hearing and writing down assignments, taking notes, or recognizing words. The skills in the processing blocks allow children to take in information, to discern its various pieces, to memorize, and to perform tasks involving symbolic learning, such as the concept that a digit stands for a number of objects. Once a child has mastered, these processing skills she ordinarily doesn't have to spend a lot of time on the mechanics of these tasks. For example, after learning to recognize a word in print, a child will usually recognize it automatically when she encounters it again in the future.

Children who struggle with learning in the early elementary grades may have difficulties in one or more of these processing blocks. One child may have trouble with visual tasks, such as those involved in remembering what a word looks like. Another may struggle with auditory tasks, such as those involved in placing letter sounds in the correct order to spell a word. Still another may do poorly with the motor aspects of learning—cutting with scissors, forming letters with a pencil, or drawing a picture. As with the foundational blocks, a child who has adequate processing skills will be able to perform various tasks, but those skills alone do not guarantee school success.

The Thinking Blocks

The thinking blocks, at the top of the pyramid, include the skills of thinking with language, images, and strategies. Thinking with language involves understanding spoken and written language, expressing ideas in reading and writing, and learning vocabulary. Thinking with images involves reproducing complex patterns, understanding and judging visual relationships, and reasoning with mathematical symbols. Thinking with strategies involves the ability to think about thinking. The ability to plan, organize, monitor, and evaluate one's own learning involves strategic learning skills. The skills in the thinking blocks help children understand meanings, comprehend relationships, and apply previously gained knowledge as they perform school tasks. For example, before writing a story or a report, a child must brainstorm and organize the relevant information she wishes to include. To solve a word problem in mathematics, a child must read the problem, sort the relevant from the irrelevant information, figure out what is being asked and how to obtain it, perform the correct calculation, and then evaluate the resulting answer to see whether it makes sense.

Fitting the Building Blocks Together

All tasks leading to good school performance depend on the ability to sit still and concentrate and the motivation to keep trying. Certain types of tasks are highly related to the thinking blocks; others are more closely aligned with the processing blocks. As we'll see, children who have difficulties within the skills of the processing blocks experience different types of learning problems than children whose difficulties are with the skills within the thinking blocks—which may be made worse by problems in the foundational blocks. These variations occur because the foundational, processing, and thinking skills play different roles in children's abilities to learn efficiently.

For example, consider the steps children must master in learning to multiply. They need skills from the processing blocks to recall the math facts or add a set of numbers repeatedly. Children also need skills from the thinking blocks to understand the sequence of steps and the procedures involved. Finally, they need skills from the foundational blocks to help them stick with the task when it becomes difficult

The Building Blocks of Learning and School Performance

Following are several examples of the relationship between the building blocks of learning and children's school performance. Each child described has strengths to draw on and weaknesses that affect performance. Your child will have both as well, and in later chapters we show you how strengths can be used to bolster and overcome weaknesses.

- Josh, a first-grade student, comes from a supportive home. His father is always telling him how creative he is. Josh has strengths in the foundational blocks of emotions, self-esteem, and environment. He experiences significant problems, however, in the foundational block of attention/impulse control, and he has great trouble paying attention during repetitive activities and those that are not immediately interesting. When his parents or teachers ask Josh to read, his eyes look everywhere but at the words. Throughout the school day, he often leaves tasks incomplete. Josh has both strengths and weaknesses in the foundational blocks that affect school performance.

- Matthew, a fifth-grade student, has no problem with tasks involving thinking skills, but he experiences difficulties on all tasks that require him to use processing skills. As long as teachers give him information orally and allow him additional time to perform, Matthew does well. For instance, when a teacher reads a passage from a book, he is able to understand. When reading independently, however, he has trouble recognizing and pronouncing words. In mathematics, Matthew can solve math story problems presented orally, because his abilities to think with images and language are strong, but he hasn't been able to memorize multiplication facts because of memory weaknesses. The situation is similar when he writes: Matthew has a lot to say, but he struggles with spelling. Matthew has strengths in the thinking blocks, but weaknesses in the processing blocks.

- Amy, a first-grade student, has no problem memorizing information that she sees or hears. Therefore, she can identify words and spell them aloud easily. In contrast, she experiences great difficulties with both large and small motor skills, and learning to write the letters of the alphabet is a real struggle. She did not learn to walk until she was 19 months old; now, at 7 years of age, she cannot ride a bicycle, even with training wheels. In preschool, Amy was diagnosed by a physical therapist as having sensory integration problems. Amy has strengths and weaknesses within the processing blocks.

- Ivan, an eighth-grade student, is a whiz at mechanical tasks such as installing a burglar alarm in his house, but when it comes to spelling or copying from the blackboard in class, he struggles. He is gifted in thinking with images, but has trouble with tasks involving visual processing skills, such as recognizing words. Like Matthew, Ivan has a lot to say but experiences difficulty with the secretarial aspects of writing. Ivan has a strength in thinking with images, but a weakness in processing visual symbols.

- Stella, a second-grade student, has neat handwriting, loves to draw, and excels on her soccer team. However, she has problems in learning to read and in understanding ideas presented orally in class. During her preschool years, Stella had speech and language problems. Now she is experiencing difficulty with all language-related skills. She has trouble memorizing words for weekly spelling tests, writing these words in sentences, and recognizing and understanding the words in second-grade texts. Stella has strengths in motor processing skills, but weaknesses in auditory processing and thinking with language.

Josh, Matthew, Amy, Ivan, and Stella excel and struggle in different ways. Each requires a different kind of help to learn.

In Chapter 2, we will show you how to evaluate your child's strengths or weaknesses in the foundational, processing, and thinking blocks, which can affect multiple areas of learning. Academic successes and difficulties are directly related to strengths and weaknesses within these building blocks—and so are the interventions that will give a child the most effective help. Chapter 2 will help you develop an understanding of how your child learns and how his or her unique strengths and weaknesses affect school performance.

▼
Chapter
2

Assessing Your Child's Learning Skills

Using the Building Blocks of Learning to Understand Your Child's Individual Learning Style

Now that you understand the concept and skills of the building blocks of learning, you are ready to evaluate your child. If the learning problems have been evident for a while, you may feel that you lack enough knowledge to do an evaluation. However, you don't have to be a trained psychologist or an education specialist to understand your child's learning strengths and weaknesses. We have found that parents are excellent observers and reporters of their children's behavior. After all, daily observation is the best way to understand a child.

The framework of the building blocks of learning will allow you to translate your observations into a clear and systematic description of your child's learning style—to identify the strengths and weaknesses and make sense of inconsistent behavior or contradictory performances. These abilities will be an advantage. Parents who are equipped with a clear knowledge of their child's strengths and weaknesses are much better prepared to advocate for their child and to explain his or her educational needs to others.

Making the Evaluation:
The Learning Questionnaire

The first step is to complete the short questionnaire that follows. If you've already been involved in assessments of your child, you may feel daunted or exhausted at the prospect of yet another form to fill out. Don't be! Most parents readily understand how to apply this framework for evaluation.

When you've completed the questionnaire, you'll be able to identify both academic and extracurricular activities at which your child may excel. Successes in these areas will, in turn, bolster your child's self-esteem. Identifying weaknesses will help you to understand why your child struggles with certain tasks, and to pinpoint the skills that need strengthening. Once you have a clear picture of your child's strengths and weaknesses, you can move on to locating appropriately helpful strategies and resources.

The questions presented for each building block will help you decide whether your child has strengths or weaknesses with skills in a specific building block. Think about each question, consider the information that accompanies it, and then place your answer on the questionnaire form. The questions are deliberately general, requiring only *yes* or *no* answers; more detailed information on specific areas of learning appears in later chapters.

If your child is currently between the ages of 4 and 8 years, you will find it easy to answer most of the questions. For an older child, try to recall the early elementary years. Can you remember a time when your child struggled to learn the ABCs and to count? Or didn't understand that a dog and a lion are both animals? Or couldn't sit still to finish a story or memorize a short list of simple words? The information you cull from your memory will help you fill in the blanks as you develop a profile of your child's strengths and weaknesses.

Block 1: Attention/Impulse Control

Does your child seem inattentive or impulsive?   A child's ability to persevere with activities that are repetitious and not immediately rewarding is an important marker of potential for school success. A good deal of formal education, particularly in the early elementary years, consists of tasks that are repetitive, seem unimportant, and are certainly less exciting than sports, games, or drawing. Can your child stick to tasks that are not necessarily interesting or are mandated rather than chosen? When there are distractions in the environment, is your child still able to work?

The Building Blocks of Learning		
Building Blocks	Yes	No
1. Attention/impulse control	_____	_____
2. Emotions and behavior	_____	_____
3. Self-esteem	_____	_____
4. Learning environment (home and school)	_____	_____
5. Visual processing	_____	_____
6. Auditory processing	_____	_____
7. Motor processing	_____	_____
8. Thinking with language	_____	_____
9. Thinking with images	_____	_____
10. Thinking with strategies	_____	_____

What about your child's impulse control? Does it appear that whatever is foremost in his or her mind is expressed verbally? Do activities that are dangerous, like playing with matches, seem to be attractive? Does your child learn from experiences but have difficulty making use of that knowledge? In other words, does your child know the difference between right and wrong actions, but become overwhelmed by the excitement of the immediate situation because of a limited capacity for self-control? Perhaps your child knows what to do, but does not stop and think before acting.

If your child seems either inattentive or impulsive, check the "Yes" box for this building block.

Block 2: Emotions and Behavior

Does your child seem unhappy or defiant?   Like the first, this is a two-part question. Although unhappy children are frequently defiant, and vice versa, the two characteristics do not go together automatically. Some children are unhappy but passive and compliant; other children can be defiant but not appear to be unhappy. Does your child seem to view the world through mud-colored glasses? Is he or she quick to be negative? Excessively pessimistic? Overly anxious about school performance? Is your child capable of experiencing pleasure and enjoyment but more likely to remember the negative rather than the positive parts of any experience?

The second part of this question deals with defiance, or what we call the "Clint Eastwood Syndrome." Is your child quick to say "No" when faced with everyday requests? Do you see behavior or attitude that is frequently negative, deliberately annoying, spiteful, vindictive, or resentful? Is there a tendency to criticize and boss around siblings or peers?

If your child seems to be unhappy, or defiant, or both, check the "Yes" box for this block.

Block 3: Self-Esteem

Does your child have low self-esteem?   Self-esteem covers many areas of life. Your child may have high self-esteem on the soccer field, but low self-esteem in the classroom. For this question, we are most concerned with how your child perceives himself or herself as a learner. Does your child often say that he or she cannot perform tasks? That a task is too difficult or requires instruction in how to do it? Does your child seem to lack self-confidence? Is he or she prone to making negative comments or self-descriptions such as "dumb" or "stupid"? Do you hear complaints about being disliked by peers and teachers or always being picked on?

Some children attempt to hide low self-esteem by wearing a mask of superiority. These children say that a task is too easy to be bothered with, or that they don't need to be held to the same standards as everyone else because they are so much more mature or proficient. If your child displays these attitudes while failing, they have probably been developed as a cover for feelings of incompetence.

If your child seems to have low self-esteem, or has few, if any, areas of real success, check the "Yes" box for this block.

Block 4: Learning Environment

Are your child's home and school environments conducive to learning?   As you answer this question, consider both your child's home and school settings. Does your child have a quiet place to do homework? Do you or your spouse take time for supplementary reading or for help with school assignments? Does your child know that you value learning?

Take a look at your child's school environment. Although all children complain about school to some degree, most parents know when their child is in real distress. Does your child seem to enjoy going to school? Are there constant complaints about school or frequent announcements of being "sick" on school days? Are the teacher and classmates described in positive terms? Does the teacher seem to like your child?

If your child is having difficulty performing school-related tasks at home or seems to dislike going to school, check "Yes" for this block.

Block 5: Visual Processing

Does (or did) your child have difficulty learning how the alphabet letters look? If your child is in the 4- to 8-year age range, this question will probably be easy for you to answer. Does your child sometimes have trouble learning and remembering letters? Do letters with similar appearance, such as *n* and *h*, or *b* and *d*, cause confusion?

If your child is older, answering the question may be more difficult. Think about whether you've noticed misreading of simple words, reversing letters when writing, or spelling all words just the way they sound. Does your child sometimes lose the word or line sequence when reading or have trouble copying from a chalkboard? Is there a tendency to write numbers in the wrong order, such as *12* for *21*?

If your child had or has these types of difficulties, check "Yes" for this block.

Block 6: Auditory Processing

Does (or did) your child have difficulty learning letter sounds?   Once again, this question will be easier to answer if your child is between the ages of 4 and 8 years. Have you noticed difficulty in identifying letter sounds or pronouncing words with several syllables? Did your child ever receive speech therapy? Were many ear infections experienced during preschool years? (If so, these may have contributed to weaknesses in the auditory block.)

If your child is older, is there difficulty in remembering letter/sound associations, putting sounds in the right sequence when spelling, or pronouncing unfamiliar words when reading? Children with weakness in the auditory block are likely to mispronounce longer words when speaking.

If your child had or has difficulties of this type, check "Yes" for this block.

Block 7: Motor Processing

Does (or did) your child have difficulty remembering how to form letters, or catching a ball?   The skills in the motor block involve both small-muscle or fine motor movements, such as those needed for writing, and large-muscle or gross movements, such as those needed for catching and throwing a ball, or riding a bike. A child may have difficulty with either fine or gross motor skills, or both, and this may affect school performance.

If your child is between the ages of 4 and 8 years, this is probably an easy question to answer. Is learning to write letters or numbers troublesome? Are the letters and numbers produced awkward in appearance? Is your child interested in drawing or learning to write?

If your child is older, consider whether there was early difficulty in learning to print letters or write in script. Is written work done at a slow rate? Is the handwriting often criticized for being sloppy, and the notebooks, for being messy and disorganized?

When your child was younger, was it difficult to develop the skills necessary for riding a bicycle? Did your child seem clumsy and uninterested in sports? Even now, does he or she prefer not to participate in physical activities?

If your child had or has difficulty with the development of either fine or gross motor skills, check "Yes" for the motor block.

Block 8: Thinking with Language

Does (or did) your child seem slow to develop spoken language?   Think back to when your child was between the ages of 3 and 6 years. Was there a slow development of spoken language and effective communication? Did your child receive services from a speech/language therapist? Was there trouble with understanding directions, expressing basic needs, or answering questions? Did your child have difficulty understanding the meaning of stories or telling you about daily activities?

If your child is older, does he or she tend to be quiet? Do lengthy explanations or long chapters in books cause confusion? Is there a tendency to use words inaccurately? When reading math story problems, does your child have trouble understanding what the problem asks?

If your child appears weak in language-related skills, check "Yes" for this block.

Block 9: Thinking with Images

Does (or did) your child have trouble working with designs, recognizing patterns, and performing spatial tasks?   Parents and teachers often overlook children's problems in thinking with images because they may not seem to be directly related to academic skills. However, children who cannot visualize story problems, for instance, may fall behind in math. Ask yourself whether your child had difficulty putting puzzles together or did not enjoy playing with construction toys as a preschooler.

Did your child struggle when learning to tell time or trying to understand basic math concepts? Is there presently a difficulty in using maps, diagrams, or graphs? Is it troublesome to work with tasks, problems, or even games that are three-dimensional? Does your child tend to have a poor sense of direction?

If your child seems to have these types of spatial weaknesses, check "Yes" for this block.

Block 10: Thinking with Strategies

Does your child have problems forming a plan and following through? Children who have problems with developing and using strategies often cannot identify the steps required to complete a task successfully. They may wait until the last minute to complete or even to start involved projects, and may be unable to develop alternative plans when something doesn't work out immediately.

To answer this question, consider whether your preschool child appeared to be unaware that some planning was necessary to complete more complex tasks. As an older child, does he or she struggle with study skills, note taking, and organization?

If your child seems to have difficulty with planning, organizing, and studying, check "Yes" for this block.

You may be unsure how to answer some of the questions in the questionnaire because we have given you the opportunity to respond only "Yes" or "No." A child may have problems with some of the skills in a learning block, but not others. If your child has now, or had earlier, *any* of the problems mentioned, check "Yes." We have limited your choice purposely, to make it easier for you to identify your child's strengths and weaknesses.

By asking for simple yes-or-no answers, we are not suggesting that the severity of a child's problem doesn't matter. Some children are much more impulsive than others, and some children experience greater difficulty remembering the sounds and shapes of letters. Children who have severe skill weaknesses may be diagnosed as having outright learning disabilities, a subject that will be covered in greater detail in Chapter 6. However, focusing on even minor struggles with these skills can provide important information that opens a window to understanding school problems. The first step, therefore, is to identify your child's learning characteristics. In the next two sections, we'll look at how two sets of parents responded to the building blocks questionnaire.

Sean's Story

Sean's mother completed the building block questionnaire when Sean was 12 years old. By then, she and Sean's father had been trying to understand their son's learning problems and get the right kind of help for him for quite some time. Sean's mother's responses to the ten building block questions, based on her recollection of Sean's school experiences, are shown at the bottom of this page.

From the time he was very little, Sean's parents were concerned about differences between Sean and his peers. Although he was clearly quite bright and had creative ideas, he did not seem particularly interested in looking at books and quickly became bored with many activities. When the parents asked about this, the family pediatrician brushed aside their worries, telling them that children develop at different rates and that Sean would be just like the other kids by the time he started school. This, however, was not the case.

In kindergarten, Sean could not pay attention for extended periods of time. Thus, Sean's mother checked the "Yes" box indicating problems with attention/impulse control. Because Sean also had difficulty remembering the letters of the alphabet and the sounds for each letter, she

Building Blocks	Yes	No
1. Attention/impulse control	✓	
2. Emotions and behavior		✓
3. Self-esteem	✓	
4. Learning environment (home and school)		✓
5. Visual processing	✓	
6. Auditory processing	✓	
7. Motor processing		✓
8. Thinking with language		✓
9. Thinking with images		✓
10. Thinking with strategies		✓

checked "Yes" for problems with visual and auditory processing. In contrast, he loved to draw and enjoyed playing soccer, so she checked "No" for problems with motor processing. But by the end of that first school year, Sean seemed to know less than when he had started. At the suggestion of his teacher, he repeated kindergarten. The second time around, he made some progress, and the teacher frequently complimented him on his excellent vocabulary and problem-solving skills. He evidenced strengths in all of the thinking blocks. Though she felt he was a little behind her other students in basic reading and writing skills, and was perhaps more active than most, his teacher was certain he would mature over the summer.

Sean's first-grade teacher commented that he could be the "poster child" for attention deficit disorder, and an evaluation by a school psychologist backed up that diagnosis. The family decided to give medication a try. Although it greatly improved his behavior and allowed Sean to be more attentive, the medication did not seem to help him bridge the gaps in reading and writing. Sean was evaluated again and diagnosed as having a learning disability as well.

Unfortunately, in the next several years, Sean's school environment worked more against than for him. One teacher announced that she did not believe in learning disabilities, and another didn't seem to understand what accommodations his learning disability required. Because of limited resources at the special education resource center, Sean received services in groups as large as twelve students. Although Sean's parents were very supportive at home, the school environment presented problems, so his mother checked that box as "Yes."

The next years were a little better. His classroom teachers spent extra time with Sean and encouraged his love of science and social studies. Using his strong abilities to transform his ideas into concrete representations, Sean was able to create experiments, games, and models that brought science and social studies concepts to life. But school proved to be an erratic experience. Several teachers were bad matches for him or did not understand what he needed, and Sean's self-esteem was slowly chipped away. Because of this, his mother checked the "Yes" box to indicate a problem with self-esteem.

Sean's profile shows that he has strengths in the thinking blocks and weaknesses in the blocks of attention and visual and auditory processing. He had a very supportive environment at home, but he was being hobbled by intermittent problems with the learning environment at school. Armed with this information, Sean's parents were able to act as his advocates and to help him manage his learning problems. When he entered middle school, they sought out the resource teacher to discuss his educational plan. Sean's classes were carefully chosen with the dual goal of placing him in classes at his level, and pairing him with teachers who would build his self-esteem. It took active intervention on the part of his parents—including many conferences with Sean's teachers and principal—to ensure that Sean was in a learning environment that was *appropriate for him,* one that recognized and built on his strengths and shored up his weaknesses.

From Sean's history and the profile his mother completed, it became clear how strengths and weaknesses within the building blocks had affected his school performance and behavior. Sean had some obvious strengths: He was quick to develop concepts and to apply his new knowledge, he learned new vocabulary quickly, and he could discuss topics ranging from the launching of the Space Shuttle to Van Gogh's most famous paintings. But his weaknesses in the attention/impulse control block and the visual and auditory processing blocks, plus a less-than-accommodating school atmosphere, combined to make his early experiences at school socially, behaviorally, and academically difficult. Eventually, the repeated school failures had a negative impact on his self-esteem as well.

Children with learning problems seldom just "grow out of them." The earlier a child's learning difficulties are identified and given appropriate interventions, the better. Had Sean's parents been able to identify his strengths and weaknesses at a younger age, his rates of reading and writing could have been accelerated, his attentional problems would have been more efficiently treated, and the subsequent wear and tear on his self-esteem would have been minimized. Sean is fortunate; he has caring parents who learned to see the world through his eyes. They had to learn the hard way how to become effective educational advocates for their child, but his future learning experiences should be more successful and gratifying.

Jamie's Story

Jamie's mother and father filled out the questionnaire when Jamie was entering second grade. After answering the ten questions as shown on page 24, they reviewed Jamie's educational history with us.

They had no trouble deciding to check the "Yes" block regarding attention and impulse control. In preschool, Jamie had trouble paying attention unless the room was totally quiet, and she reacted to sounds most people are able to ignore: the motor in the refrigerator, a bird chirping

Building Blocks	Yes	No
1. Attention/impulse control	x	
2. Emotions and behavior		x
3. Self-esteem		x
4. Learning environment (home and school)		x
5. Visual processing	?	
6. Auditory processing	?	
7. Motor processing	x	
8. Thinking with language		x
9. Thinking with images		x
10. Thinking with strategies		x

outside, a car passing by. Jamie was also extremely sensitive to touch. If someone bumped into her accidentally, she would hit back instinctively.

Most of her parents' concerns centered on the Motor Processing block. Jamie did not crawl until after her first birthday, and she did not walk until she was 2 years old. She also had trouble developing fine motor skills. When she went to kindergarten, she could not yet cut with scissors or color without scribbling, nor could she color while sitting. The family's pediatrician had diagnosed low muscle tone, and prescribed lots of sports and physical therapy. Because of her many motor problems, including an inability to sit still and to stick with any task, Jamie was also diagnosed as having "sensory integration dysfunction." To counteract these problems, Jamie underwent visual training to learn to track with her eyes, vertically and horizontally, and to use biofeedback to help her physical development.

In first grade, she was tested for learning disabilities and was diagnosed as having an auditory processing dysfunction. However, she also continued to have problems paying attention, and Jamie's parents wondered whether these difficulties were related more to inattention than to true skill weaknesses. Thus, they put question marks in the boxes for visual and auditory processing.

Jamie's parents' major concerns continue to be her motor development and her inability to pay adequate attention. Now in second grade, Jamie plays on a soccer team, but she often runs away from the ball rather than toward it, and she still cannot ride a bike. Her printing is still very disjointed. She often stops writing in the middle of a word to try to fix a letter. Because she is easily distracted by any extraneous noise, Jamie does not get very much work done in class. She brings classwork home to do each night.

Jamie's parents observed that she also has some real strengths, such as an excellent memory when she does pay attention. She loves to talk and is intensely curious about everything in the environment. Jamie also enjoys listening to music and she is attentive when books are read to her. She is learning to read and spell. She has many friends and is a real leader in most activities. Thus, she has strengths in the areas of emotion and behavior, self-esteem, and all the thinking blocks.

Although they still need a treatment plan to address their concerns about her motor development and attention, the assessment of Jamie's learning strengths and weaknesses has allowed Jamie's parents to intervene early. They understand their daughter's needs and are doing everything they can to help her succeed, including working with her teachers to make sure that the school environment is helpful to her. Because of this strategy, they are heading off problems with self-esteem. However, Jamie's path, like those of many children with learning problems, is likely to have its ups and downs, and her education will require constant attention and fine tuning if she is to continue to succeed.

Common Profiles

As you think about your own responses to the ten building block questions, keep in mind that weaknesses in foundational skills can both cause school problems or be caused by school problems, as was the case with Sean. Weaknesses in the visual, auditory, or motor processing blocks, combined with attention and impulse control problems, contribute to emotional and behavioral difficulties, as well as low self-esteem. Problems in behavior and self-esteem are then likely to have a negative impact on the home environment.

When you consider the framework of the building blocks of learning, you can see that many different combinations are possible. Some children have a specific pattern of strengths and weaknesses; other children have a weakness in only one of the building blocks. As we have worked with children, we have encountered a number of frequently occurring profiles of strengths and weaknesses. In the following section, we briefly describe five of the most typical learning block profiles. Consider whether your child fits one of these.

1. Strengths in the Thinking and Processing Blocks, Weaknesses in the Foundational Blocks

Some children's school difficulties are linked directly to weaknesses in the foundational blocks. Children who cannot pay attention, or who have emotional problems, low self-esteem, or an impoverished or inappropriate learning environment, may have the intellectual skills needed to succeed in school, but not the supportive system that makes sustained success possible. For example, a child who is being raised in a chaotic or extremely stressful environment may possess processing and thinking skills that are adequate for school success, but may subsequently develop behavioral or emotional problems as an effect of life experiences. Similarly, a child with an untreated attentional problem often falls further and further behind in school and becomes increasingly more alienated from peers and family. Once their attentional, emotional, and social issues are addressed, these children are able to succeed in school. If the problems are not addressed, however, these children find themselves trapped in a downward spiral that often leads to delinquency, clinical depression, and more serious conduct disorders.

2. Strengths in the Thinking and Foundational Blocks, Weaknesses in the Processing Blocks

Despite good thinking skills, a good environment, and the ability to pay sufficient attention, children with weaknesses in the processing blocks struggle in school with tasks that require rote learning, such as memorizing the alphabet, learning the letter sounds and/or words by sight, remembering how to spell, and copying from a blackboard. These children are often a puzzle to their teachers and parents because they are well adjusted and well behaved, and seem capable in many ways. Although problems with the auditory processing block are the most common, children experiencing problems with one processing block often experience at least mild difficulties with the other two as well. With appropriate, and sometimes intensive, educational interventions, these children can and do succeed in school.

3. Strengths in the Thinking Blocks, Weaknesses in the Processing and Foundational Blocks

Some children with strengths in the thinking blocks but weaknesses in the processing blocks often have problems with attention and impulse control as well. When they do not receive early or appropriate treatment, as was the case with Sean, they may develop emotional problems and poor self-esteem. Fortunately, with effective treatment, these children often understand that they are smart and capable and that there are strategies that they can use to circumvent their difficulties and succeed in school and life.

4. Strengths in the Foundational and Processing Blocks, Weaknesses in the Thinking Blocks

Children with severe weaknesses in the thinking blocks have difficulty with tasks involving reasoning and language. Fortunately, parents and teachers of children with weaknesses in the thinking block of language usually identify them during their preschool years because problems with language tend to be obvious. Detecting less pronounced weaknesses in the thinking blocks is often more of a challenge. Parents of children with these less severe weaknesses are often surprised, because the school problems seem to come out of nowhere. The child usually does well in preschool and first grade, showing no difficulties in learning to read. By the second grade, however, the child develops a difficulty in reading for comprehension. By the middle or late elementary school years, children with problems in the thinking blocks have difficulties with most school subjects, particularly with tasks involving reading comprehension, problem solving, and expression of ideas. Like those who have weaknesses in processing, these children may develop emotional and behavioral problems as well as poor self-esteem. By working to increase language development, and with instruction in the use of strategies to aid thinking, however, they can improve their problem-solving skills and their chances for school success.

5. A Significant Weakness within One Block

Some children have a significant weakness in only one block. If the problem is severe enough, these children are usually identified as being in need of special services. Many receive educational or mental health diagnoses. For example, a child with severe problems in the foundational block of attention and impulse control is likely to be diagnosed as having attention deficit/hyperactivity disorder (ADHD). A child with a severe weakness in the visual or auditory processing blocks may be identified as having a learning disability or dyslexia. A child with severe emotional and behavioral problems may be identified as having a conduct disorder. A child with a severe weakness in the thinking block of language may be identified as having a language impairment, whereas a child with marked weaknesses in all of the thinking blocks may be identified as having mental retardation or developmental delays.

Children with a significant weakness in one or more blocks require support from both family and school. Without this support, problems usually develop in the foundational blocks of emotions and self-esteem as well.

Your Child's Profile

You are ready now to learn more about the specifics of your child's learning profile. If you have identified specific strengths and weakness, you may want to move on to the parts of the book that address your most immediate concerns. In most chapters, we present some additional questions to help you develop a more comprehensive picture of your child's skills within a specific learning block.

If your child has problems in any of the foundational blocks, we suggest you read each of the chapters in Part II and answer the additional questions given there. Chapter 5, on self-esteem, is especially important. If your child has problems in any of the processing blocks (visual, auditory, or motor) or thinking blocks (language, images, or strategies), turn to the introduction to Part III, and locate the additional questions about your child's skills and abilities. Once you've answered them, you'll have a better idea of why your child is struggling with particular kinds of learning, whether in basic skills—such as learning to read or to do basic math calculations—or in tasks that involve higher thinking, such as reading comprehension, writing, or doing math story problems. Read the most relevant chapters. If your child's weaknesses occur in a number of areas, or you would like to gain a better understanding of how to help with many facets of school behavior and performance, you will find helpful information throughout the book. The strategies we offer in each chapter can benefit any child.

◀ Part II ▶

FOUNDATIONAL BLOCKS: THE LEARNING SUPPORT SYSTEM

In the next four chapters, we explore the skills of the foundational building blocks of learning: attention and impulse control, emotions and behavior, self-esteem, and the home and school learning environment. These foundational blocks are important for all children. Although children with weaknesses in these blocks can and do learn, they are, in effect, swimming against a strong current and must work harder to succeed; conversely, a child with strengths in the foundational blocks has the advantage that comes from swimming with a strong current: the distance may be long, but there is consistent help along the way.

If the assessment in Part I showed that your child has weaknesses in several of the foundational blocks, you may want to read all of the chapters in Part II. If your child has a weakness in one particular foundational block, you may want to turn to that specific chapter. Because all children with school problems receive more criticism than their peers who have no problems, and thus are more likely to develop a poor self-image, we urge you to read Chapter Five, which discusses the foundational block of self-esteem.

▼
Chapter

3

Attention and Impulse Control

What to Do When Your Child Can't Concentrate or Lacks Enough Self-Control to Learn

As a parent of a child whose behavior is impulsive or inattentive, you're not alone. No set of problems creates more difficulty for parents, teachers, and the children themselves than children's inability to sit still, to pay attention, to complete required tasks, and to think before they act. In fact, over half of all children's referrals to mental health clinics and special education programs stem from complaints about inattentive or impulsive behavior.

These problems must be managed day in and day out—first by the adults in the children's lives, and eventually by the children themselves. This chapter provides you with a better understanding of your child's attentional and impulse problems, thus helping you to be more effective as an advocate and educational case manager. It also offers a variety of changes you can make at home and at school to minimize the impact of factors that affect your child's ability to learn.

Children's problems with attention and impulse control vary widely. One child may be a good student but unable to sit still—fidgeting, climbing up to kneel on the desk, calling out the answer to a teacher's question before his or her raised hand is acknowledged. Another child may be unable to finish class assignments or homework but has no difficulty spending long hours playing with favorite toys. Still another may misbehave repeatedly, in spite of knowing what is correct or appropriate behavior. A child's problems with inattention and impulsivity may show up in the form of a desk that is messy and crammed full of long-lost homework assignments, or in rough and unpredictable playground behavior that scares off other children. All of these behaviors stem from a weakness in the building block of attention and impulse control.

Health and education professionals agree that there are children in every classroom who experience problems because of inattentiveness, impulsivity, or hyperactivity, although only 2 to 5 percent of all students meet the criteria for a formal diagnosis of attention deficit/hyperactivity disorder (ADHD; see pages 35–39). Because a child can experience attentional problems that interfere with learning even in the absence of a clinical diagnosis, and because there is no consensus on the cause of these problems, it's best to focus your efforts on determining how a weakness in the block of attention and impulse control affects your child's school performance. Once you have a good understanding of the problem, you'll be in a position to help. There are no perfect solutions, but there are many effective interventions, including behavior management, skill building, and the appropriate use of medications such as Ritalin.®

The ten characteristics in the chart on page 33 will provide you with an in-depth look at your child's strengths and weaknesses in the foundational block of attention and impulse control. Children become better at sticking to tasks, paying attention, and controlling their impulses as they mature, so compare your child's behavior to that of children of the same age or to siblings when they were that age.

If you checked "Yes" to several of the descriptions above, it is likely that your child is weak in a number of skills related to attention and impulse control. There is also a strong likelihood that temperament—the inborn psychological qualities children bring with them at birth—may interfere with the ability to succeed at school.

Inattentiveness, restlessness, excessive activity, overly emotional and impulsive behavior, and difficulty in delaying rewards affect children's interactions with their entire world. Unpredictable behavior—grabbing toys, shoving to be first in line, or continually violating household rules—can damage relationships with parents, teachers, brothers, sisters, and friends. It can also derail academic progress, even in children who have strengths in processing and thinking skills.

As they progress into higher grades, impulsive and inattentive children often struggle with handwriting, spelling, memorizing math facts, and completing written assignments. Because self-esteem and other personality

Attention/Impulse Control	Yes	No
1. Restless in a squirmy sense	_____	_____
2. Distractive or inattentive	_____	_____
3. Always up and on the go	_____	_____
4. Prone to acting before thinking	_____	_____
5. More likely not to finish things than to finish them	_____	_____
6. Easily frustrated	_____	_____
7. Unable to work independently	_____	_____
8. Unable to persist with tasks for reasonable amounts of time	_____	_____
9. Poor at listening	_____	_____
10. Prone to difficulties when organizing tasks and materials	_____	_____

factors are significantly affected by impulsive and inattentive behavior, these children are considered "at risk"—vulnerable to experiencing other problems, such as substance abuse and depression, in the future.

The profile of 9-year-old Michael is typical of a child with attention and impulse problems. Michael has boundless energy, but he often acts before thinking. His impulsive and inattentive behavior causes significant problems at home and school. Michael often leaves his schoolwork unfinished, and he tends to forget to turn in the homework he does complete—or he loses it in his chaotic desk. His classmates generally steer clear of him, especially during academic tasks requiring group cooperation, and his brothers and sisters are frequently unhappy with the way he treats them, their friends, and their possessions. Michael is often unable to follow the rules of games or to get along well with groups of other children on the playground. However, because he is daring and often does not weigh the consequences of his acts, his classmates and friends seek him out when they need someone to chase a ball over a fence or across a busy street. Michael's parents are frustrated with his seemingly irresponsible behavior; no amount of scolding, nagging, punishment, or cajoling appears to have any impact on him. His teachers are also frustrated by his inattentive, impulsive style. They complain about his poor work habits and note that even though he often knows what to do, he does not follow through.

Although Michael's problems cause him, his family, his teachers, and his classmates difficulties, his impulsivity and inattentiveness do not constitute abnormal behavior or mental illness. Instead, they represent a bad fit between what Michael does and what his environment requires. For most affected children, inattention and impulsivity are due to inborn temperament. Researchers believe that these qualities are inherited and may be the result of a specific imbalance in brain structure or chemistry. Nonetheless, as child psychiatry pioneer Dr. John Werry noted, "Biology is not destiny."[1] Some children are at greater-than-average risk for impulsive and inattentive behaviors, but the day-in, day-out quality of their lives and their educational experiences provide enough support to help them avoid the development of significant problems.

Children may exhibit problems with attention for reasons besides inborn temperament. Some children are impulsive or inattentive because of anxiety, frustration, depression, or ineffective parenting; others behave this way because of the stressful effects of other learning difficulties.

Whatever the reason for your child's problems, by the time a teacher, friend, or physician suggests that a greater-than-average problem with inattentiveness or impulsivity is a possibility, you are likely to be coping with a complex set of difficulties that affects all areas of your child's life. These problems can be made worse by such factors as health, diet, friends, learning problems, interactions with siblings, and even your own emotional responses to your child. For example, if you are in a bad mood after a difficult day at work, you may overreact to any minor problem. If, on top of this, your child is inattentive and unable to stick to an assigned homework task, you may find yourself ranting and raving, which is unlikely to help the situation.

Evaluating a Child with Impulsivity or Inattention

Professional evaluation for problems with attention and impulsivity is complicated. There is no absolute diagnostic test for overly impulsive behavior, no firm standard that defines a short attention span. Assessing these problems requires a careful collection of information from parents, teachers, and pediatricians, drawing on questionnaires, interviews, and testing. Certain early childhood developmental problems, such as difficulty going to sleep, seem to indicate that a child is at risk, but these markers are not infallible and do not absolutely predict temperamental inattention and impulsivity.

Inattentiveness and impulsivity reflect *inconsistency* in age-appropriate behavior; a child may act too quickly in one situation or be inattentive in another, but, at other times, may behave quite appropriately. However, the amount of trouble an impulsive child gets into is partly determined by the circumstances. For instance, some children do well when playing alone or with one friend, but their limited capacity for self-control is overwhelmed when they are in a group, and they become uncooperative and impatient. Impulsivity and inattention may cause a cluster of problems of different levels of intensity, severity, and persistence as these children grow, and their school performance is then likely to be uneven.

It is both untrue and unfair to say that an inattentive child can never pay attention, an impulsive child can never stick to a plan, or a restless child can never sit still. These problems result from *inconsistency* in performance rather than a child's inability to perform. Most impulsive and inattentive children know what to do but do not consistently act on what they know. In one situation, they pay attention; in another, they seemingly cannot. One minute, they are attending to the teacher; a few minutes later, they are completely distracted by the sounds of a garbage truck going down the street. Daily life for these children is a series of challenges brought about by their inability to meet the demands and expectations of their environment. Although children described as impulsive and inattentive share similar weaknesses, they may experience very different life problems because they have different parents, teachers, siblings, other levels of skills, and so on.

A century ago, a teacher's usual approach for dealing with these difficulties was to whack the child soundly with a ruler. If the ruler broke before the child's behavior changed, the school authorities suggested the child not return to school, thus "solving" the problem. Today, all children are encouraged to attend and finish school, regardless of the severity of their problems. But education within the school setting requires that even young children pay attention, manage their impulses, and plan and finish projects. Unable to meet these demands, the inattentive or impulsive child is an immediate candidate for many learning problems, and they are compounded if the child also experiences processing and thinking skill weaknesses.

Attention Deficit/Hyperactivity Disorder (ADHD)

A formal diagnosis of attention deficit/hyperactivity disorder (ADHD) is given to children who have severe problems with inattention and/or impulsivity. The diagnosis includes three groups who have common variations of this problem: children who primarily have difficulty with attention and organization; children who primarily have difficulty with impulsivity and hyperactivity, and children who experience both.

Children in the second and third groups tend to get referred for treatment much more quickly than children in the first group. This is partly because impulsivity—the inability to stop and think before acting or speaking—is the core problem for most children receiving a diagnosis of ADHD. As educator Rick Lavoie has noted, these children demonstrate the "OTM-OTM syndrome"—what's on the mind comes immediately out the mouth. They have difficulty separating thought from action and experience from response. They do not analyze problem situations well or consider alternatives before acting; in fact, they appear to spend the majority of their lives reacting rather than planning.

The parents of children with these problems may overestimate their severity because of their disruptive nature, and the parents of children whose problems are attentional but not disruptive may underestimate their severity because they do not leap out at the observer. Children with impulsivity and hyperactivity problems seldom go unnoticed because their behavior tends to have a large impact on the adults in their lives—they cause annoyance and throw family and school life into turmoil. In contrast, the problems of children with attentional problems, who daydream or lose or forget about their homework, tend to get shorter shrift because, although these problems cause worry, they are seldom disruptive. In fact, children with nondisruptive attentional problems may have more serious learning difficulties and end up with more serious school problems because they are less likely to be referred for early evaluation and treatment than children with impulsivity problems.

Impulsivity versus Inattentiveness

Are there differences between the impulsive and the inattentive child? A large volume of scientific literature suggests that there are. Impulsive children have much greater difficulty with aggression and are often unpopular socially. They often experience conduct problems and are much more likely to become oppositional or delinquent. (See Chapter 4.) Inattentive children, by contrast, are seldom referred for behavioral problems, but may have more difficulties with learning. They are often described as shy, socially isolated and moderately unpopular, and poor at sports. However, they are likely to have at least a few friends and do not disrupt their families' lives. Their difficulty with sports may arise not from a lack of

How Widespread Are Problems with Impulsivity and Inattention?

Recent studies have suggested that as many as 20 percent of school-age children experience problems with impulsivity or inattention. However, not all of these children receive a formal diagnosis of ADHD, which is made only when there is an observation of consistent problems in a variety of settings—at home and at school—and there is agreement among parents, teachers, and mental health professionals. When all evaluation criteria are met, the presence of ADHD in childhood is approximately 2 to 5 percent. Higher percentages occur in certain populations, such as children from low-income families. Approximately 30 percent of children receiving a diagnosis of ADHD are also diagnosed with a specific learning disability. However, the majority of children with learning disabilities are not inattentive or impulsive, and the majority of children receiving a diagnosis of ADHD do not have a specific learning disability.

ADHD is a more common categorical diagnosis for boys than girls. Some studies have suggested that boys have greater problems with impulsivity and aggression, whereas girls with ADHD experience more problems with mood, emotion, and language development.

physical ability but from a tendency to lose focus during organized activities—to be on the other side of the soccer field watching the clouds go by as other children play the game. In contrast to the inattentive child, the impulsive child may be right in the middle of the game but may thoughtlessly kick the ball into the wrong goal.

Dealing with an impulsive child can be exasperating. This has certainly been the case for Jared, an 8-year-old second grader who has been a challenge to his parents, relatives, and teachers for years. Although he was the same size as other children and had had two years of preschool, he was frequently described by his kindergarten teacher as immature. He did not pay attention, nor did he finish even simple tasks consistently. He was restless and fidgety and often crawled under his desk. He was overly emotional, became overexcited easily, and cried frequently—and consequently drew attention to himself in a negative way. At home, his behavior was self-centered and often resulted in conflicts with siblings. He did not seem to learn from his experiences, and neither punishments nor rewards seemed to alter the negative course of his development.

Although Jared tested as a capable learner, he frequently failed to finish his classwork and appeared to his first-grade teacher to be slow to grasp new academic concepts. When playing with other children, Jared was impulsive, frequently behaved inappropriately, and was soon excluded from most social activities. By second grade, this pattern had intensified. Because he could not stay on task, he frequently sought reasons for not completing schoolwork and became the class clown. He continued to have problems with other children and got involved in a number of fights at school and in the neighborhood. Recently, Jared has become increasingly aware of his problems and has started to say things like "No one likes me" and "I'm stupid." His family and teachers have exhausted themselves and their resources in an attempt to understand and help him succeed.

Where Jared is impulsive, Ellen exemplifies the child with attentional problems. Her father affectionately calls her "the great dreamer," because she is so often lost in thoughts and daydreams rather than paying attention to the task at hand. Her brothers and sisters, on the other hand, describe her as "an airhead" who would lose her head if it weren't attached. Ellen has always been described as a pleasant girl, but her teachers complain about her messy desk and lost assignments. Her few close friends often become upset because she is so disorganized and forgets important things, and her family knows that they have to allow extra time for Ellen's customary frantic search for a schoolbook, an article of clothing, or an important possession before leaving the house.

Ellen has a number of strengths: she is a good reader and a good athlete, and she scores quite well on achievement tests. Her teachers marvel at her ability to learn even though she often appears not to be listening in class. Ellen doesn't have a learning disability; she is intelligent and able to comprehend. However, her grades suffer because she is so disorganized and often does not turn in her work. Ellen presents a less common pattern: inattentiveness in the absence of hyperactivity and impulsivity. This pattern occurs in approximately one out of nine boys given the diagnosis of ADHD, but more frequently (one out of three) in girls given that same diagnosis.

Children with problems of either inattention or impulsivity are more likely to develop depression or anxiety, other disruptive behaviors, and academic problems. They also have more problems with friends and poorer self-concepts, and are at greater risk for adult personality and substance abuse problems than other children.

Common Sense and Attentional Problems

In severe cases, it is not difficult to decide whether a child has ADHD. In mild to moderate cases of overactivity and inattentiveness, however, it is often not clear whether the child has ADHD or is just more active or more of a daydreamer than others. In our experience, obtaining a diagnosis of ADHD for a child is not the critical step. However, it is critical that parents recognize whether impulsive and inattentive behaviors impair a child's ability to succeed at school. The following four commonsense descriptions should help in making this determination:

1. *Impulsivity.* Impulsive children often act before thinking. They are not good at following rules; even when they understand and know them, their need to act quickly overwhelms their limited capacity for self-control. Thus, impulsive children are frequently "repeat offenders," unable to benefit from experience even after a third or fourth repetition of engaging in forbidden behavior and being on the receiving end of their caretakers' anger and punishment. They require more supervision and are quite frustrating to parents and teachers, who often view their behavior as purposeful, naughty, noncaring, or oppositional. However, these children's problems usually stem from temperamental difficulty rather than from intentional disobedience.

2. *Inattentiveness.* Inattentive children have difficulty sticking with repetitive, relatively uninteresting activities that require effort and are not of their choosing. Unfortunately, that describes half of what children are asked to do at school and at home! Thus, the more uninteresting or repetitive a task, the more difficult it is for these children. Attention is a complex process consisting of different skills. To function effectively in a classroom, children must be able to focus attention appropriately, begin an assigned task, and sustain attention long enough to complete it, ignoring distractions. They must also be able to do two things at the same time, such as taking notes and listening to the teacher, and they have to be ready to respond during group activities. Weaknesses at any point in the attentional chain undermine their ability to perform.

3. *Overarousal.* Children described as impulsive are also often described as hyperactive—excessively restless, overactive, or easily provoked to excessive emotion. They have difficulty controlling their bodies when

they are required to sit still for a long time. In addition, their emotional reactions are more intense and more frequent than those of other children, regardless of the emotion being expressed—anger, frustration, happiness, or sadness. Impulsive children often wear their emotions on their sleeves. The term that professionals use to describe these tendencies is "overaroused."

4. *Difficulty working toward long-term goals or rewards.* Inattentive and impulsive children frequently have difficulty working toward long-term goals. To stick with a task, they require repeated short-term payoffs rather than a single end-of-task reward. Some researchers have suggested that these children may have a motivational deficit. Instead, the problem may be that they require a larger-than-usual number of trials to develop proficiency in any skill.

TRIALS AND REWARDS

How many trials does it take for a child to learn something? Consider the problem of teaching daily toothbrushing to two children: Stella, described as "normal," and Cindy, described as "impulsive." At the beginning, neither child brushes her teeth on a routine basis. Both are offered an immediate, frequent, predictable payoff of 50 cents for brushing their teeth daily. Both children undertake the task with great enthusiasm.

For the following few weeks, during which reminders are offered and rewards are given, both children brush their teeth. However, when the reward is removed after a few weeks of success, Stella continues brushing fairly regularly; Cindy does not. Stella's behavior has gone from being motivated by an external reward to being internally directed—she has formed a habit. When she gets up each morning, entering the bathroom is a cue reminding her to brush her teeth. In contrast, Cindy's behavior on the day the reward is stopped reverts to her behavior on the day before the whole effort started: Entering the bathroom provides no clue, and she doesn't brush her teeth. Her parents then accuse her of purposeful misbehavior.

TRIALS AND REWARDS (CONTINUED)

In all likelihood, the real problem is that the number of trials was insufficient for Cindy to consistently demonstrate the behavior that she knows is desired. Developing a daily toothbrushing habit for Cindy appears to require many, many more successful trials before she will consistently brush her teeth on an independent basis. Some impulsive children may need as many as ten times the usual number of trials! Thus, if it takes a "normal" child 30 consistent days of brushing and reinforcement to develop the habit, it may take an impulsive child 300 days!

As parents, most of us equate learning and acquisition of a behavior with consistent demonstration of it. Though this may be the case for most children, it is not true for impulsive and inattentive children. We get them started on the right track by providing reinforcement, but by withdrawing that reinforcement just as they begin to demonstrate the behavior consistently, we fail to give them a sufficient number of successful experiences to gain mastery and independent control over the behavior. The impulsive and inattentive child learns what to do but does not do consistently what has been learned. Repetition through practice, patience, and, most importantly, success are critical if impulsive children are to gain better control over their behavior.

If your child is inattentive and impulsive, regardless of whether a clinical diagnosis has been given, the secret to success lies in your ability to make tasks more interesting and payoffs for completing them more valuable. This is not blackmail or extortion. In rewarding your child, you are not doing something immoral. You are simply recognizing that this very young human being requires more immediate, frequent, and predictable rewards, and more interesting and engaging activities. By providing structure and increased motivation, you can have a dramatic, positive impact on your child's school and home performance.

THE PERILS OF NEGATIVE REINFORCEMENT

Children with attentional and impulse problems may be "wired" to have more difficulty in working toward rewards and forming desirable habits, but this problem also has a learned component— what psychologists call *negative reinforcement*. Negative reinforcement is anything aversive or unpleasant that you do—from scolding, to yelling, to a denial of privileges—in an effort to motivate a specific behavior. In positive reinforcement, by contrast, you reward behavior that you wish to strengthen after it occurs.

The behavior of children with impulsivity, hyperactivity, or learning disabilities typically results in a large amount of negative reinforcement. Parents end up spending excessive time nagging and cajoling their child. The child ultimately complies with their requests not because of a wish to complete the task, which is seen as boring or difficult, but to gain freedom from the aversive consequence—the parents' angry attention.

For example, Sam finds getting dressed a repetitive, effortful, and uninteresting task. His mother might come into his room when he is supposed to be dressing and remind him to stop playing until he is dressed. When she walks out of the room, however, Sam loses focus and stops dressing. When she comes back, he still has not put on his socks and shoes. This time, his mother yells. As long as his mother watches him, Sam continues dressing, but the second she leaves, he resumes playing with his toys. Sam finds it difficult to get dressed during the school week, because there is no positive reinforcement, only negative. In addition, he may perceive going to school as an effortful, uninteresting, and repetitive behavior. During the week, Sam dresses only when supervised. He does not, however, have a problem getting dressed on the weekend, because doing so allows him to move on to something he wishes to do. In fact, on weekends, he is often dressed and playing outside before anyone else in the family is awake.

What has happened is that his mother has become a negative reinforcer. A better solution than scolding or yelling would be for her to reinforce him with praise or some other reward as long as he is dressing, and ignore him when he is not. She could sit in his room until Sam has completed dressing, or she could use a timer

THE PERILS OF NEGATIVE REINFORCEMENT (CONTINUED)

and send him off to school with a bag of clothes if he is not ready when the time is up.

Negative reinforcement is less effective, for everyone, than positive reinforcement. Impulsive and inattentive children get a double whammy because eight out of ten of their interactions with adults are negative. Too often, they begin to view the world as a place where you work to get rid of the things you don't want—parents' or teachers' angry attention—rather than a place where you strive to earn things you desire.

Impulsivity and Attentional Problems and Childhood

Parents frequently ask: At what age can a child's problems with impulsiveness and inattentiveness be accurately identified? Because early intervention—including refining and adjusting basic parenting skills—may go a long way toward reducing a wide variety of secondary problems that many impulsive children experience, this is a reasonable question. There are no hard and fast rules, but there are general patterns that many children with these problems display from an early age.

Infants

As parents have long known and research has now begun to support, some children are just plain "born difficult." Approximately 5 to 10 percent of infants appear to have difficult temperaments. They have negative moods and intense reactions to minor events, and they do not adapt easily to changes in their environment. They often have high activity levels, are restless in sleep, and are a challenge to bathe and diaper. They may be excessively irritable and difficult to comfort, and they may frequently appear to be unhappy. They may also be stubborn and picky eaters.

Temperamentally difficult infants are hard to parent effectively. Feeling guilty about their inability to calm or comfort them, new parents may become overly permissive or solicitous, which interferes with the infants' ability to develop a sense of self-control. Other parents may feel angry and consciously or unconsciously reject these difficult children. Unfortunately, just as temperamentally "easy" children are perceived as good and normal, temperamentally "difficult" children are perceived as bad and abnormal. These labels are not only inaccurate, but they contribute to impaired parent–child relationships. Many years ago, the renowned English child psychiatrist, Dr. D. W. Winicott, wrote that "most mothers are good enough for most children." Temperamentally difficult children are a challenge, even to the best and most competent parents.

Are all of these difficult infants destined for a life of school problems? No! However, these early signs of developmental difficulty do increase the risk of later childhood problems. As they mature, difficult infants as a group appear to experience more problems with learning, behavior, socialization, impulsivity, and inattention than others; some experience a combination of these problems. However, some infants pass through this period of difficulty and do not develop later childhood problems. Therefore, temperamentally difficult infants are best described as at risk for or susceptible to later difficulties, rather than destined for a lifetime of problems.

Preschoolers

"Normal" behavior in toddlers and preschoolers is difficult to define because what is considered normal or acceptable varies with the environment. Three-year-olds are typically curious and explore their environment readily; their behavior is vigorous, unrestrained, and playful. They have boundless energy, are enthusiastic and exuberant, and attend to new stimulation. Thus, it is often difficult to determine when a young child's pattern of behavior crosses the invisible line that suggests impulsiveness or inattentiveness, to a clinically significant degree.

A past trend in psychology suggested that any struggles that preschool children experience are temporary, reflecting stages the children may be passing through rather than the early signs of a lifetime problem. However, some problems are serious and frequent, and they provide important early warnings of greater-than-average risk. Ignoring these early signs, especially when they last more than 12 months and are not caused by other life difficulties, can result in the loss of valuable treatment time and cause a child's difficulties to be set in cement.

Joey is a typical ADHD preschooler. His parents describe him as difficult and frustrating. As an infant, he was often irritable, overactive, and moody. He had trouble fitting into routines, and his high-pitched crying frequently caused his parents to curtail family outings. At age 4 years, Joey rarely sits still. He is very impulsive, and his risk-taking behavior has resulted in numerous bumps and bruises and a half-dozen trips to the hospital emergency room. Joey is extremely aggressive around his brothers and friends. His aggression does not appear premeditated; rather, it is an impulsive response to frustration. He throws tantrums on a daily basis, and his parents have been asked to remove him from two preschools. Teachers report that Joey has shown little interest in preacademic activities. His problems are unlike any that his parents experienced with their other two children, and they are angry, frustrated, and unhappy, taking little pleasure in parenting him. Despite all of his struggles, Joey at times expresses awareness that his behavior is out of control and inappropriate. After one tantrum, he told his mother, "I'm sorry, but I just can't help it."

Early treatments for children such as Joey are critical. Involving impulsive children in structured preschool programs, teaching them acceptable social and problem-solving skills, improving the parenting skills practiced in the home, and providing early preacademic training can go a long way toward avoiding and minimizing the many secondary problems these children may develop.

IMPULSIVITY, INATTENTIVENESS, AND LANGUAGE

Research shows that toddlers and preschoolers with impulsive and inattentive behavior also appear to have a higher rate of weaknesses in the thinking block of language. In some studies, as many as 50 to 70 percent of young children with hyperactivity were experiencing problems in understanding or expressing ideas with language. These children also had a high rate of learning disabilities in school. It is unclear whether (a) their temperament contributes to delayed language or (b) delayed language contributes to their difficult temperament.

Before they learn to speak and begin to attach verbal labels to things, infants must touch, feel, and taste as a means of gaining information about the world. Once they learn to use language effectively, words replace touch. Impulsive toddlers often have difficulty making this transition. Typically, they continue to need to touch and feel things, possibly as a means of gaining sensory input from their world.

(continued)

IMPULSIVITY, INATTENTIVENESS, AND LANGUAGE (CONTINUED)

In long-term studies, Dr. Walter Mischel and colleagues* found a most interesting relationship between a young child's ability to use language skills during a wait for rewards, and later success as a teenager and young adult. In Dr. Mischel's study, a group of preschool children were given a snack and asked to wait a period of time before eating it. Some were able to wait, others ate the snack immediately. The children were then given a second snack and told that if they could delay eating it for a specific period of time, they would be rewarded with additional snacks. Again, some children immediately ate the snack and some did not. Dr. Mischel discovered that those who were able to wait talked to themselves and convinced themselves that waiting was worthwhile. In other words, they used language to delay gratification. The children who could not wait simply did not use these verbal strategies. He attempted to teach these children verbal strategies, but they could not implement them independently.

Both groups of children were followed as they grew up. As teenagers, the group that had been able to delay eating a snack was doing significantly better in many areas, including academic achievement, college entrance exams, and general behavior, than the group that could not wait. While the snack test is certainly not a clinical measure and would not be expected to be an accurate predictor of future behavior for each child, findings from this research are important. They help us understand the relationship among language, the ability to wait for rewards, and future success. Impulsive children, unfortunately, appear to have greater problems using the skills in the thinking block of language. One of their core problems becomes their inability to delay rewards. If they experience specific learning problems as well, academic tasks are likely to be more frustrating, to require more practice for proficiency, and, consequently, to result in a longer delay of gratification. This poor combination of experiences magnifies their problems.

---

*Mischel, W., Shoda. Y., & Rodriguez, M. L. (1989). Delay of gratification in children. Science, 224, 933–938.

Children in Primary School

School-age children must learn to deal with the rules, structure, and limits set by society at home, in the community, and in the classroom. Impulsive or immature behavior once accepted as cute is no longer tolerated. A child with impulsivity problems quickly attracts negative attention from the teacher and takes up a disproportionately large percentage of classroom time. If the behavior persists, the classroom is further disrupted, and eventually the child is labeled as a classroom problem.

Because neither the threat of punishment nor the promise of reward has an impact on an impulsive child's behavior, family life is often stressed and tense. Disruptive behavior is frustrating to parents and teachers, but it is important to understand that these are problems of difficult temperament and do not result from purposeful noncompliance.

Many impulsive children experience social difficulties, and these social problems often increase with age. Clinician and researcher Dr. Russell Barkley has found that nearly 80 percent of parents of children described as impulsive and hyperactive report that their children have serious problems playing with others;[2] a similar report is made by less than 10 percent of parents of normal children. Impulsive children's problems may stem from an occasional impulsive act rather than from continuous unacceptable behavior, but the fact is, a child doesn't have to hit someone more than once or twice before others keep their distance. An immediate need for gratification and an inability to stop and think create escalating negative attention and conflicts at home and in school. Inattentive children, by contrast, tend to experience social problems because of their persistent awkward behaviors, such as not knowing how to start conversations, join ongoing groups, or stay focused during games.

Their school performance has led some researchers to suggest that hyperactive and impulsive children are simply not as intelligent as other children. But the majority of children with school problems demonstrate competence and skill in a number of other areas, indicating that the problem is not a lack of intelligence. In some instances, problems with inattentiveness and impulsivity are linked with learning disabilities—for example, weaknesses in the skills of the processing blocks or, in some cases, weaknesses in the thinking blocks. The combination of these problems makes learning that much more difficult.

Adolescence and Beyond

Inattentive and impulsive children continue to evidence many of these same traits throughout their life span; almost as many teenagers experience inattention and impulsivity as do younger children. As your child reaches adolescence, it is important to keep in mind the stages of normal adolescent development. When teenagers assert their independence, conflict is normal. Parents of impulsive or inattentive teens need to guard themselves against unrealistic expectations. It is realistic to expect these teens to obtain satisfactory grades, exert effort at home and school, and adhere to society's and the family's rules. It is unrealistic, however, to expect them to behave perfectly or to act consistently on their knowledge.

Attention and impulse problems in early childhood, combined with school failure, greatly increase adolescents' risk for substance abuse, delinquency, and depression. However, not every impulsive and inattentive child experiences significant problems in adolescence or will grow up to become an impulsive and inattentive adult. Success in school, self-esteem, and a sense of emotional security are critical protective factors. It's important to provide a strong base of early, successful life experiences to build self-confidence, resilience, and coping skills.

Helping Your Inattentive or Impulsive Child

In this section, we will discuss suggestions for helping your child. In Chapters 4, 5, and 6 we provide additional advice, such as methods for behavior management and discipline, that can be used in the home and the school. These chapters are relevant because many children who have problems with inattention or impulsivity develop problems in the foundational blocks of emotions and behavior (Chapter 4), self-esteem (Chapter 5), and the learning environment (Chapter 6).

Help At Home

Medication If your child has received the diagnosis of ADHD, the question of medical intervention, usually with a psychostimulant drug such as Ritalin®, is likely to arise. The use of medications as an effective means to help children with ADHD problems is well established, and their use has increased dramatically in recent years. Studies involving thousands of children treated with stimulant medications have shown that medication is effective more than 70 percent of the time. However, a few children, such as those with motor tics or anxiety disorders, may not respond well to psychostimulants. They are sometimes treated with antidepressant drugs instead.

Parents may worry that the drugs will sedate the child, but this is not the case unless the dosage is too high. Instead, they help the child with ADHD to focus attention, think before acting, control impulses, and self-regulate their level of activity. The exact mechanism of their action is not well understood, but Ritalin and similar medications actually appear to stimulate parts of the child's brain that are understimulated. The drugs do not just mask the symptoms of ADHD, as some suggest, but act directly on a cause of the problem by adjusting a biochemical condition that interferes with the ability to control impulses and focus attention.

It is estimated that over two million children now receive stimulant medication for ADHD. There is no conclusive evidence that treatment leads to chemical dependence or addiction, or negatively affects a child's potential height or weight, or causes long-term personality change or other serious illnesses. The most common negative side effects, for some children, are loss of appetite, and/or irritability and insomnia as the medicine wears off. There is increasing recognition of the effectiveness of stimulant medications for adolescents and adults with ADHD.

We believe that the use of stimulant medications to treat children with ADHD is an integral part of the treatment plan for most children with this disorder. However, *pills won't substitute for skills.* A medicine may help improve a child's ability to remain on task and therefore be more available for learning, but it will not magically fix a poor classroom, defiant behavior or learning problems. Other interventions are necessary as well.

After a careful review of history and characteristics, if your child receives a diagnosis of ADHD we strongly urge you to learn everything you can about all kinds of treatments, including the use of medications. Consider reading *Hyperactivity: Why Won't My Child Pay Attention?* (John Wiley & Sons) by Sam Goldstein, PhD and Michael Goldstein, MD, and *Taking Charge of ADHD* (Guilford Press) by Russell Barkley, PhD.

Strategies for Intervention at Home To help your inattentive and impulsive child, you must be an effective manager. Your interactions with your child must be consistent and predictable; at the same time, you must recognize that changes *will* occur but they take time. Following are some essential guidelines for the help you can give at home.

- *Educate yourself.* You must understand how problems of poor impulse control and difficulty paying attention affect your child day in and day out. Knowledge is your best ally when neighbors, teachers, friends, and others offer their opinions and advice. Educate yourself on the subject: read, join groups, talk to educators.

- *Remember the difference between "I can't" and "I won't."* To cut down on frustration, you must understand the difference between problems of incompetence ("I can't"), which result from your child's inconsistent ability to control impulses and pay attention, and problems of noncompliance, which occur when your child doesn't wish to do as he or she is asked ("I won't"). Remember that your child's behavior often looks as though it stems from irresponsibility or bad attitudes, but it doesn't. We once heard a speaker say that one of the major problems of children with learning difficulties, especially ADHD, "is that they have one good day." From that time on, the adults in their world hold these children to this one-good-day standard and assume that, if they were only willing, they could behave that way again. But this is not the case. For children with learning difficulties, trying does not guarantee success.

- *Give explicit, positive directions.* When giving instructions to your child, explain briefly, but explicitly, *what to do* rather than *what not to do.* If you want to end some running inside the house, avoid long discussions about not skipping, dancing, hopping, and so on. Instead, be positive and precise: "*Walk* in the house." Similarly, say "Get your jacket and backpack together now" rather than "Don't dawdle." Given a brief, positive direction, your child will become more willing to respond. Do not give more than one or two instructions at a time. Break complex tasks into smaller parts, and guide each task separately. Ask your child to look at you and repeat the instructions. Give praise when they are followed correctly.

- *Offer rewards rather than punishments.* For children who have problems with attention or impulsivity, punishment is not usually effective in changing behavior. In contrast, by making tasks more interesting and giving more valuable payoffs for completing tasks, you increase the likelihood that your child will start and stick with assigned tasks. To reinforce the behavior you want, provide frequent, consistent, and meaningful rewards—not only praise but tangible rewards such as toys, treats, and privileges. If your child forgets homework because of impulsive or inattentive behavior, the most effective intervention is to provide strategies for remembering it next time.

- *Give immediate feedback.* Children with problems of inattention and impulsivity have trouble waiting for rewards and working toward long-term goals. They need *immediate* feedback. Reinforcements—rewards and punishments—must be provided consistently and as soon as possible following the desired or undesired behavior.

- *Use the procedure of "response cost."* The concept of response cost involves losing, for poor behavior, something that has been earned for good behavior. Impulsive and inattentive children work better when they start out with a full plate and must work to keep it full rather than when they start with an empty plate and must work to fill it. For example, when John was learning to speak in an "inside voice" at home, his mother placed twenty nickels in a jar each day. Every time John raised his voice, a nickel was removed from the jar. At the end of the day, John received the nickels that were remaining in the jar.

- *Take time for planning, and offer supervision and structure for your child.* Think ahead. Avoid placing your child in situations where there is a strong likelihood that any inattention or impulsivity will result in problems. Your child needs closer supervision and more structure than most of his or her peers. Changes in schedule are disturbing to impulsive children, so it's important to be as consistent as possible.

  — Set up a regular schedule for waking, chores, homework, playtime, TV time, dinner, and bedtime. Minimize the effects of changes in routine by announcing them ahead of time so that your child understands and can anticipate them. For example, before field trips, review the rules for behavior when riding a bus, visiting a museum, waiting in line, and so on.

  — Provide supervision during times of transition, such as leaving the house or doing errands, by staying physically close to your child. Alert the teacher to this strategy as well.

  — Consider using a timer for small chores and other activities, to give your child a sense of passing time.

  — Write down family rules, the consequences for breaking them, and the rewards for appropriate behavior, and post the notice in a prominent place. If a rule is broken, follow through with the agreed-on consequence every time. Consistency is key—for rewards and for punishments.

  — Try to keep your child's stimulation level as low as possible. Arrange for play with one child at a time, or involvement in one activity at a time. Cut down on unnecessary background noise, and remove unused toys, games, or books from the activity area.

  — Designate a special spot for academic work or quiet play. Remember, however, that unless the task is interesting or the payoff for completing the task is motivating, even the quiet spot may not keep your child on task.

- *Use and model a problem-solving approach.* If your child is short on attention and doesn't seem to know how to solve problems, the best thing you can do is *show* the solution—what psychologists call "modeling" the behavior. A problem-solving approach involves the following steps:

  — Define the problem. Make sure that everyone agrees on the definition.

  — Generate ideas to solve the problem. Try to come up with a minimum of three ideas; more is better.

  — Choose the best plan. Make sure everyone gets input and agrees.

  — Put the plan into action.

  — Evaluate whether the plan is effective.

Here's an example of problem solving in action. Susan, a fourth-grade student, had a hard time being ready when the bus came to pick her up for school each morning. Consequently, school mornings became extremely stressful. Susan and her mother sat down and defined the problem in writing: Susan was not prepared to leave for school in time to catch the bus. Together, they then made a list of possible solutions. Her mother started by suggesting that Susan might sleep in her clothes so that she would have one less thing to do each morning. The idea made them both laugh. They then wrote down the following ideas. On the evening before a school day, Susan could shower, select and lay out her clothes, and collect her books and backpack and place them by the door of her room. She could also get up 15 minutes earlier each morning. Susan and her mother decided that, with these activity changes, Susan would be ready for school each day. When they put the plan into action, Susan's mother also offered an incentive—a night out at the movies at the end of the week if the plan was successful. Over the next two weeks, Susan was ready to get on the bus on time. Not only did the plan solve the problem, but Susan and her mother enjoyed two movies together.

- *Count on the need for more trials for successful learning.* Remember, inattentive and impulsive children learn just as everyone else does, but they need more practice before they perform consistently. Most children master a particular behavior after just a few weeks of reinforcement; impulsive and inattentive children may require hundreds of days of reinforcement before a habit takes hold.

- *Praise appropriate behavior.* Instead of focusing on a child's annoying behavior, make a point of staying alert to the times when behavior is appropriate or tasks are completed. Make certain that your child understands what is expected and can do what is asked, then give praise when it is done correctly. When you must order corrections, be conscious of separating the child from the irritating or inappropriate behavior: "I like you, but I don't like you to track mud through the house."

- *Help your child develop self-control and verbal communication skills.* As your child matures, teach behavior management by allowing (a) choices within the limits you set, and (b) expression of wants and needs in acceptable and useful ways. Remember, children use their behavior to communicate a variety of emotions—anger, depression, a sense of hopelessness, or even a desire for revenge. If the behavior is the result of impulsiveness, your child may be trying to communicate something but has not thought out the response adequately. Michael, for instance, became very frustrated after spending an entire Saturday working on a big social studies project. He insisted on working alone, reminding his parents that the teacher had said that the children were to complete the project themselves. When his efforts to put all the information on a large chart ended in repeated failures, and his parents made him stop for dinner, he began crying and accused them of not giving him enough time to finish the work. Michael's mother asked him to think about what he had said. Although he needed to finish the report, he also needed to eat dinner. After a few minutes, Michael apologized for his outburst and asked for his parents' assistance in figuring out how to make the chart. Michael needed to step back, control his frustration, consider what he needed, and ask for help.

- *Act, don't yak!* Continually repeating messages, directions, and requests is often inefficient and ineffective. Say what you need to say, but say it *once*—briefly, clearly, completely, firmly, and calmly. Try to keep your voice quiet, slow, and deliberate. If your child persists in inappropriate behavior, follow through with a logical consequence (see Chapter 6) or redirection.

- *Stay positive and calm.* The emotional waves of the family are often carried on the tides of an inattentive or impulsive child's behavior. It is important to recognize the impact these tides may have on your family, to prevent problems when possible, and to deal with unavoidable outcomes in a positive way. Monitor yourself; when you have exceeded your tolerance level, your comments are likely to become frustrated, angry, and negative. Take five minutes of personal time to regain your equilibrium. When your child is getting more and more wound up emotionally, stay calm to encourage a wind-down. If your child says, "I wish you would just go away," try not to answer with, "I wish I could go away." Instead, stick to the main subject: "I'm just reminding you to get ready." Try not to argue with your child. In Chapter 4 we present several techniques for minimizing oppositional behavior and reducing family arguments.

Help at School

The most frequent complaints made or heard by parents of children with weaknesses of inattention and impulsivity are about school problems. A child whose behavior at home may be problematic will begin to feel helpless and frustrated at school. These problems affect all of learning, and if you're hearing near-constant complaints about your child's behavior, it's easy to feel discouraged.

If you persist, you *can* make a difference. But you must be willing to educate teachers about the problems of inattention and impulsivity, offer resources, and provide understanding and support. You must learn to advocate, negotiate, compromise when necessary, and recognize the kinds of interventions that are feasible for teachers to provide. Homework can be your chief intervention at home. Remember, no single set of guidelines and suggestions will work for every teacher with every hyperactive and impulsive child. Many different interventions might have to be tried before you hit on a combination that works.

The Right Classroom and the Right Teacher

As an advocate for your inattentive or impulsive child at school, you need a clear idea of what constitutes the best educational environment. Chapter 6 offers comprehensive general guidelines for selecting a classroom and teacher for your child. For now, consider the following:

- The teacher should be knowledgeable about inattention and impulsivity in childhood, and willing to acknowledge that these problems have a significant impact on your child in the classroom. The teacher should also understand the issue of incompetence ("I can't") versus noncompliance ("I won't") and learn to discriminate between the two problems.

- To be effective for inattentive and impulsive children, classrooms should be organized and structured, with separate desks, clear rules, and a predictable schedule.

- The teacher should prepare all the students for changes in routines and provide close supervision at regular transition times— when changing classes, going to lunch or recess, and ending the school day—as well as during special activities such as assemblies and field trips.

- Teacher feedback should be frequent and immediate. Brief, timely corrections should be employed when a child disrupts the work of others.

- Rewards should be given consistently and frequently. A response cost reinforcement program, using points or tokens, should be an integral part of the classroom. (See Chapter 4.)

- Academic materials should be matched to your child's abilities, and expectations should be adjusted to meet his or her skill level. Strategies that increase the ability to remain on task should be taught. Tasks should vary but generally be interesting. The best teacher for a child with attentional problems is one who is willing to intersperse high- and low-interest activities throughout the day rather than having students complete all work in the morning by performing one repetitive task after another.

- The teacher should accept responsibility for ongoing communication with you, ideally sending home a daily note summarizing your child's general behavior and the quality of work each day. (Weekly progress notes are generally enough for junior and senior high school students.)

- The teacher should be willing to help your child learn and practice organizational skills through the use of a written record of both daily and long-term assignments, and through a daily monitoring of whether the homework assignment is being taken home.

Teachers need to be able to find positive, good, and worthwhile characteristics in your child, and they should be aware of the potential for negatively reinforcing the impulsive and inattentive behaviors that are the reason for complaints. Most importantly, they should be able to see your child's strengths as well as weaknesses, and to value who your child is rather than what your child can do or produce at a given moment.

A careful review of the school history of impulsive and inattentive children often demonstrates that, in successful years, the children's teachers had the ability to understand and intervene effectively in a positive way. In less successful years, the teachers' use of punitive, often negative reinforcing methods for managing problems of incompetence resulted in things getting worse rather than better. This was clearly the case for Karen, a highly energetic second-grade student who experienced difficulties because of her erratic and impulsive behavior. As early as preschool, the notes about Karen's day were always negative:

- "Today, Karen took the goldfish out of the bowl. She said she just wanted to see what it felt like."
- "Today, Karen threw Jamie's doll over the fence."
- "Today, Karen grabbed the barrette from Lisa's hair. Please buy her a new barrette and bring it to school tomorrow."

Karen's mother had quickly become apprehensive about the summary she would receive when she picked up her daughter each day.

When Karen's second-grade teacher made contact with her mother, the first thing the teacher said was: "I really like Karen. She has some very creative ideas." Karen's mother sighed with relief, knowing from this comment that this teacher would help her daughter have a positive year in school.

Another crucial factor in your child's success at school is the teacher's ability to make modifications to manage problems. Sometimes, only reframing is needed, such as offering a reward for desired behavior rather than a penalty when the behavior doesn't take place. For instance, Andy's second-grade teacher did not like Andy's habit of tipping back and rocking in his chair during class instruction. To solve this problem, she taped down four Xs on the floor, one for each leg of his chair. Originally, she penalized Andy; whenever she looked over and a leg of the chair was off the ground, he was given a negative point. If he had 5 points, he would miss recess; if he had 10 points by noontime, he would have to stay in and eat his lunch in the classroom. However, she soon recognized that this approach wasn't working. She decided to reframe the situation and use a response cost reinforcement program instead. She started Andy off each

COMMUNICATING WITH YOUR CHILD'S TEACHER

When your child has problems with attentiveness and impulsivity, it's especially important for you to work closely with your child's teacher so that you know what's going on in the classroom. To make this easier, Diana L. McDonald developed the form letter shown below, for use by parents and teachers. The child brings the letter to the teacher, who fills it in and signs it before giving it to the child to return to the parents.

Date _____

To: ___(teacher's name)___   From: ___(parent's name)___

Student: _____   Regarding: _____

WHAT HAVE BEEN YOUR THOUGHTS?   Y = yes   N = no

Has ___(child's name)___ been: _____

completing work in class	_____	turning in homework	_____
exhibiting a positive attitude	_____	behaving appropriately	_____
on time	_____	cooperating, taking turns	_____
following procedures	_____	staying on task	_____
working hard without		asking questions when	
complaints	_____	necessary	_____
actively participating	_____	getting along with peers	_____
speaking only when		sitting at desk when	
appropriate	_____	required	_____

Do you think we need to meet?   Yes   No

If Yes, when would be convenient for you? Time(s): _____ Date(s): _____

Are there any upcoming special assignments and/or events that I should be aware of?

Yes/No: _____

_____

Have you witnessed any improvements? If so, in what areas? Yes/No: _____

_____

Do you have specific concerns? Yes/No: _____

_____

Any additional comments/thoughts or things we should be doing at home?

Yes/No _____

_____

_____

Thanks.

     Teacher's Signature _____

morning with a fixed number of points that he would work to keep. If she saw that a leg of the chair was off the ground, he would lose a point; he would earn a point each time she looked over and his chair was standing properly. Andy could trade the remaining points for free time, extra time on the computer, or skipping an evening's homework assignment. Such reframing reinforced the desired behavior, and Andy gained from the intervention, rather than feeling punished and deprived.

Homework and the Child with Attentional Weaknesses

As a parent of a child with attentional or impulsivity problems, you've probably heard the panicky cry: "Mom, Dad—I lost my homework." And your child's teacher may tell you that completed homework hasn't been turned in, or that pencils, notebooks, and important papers get lost within your child's desk, which is often messy. Not surprisingly, researchers have verified that children with attentional and impulsivity problems tend to misplace homework; lose books, pencils, and other school supplies; and have trouble organizing and even locating their work both at home and in school. In Chapter 6, we deal with homework strategies in some detail, and offer many interventions. Meanwhile, here are some basics:

- Urge your child's teacher to try a cooperative homework "buddy" or "team" approach. The partners or team members call to remind one another of homework assignments or to help if needed. Some schools already encourage this approach, and student teams are awarded prizes for improvements in the rate of homework turned in on time.

- Use positive reinforcements with immediate consequences; written contracts that specify consequences may also be of help. (See Chapter 4 for a model contract.)

- Use assignment folders with inside pockets—one pocket for work to be done, the other for work that is finished and ready to be handed in. Separate color-coded folders, daily homework planners, and checklists of which books and files need to be brought home and back to school each day are also helpful.

- Designate one part of your home as the homework spot, and keep all supplies there.

IF YOUR CHILD IS A CHIP OFF THE OLD BLOCK . . .

As you have read this chapter, you may have felt that many of the same issues affected your own childhood and are even present in your adult life today. This would not be surprising; problems with inattention and impulsivity are often hereditary. If you continue to experience these types of problems as an adult, getting help for yourself is a critical step in helping your child. Long-term studies clearly show that parents' availability, competence, and persistence are key factors in predicting good life outcomes for their children. By taking care of your problems, you will be easing your child's problems.

Cutbacks in educational funding and the widespread problem of overcrowded classroom may make some of these guidelines difficult to attain. Don't give up. Good classroom situations are built on good attitudes and a trusting, respectful relationship between you and your child's teachers. When parents and teachers join the educational journey together, good things happen—even when there are limited resources and crowded classrooms. However, should you have to swim against the tide to obtain services you feel are needed for your child, it is best to be a calm and knowledgeable advocate. In Chapter 6, we offer an outline of children's educational rights. It is essential for you to understand this information, especially if you feel that your child is not being provided with appropriate services.

Chapter 4

Emotions and Behavior

Reducing the Impact of Anxiety, Depression, and Behavior Problems on Your Child's School Performance

A child who struggles with school performance is likely to experience some type of emotional or behavioral problem during the school years.

In this chapter, we focus on the symptoms of oppositional behavior and conduct disorder, and on anxiety and depression in children—the main problems that affect the building block of emotional and behavioral skills. It is important for you to be aware of the symptoms of these problems because they frequently occur with underachievement in school, and in some cases can be its primary cause. Because self-esteem is such a large part of good mental health and is essential for learning, we discuss it in detail in Chapter 5.

Many children who have problems at school also experience emotional or behavioral problems, so it's natural to ask whether the emotional problems or the academic difficulties came first. As with the proverbial chicken and egg, a relationship can exist in both directions. When you evaluate the ten characteristics related to your child's behavior and emotions, listed on page 62, ask yourself: Have problems been slowly escalating or has the situation remained fairly steady throughout your child's school life?

In recent years, research has verified what many parents have long known: Children come into the world with a dominant temperament—an inborn disposition, habitual mood, or character—that influences their ability to cope with stress. For example, from a very young age, one child may see the world through mud-colored glasses, be unhappy and easily frustrated, and wake up most days with a scowl rather than a smile. As a matter of temperament, this child may focus almost exclusively on the downside of life, and any school problems encountered become a part of this pattern. Another child may be quite happy and may enjoy school until academic problems arise. The child may then become moody, complain of illness on school days, and worry about being held back and losing all the classmate-friends. Both children have emotional difficulties. Yet the second child's emotional problems appear to be a consequence of academic struggles, whereas unhappiness appears to be a way of life for the first child. This is an important distinction because the interventions that work well for one may not be effective for the other.

Emotional distress unrelated to temperament or academic challenges can also lead to school difficulties. A depressed or unhappy child is likely to have little motivation to work hard in school. A worried, anxious child may not focus on academics. An angry child will not invest very much time in completing schoolwork. Children may become distressed for a variety of reasons—illness or divorce in the family, a move to a new neighborhood or school, news coverage of a natural disaster—and these upsets can cause downturns in behavior and school performance. When such events happen, parents should make a point of talking with their child's teacher. With an understanding of what is going on, school personnel can offer support. When they receive empathy and support from their parents and teachers, children usually rebound rather rapidly. If the problems persist over a long period, or if the child does not receive adequate support, the results can be longer-lasting changes in school performance and serious behavioral or emotional difficulties. In other words, what's important is not whether the emotional problems or changes are due to a specific event, but whether they become chronic.

A Closer Look at Your Child's Emotions and Behavior

In the assessment in Chapter 2, we asked you to consider whether your child is generally defiant or unhappy. Now it's time to examine these issues in greater detail. As you review the list of characteristics on page 62 to determine whether your child's emotional and behavioral problems represent a core reason for difficulties in school, think back over the school

Emotions and Behavior	Yes	No
1. Cries frequently	_____	_____
2. Becomes angry quickly	_____	_____
3. Complains of boredom	_____	_____
4. Has frequent temper outbursts and behaves unpredictably	_____	_____
5. Changes moods quickly	_____	_____
6. Often seems unhappy	_____	_____
7. Has difficulty falling asleep at night or complains of fears	_____	_____
8. Worries excessively		
9. Has a low energy level	_____	_____
10. Expresses suicidal thought	_____	_____

career to date. If your child functioned well in school until a specific event or stressful episode occurred, it's likely that, with enough support and understanding, the subsequent changes in behavior or school performance will not be permanent. We will discuss shorter-term problems and offer suggestions for solutions, but our primary focus in this chapter is problems with or changes in a child's emotional and behavioral coping skills that reflect a long-term pattern (lasting more than eight weeks) and have a significant impact on his or her daily life.

The first five characteristics in the chart on this page have to do with anger and disruptive behavior; the rest involve issues that reflect anxiety, depression, or general unhappiness—what is referred to as emotional distress. Both disruptive behavior and emotional distress can affect your child's school performance, so if you checked "Yes" for a number of these characteristics, you'll want to read this chapter carefully.

As you do so, you may find yourself saying, "But my child isn't clinically depressed; he's just got a gloomy outlook," or "She's anxious, but I don't think she needs psychiatric help." Similarly, you may feel that your child's main problem is too much "rebelliousness" or "a bad attitude" rather than a diagnosable emotional or behavioral problem. However, the fact that the problem may not be severe enough to rate a formal clinical diagnosis doesn't mean you shouldn't intervene! Even children with only a few symptoms of depression or anxiety will benefit from help or assistance, and *all* children benefit from consistent parenting and discipline. Nor should you automatically assume that your child's behavioral or emotional problems are caused exclusively by academic difficulties and thus can safely be ignored while you focus on helping with learning difficulties.

Remember, you know your child best. If you find his or her behavior worrisome, don't be too quick to dismiss your concerns. Research has consistently demonstrated that parents are accurate reporters of their children's behavior and are intuitively aware when their children are struggling.

Oppositional Behavior Problems

All children misbehave occasionally. This is called *oppositional* behavior, and it goes hand in hand with developing independence. But most parents recognize when a child's defiant behavior is not the normal and predictable assertion of independence but arises instead from resentment, anger, or unhappiness. Mental health professionals note that excessively oppositional children are very negative and provocative in their behavior, and at times are spiteful or vindictive. They lose their temper frequently and without good reason, argue with adults, appear angry and resentful, and are easily irritated. They often blame others for their mistakes, defy rules, deliberately annoy other people, and use obscene language. Some of them exhibit what has been called passive aggressive behavior, agreeing to comply with rules, but never following through.

Oppositional behavior and delinquent behavior are not the same. Although their attitudes may be negative and even hostile, children with oppositional problems tend to direct their negative behaviors toward adults and children with whom they interact on a regular basis both at home and at school. Delinquent children, by contrast, behave badly toward unfamiliar adults and children as well as their families, and they often do so in a public setting.

More often than not, when children have school problems, they also have emotional or behavioral problems at home. However, they are much more likely to "let it all hang out" at home, where they feel comfortable, rather than at school, where a teacher might think badly of them. When called by the school to discuss their child's academic problems, parents may come away with the distinct impression that the conference was about two entirely different children: the well-behaved, timid, and cooperative student the teacher sees at school, and the defiant, angry, and temperamental child the parents see at home. This is especially true of anxious children, most of whom would never consider misbehaving in school; at home, however, their anxiety and anger translate into negative behavior. When children do act out in school, they have usually crossed a line emotionally and are displaying a willingness to let the world see their problems and their unhappiness. A significant number appear to be at great risk for developing outright delinquent behaviors.

It is not clear why children become excessively oppositional. Some research suggests that defiant behavior is caused or encouraged by environmental factors. However, many oppositional youngsters appear to be looking for a fight almost from the moment of birth. Researchers report that some adopted children, even though they live with calm and accommodating adoptive parents in a supportive environment, behave in an oppositional manner that closely resembles the behavior of their birth parents.

The fact is, some children seem to come into the world "wired" to be oppositional. As infants, they are fussy and difficult to comfort, and their "terrible two" stages are truly terrible, with every frustration leading to a tantrum. As they get older, they continue to be quick to anger and do not seem to care about the feelings of others. When they are defiant at school, it is clear that they brought their oppositionality to school with them. Other children seem to be easygoing until they begin to have school problems; at that point, they become angry, negative, deliberately provocative, and oppositional at home as well as at school. After years of being calm and easy to please, they suddenly seem to be "spoiling for a fight."

It is not surprising that many children who struggle at school frequently develop defiant patterns of behavior. Because their academic performance does not meet the expectations of the adults in their world, they regularly receive huge doses of criticism. Eventually, this constant flow of negative feedback leads to frustration, and they start pushing back in retaliation. Parents may come to believe that these children are merely being disobedient and that this disobedience is the cause rather than the consequence of school problems. Closer scrutiny frequently reveals, however, that the behavior has followed rather than preceded poor school performance.

Helping Your Child with Oppositional Behaviors

If your child is oppositional, it is important to determine whether the oppositionality preceded or followed school problems. If it followed the appearance of school problems, it's wise to focus your efforts on improving your child's ability to succeed at school. (See Chapter 2 for information on the specific chapters in this book that address your child's individual learning weaknesses.) If the oppositional behavior preceded the school problems, your best move is to develop a set of parenting strategies to prevent the oppositional behavior from escalating.

Children usually misbehave for one of four reasons: (a) attention, (b) revenge, (c) control, or (d) as a sign of giving up. Children with school problems often become frustrated and feel the need to express one or more of these purposes through their behavior.

You need to recognize that, besides outright disobedience, behaviors such as quitting, avoiding, clowning, and denying, are all forms of oppositionality. These behaviors are problematic, but they are more likely to be the result of children's losing the battle to meet adult expectations for academic success than the primary causes of poor school performance. They are signs of low self-esteem. (In Chapter 5, we will review a variety of long-term strategies to deal with these behaviors and build self-esteem.)

Annoying though it may be, your child's behavior results from a parent–child interaction and can be controlled by a variety of means. It is not set in stone. Because oppositional behavior is often (but not always) within your child's control, your most effective response is likely to be a consistent but fair program of intervention.

Time out, the 1-2-3 Magic procedure, and the Broken Record technique are three easy, practical, and effective tactics for dealing with day-to-day oppositional behavior.

Time Out Assigning a "time out" allows you to respond to your child's negative or inappropriate behavior without anger, pain, or humiliation. Time out involves isolating your child for a few minutes immediately following a misbehavior. It requires no special equipment: a chair in the dining room, your child's bedroom, the back stairs, or an unoccupied corner will all serve nicely as time-out areas. The time-out area should contain no diversions or interesting toys; they would defeat the purpose of stopping *all* reinforcements, positive or negative, and allowing the child to calm down and think.

Time out isn't a punishment and shouldn't be presented that way. Instead, explain to your child that time out is "quiet time," a few minutes in which to think about an unacceptable behavior and come up with good ideas about how to handle things the next time. After the time out, which should last only a few minutes, the child may resume normal activities.

In *S.O.S. Help for Parents,*[1] Lynn Clark offers parents an extensive set of ideas and strategies for using time out. He notes that time out has many advantages: it quickly weakens many types of bad behaviors; it is easy for parents to learn and use; it gives parents a rational and nonaggressive means of dealing with childhood problems; it is usually not time-consuming; and it can also be adapted for use with children of different ages.

1-2-3 Magic   Time out is an effective way of dealing with oppositional behavior because it provides you and your child with an opportunity to cool off. However, it is something of an all-or-nothing approach: the child is or is not sent to time out. And if time out is used for every little infraction, the procedure will lose its effectiveness and you will spend your entire day supervising it. On the other hand, if you do not intervene early in an oppositional cycle, it is only a matter of time before a time out will be necessary. So what can you do when you see trouble brewing but your child has not actually done anything to merit time out—yet? The most effective procedure is to deliver a verbal warning before declaring a time out, and that is where the 1-2-3 Magic,[2] an adaptation of time out developed by Dr. Tom Phelan, comes in.

The 1-2-3 Magic intervention doesn't involve nagging or threats, and it helps you avoid power struggles or arguments with your child. Instead, you warn that you do not approve of a particular behavior, you tell what you would like done instead, and you state the consequences if your child does not do as you request.

The rules and the consequences are consistent. When bad behavior is brewing, you hold up one finger, then tell your child, "That's one." You state what you want stopped and what should be done instead. If the behavior does not stop within a few seconds, you say, "That's two." If the behavior still persists, you say, "That's three" and send the child to time out.

This technique works very well with children who are oppositional. One mother told us that she kept trying to bargain with her son, promising that if he would just start listening, she in turn would stop yelling at him. The deal never worked. She then implemented the 1-2-3 Magic system and found that not only did her son start to listen, but she no longer needed to resort to yelling to get his attention.

The Broken Record Technique   Sometimes a child persists in trying to start an argument. It is important to realize that once you engage in an argument with your child, you have already lost control of the situation. Each side will angrily reiterate its position, the problem will escalate, and nothing will be gained. Power struggles are ineffective for resolving or reducing conflicts. Educator Rick Lavoie[3] describes a very simple and effective strategy, called the Broken Record Technique, for dealing with argumentative children. It works like this: Each time the child objects to your request, you softly, firmly, and calmly repeat the rule or policy, as many times as needed, without engaging in discussion.

- Mary is eating a snack in the living room, which is against the family rules. Mary's mother asks her not to eat in the living room. Mary responds: "But I want to eat in here." Her mother repeats: "We do not eat in the living room." Mary replies: "But Tom ate some pizza in here yesterday." Her mother repeats: "We do not eat in the living room." At his point, Mary, realizing her mother is not going to alter her position or engage in debate, carries her snack into the kitchen.

- Jim says he is ready for school. He is dressed in a T-shirt and ripped gym shorts. His dad states: "You cannot go to school wearing those shorts." Jim replies: "Why not? All the other kids wear clothes like this." His dad reiterates: "You cannot go to school wearing those shorts." Jim retorts: "What's wrong with these shorts anyway?" Once again, his dad repeats his statement. Jim returns to his room and changes into another pair of pants.

- Danny wants a piece of candy before dinner. His mother states: "You may have a piece *after* dinner." He angrily replies, "I want candy now," and begins to cry. His mother repeats: "You may have a piece of candy *after* dinner." Danny threatens: "Then I just won't eat dinner." His mother repeats her statement and then walks away. Danny whines for a minute more, then resumes playing with his toys.

In these three situations, the parent remained in control and calmly repeated the request or the house rule without engaging in an argument. In most instances, you will not need to repeat your request more than three times before you child stops raising objections and complies with your wishes without an upsetting and unfruitful argument. The Broken Record Technique is particularly effective in situations that you know are nonnegotiable.

Conduct Disorder

Mental health professionals reserve a diagnosis of *conduct disorder* for children who seriously and persistently ignore the rules of daily living.

Children with conduct problems take oppositional behavior one step beyond tolerance: they violate major rules, infringing on the basic rights of others. Children with conduct problems are often aggressive, cruel, violent, and destructive of property. As adolescents, they are truants and get involved in substance abuse and sexual misconduct. A conduct disorder is much more serious than simple oppositional behavior and is often accompanied by significant home problems.

Most children with conduct disorder do poorly in school. A frequent overlap of conduct difficulties and school problems should not be surprising. A child who is aggressive or destructive in school has concerns other than schoolwork, and a child who is frustrated with school problems may express that frustration quite negatively. (Although problems with impulse control and hyperactivity may influence conduct disorder, these are separate childhood problems having different causes and courses of development. See Chapter 3 for an in-depth discussion of these problems.)

Jason presented a typical case of conduct disorder. He had long been defiant and was diagnosed with conduct disorder in second grade. By third grade, his major problems were chronic stealing and lying. Parents of other students frequently called the school to complain that Jason had taken their child's lunch money or had stolen a pencil box or bracelet. His teachers had to check his backpack, lunch box, and pockets each day to ensure that he was not departing with possessions taken from his classmates. He would even take things that had little value, such as the door jambs from the school's classrooms. When caught with the goods, Jason would deny that he had taken them and would fabricate stories that blamed someone else. While he was in high school, he was arrested several times for stealing cars. He was eventually assigned to a residential treatment center surrounded by a high, barbed-wire fence. Years earlier, Jason's first-grade teacher had commented: "No matter what we do, I think this child is going to wind up in jail."

Many youngsters like Jason, who qualify for the diagnosis of conduct disorder and are considered juvenile delinquents by their parents and the community, continue to engage in antisocial behavior and wind up in correctional facilities. They may have poor interpersonal relationships and suffer from a variety of psychiatric problems, including alcoholism, drug abuse, and mood disorders. However, it's important to recognize that many children who are identified as having conduct disorders also settle down in their adult years and become reasonably stable and productive citizens.

The children at the greatest risk for problems in adult life are those who engage in violent and aggressive behaviors at an early age. Children who grow up in families with histories of antisocial behavior, alcoholism, or violence are also at great risk for continuing problems. However, youngsters whose misbehavior runs to relatively minor infractions, such as truancy, appear to have a much better chance of outgrowing their difficulties.

The best ally of a child who has a conduct disorder is a parent who is patient and persistent, who keeps the lines of communication open, and who develops strategies to resolve conflicts. The general use of logical consequences (discussed in Chapter 6) and penalty and reward systems, including contracts and a token economy (discussed below), are examples of conflict-resolving strategies.

Contracts

A contract is an agreement between two parties to behave in certain specified ways or to perform certain specified services. Drawing up a contract between parent and child or teacher and child is an effective method for reinforcing desired behavior, particularly with younger children. The contract need not be elaborate or complex; all that is needed is a simple, straightforward document encompassing the desired behavior, some ways of helping the child achieve it, what the specific agreement is, and a section on rewards and consequences. Because both the child and the parent or teacher sign it, there is mutual commitment to the promises or the project. And because the agreement is spelled out, the consequences and rewards are very clear, which short-circuits arguments about what has been agreed to. A sample parent–child contract is given on page 70.

Some children find it helpful to specify ways for them to get help in abiding by the agreement, adding clauses like "I will help myself by. . ." or "My dad will help me by. . . . " This kind of assistance teaches advance planning and lets children know that they are not alone in trying to change their behavior.

Token Economy

Another effective means of establishing motivated behavior and teaching self-discipline is to use a token economy—essentially, a contract between you and your child stating that certain behavior will earn certain rewards and/or privileges. In drawing up this contract, you are not doing something immoral, or endorsing blackmail or extortion. You are simply recognizing that, in order to learn self-discipline, your child requires frequent and predictable feedback on his or her behavior.

Dr. Harvey Parker, a respected expert in the field of parent training, offers the following outline for developing a token economy at home.[4] For

---

CONTRACT

Date _____

This contract is an agreement between _____JOHN_____

and _____DAD_____.

_____JOHN_____ will __FINISH HIS HOMEWORK EVERY DAY__

___THIS WEEK___.

If the above is performed promptly,

_____DAD_____ will __TAKE JOHN TO RACE GO-KARTS ON__

SATURDAY AFTERNOON.

If the above is not performed,

_____JOHN_____ will __FORFEIT THE EVENINGS' TV TIME__.

Signed by _____ and _____
          JOHN   DAD

---

children with school problems, the introduction of a home token economy often is helpful in developing a routine related to schoolwork and in managing behavior at home.

To start, examine your child's behaviors and decide which are acceptable to you and which are not. Put these expectations down in writing so that there is a clear understanding of what you expect. Keep in mind, however, that clear expectations alone do not produce changes in behavior. Many children know what their parents expect of them, but misbehave anyway. What's needed is motivation.

With a token reward system, you motivate your child to behave appropriately by offering incentives. Your child is given the opportunity to earn tokens that can be exchanged for rewards and privileges. Young children (below age 7 years) may be given tokens such as poker chips, stickers, play money, and so on, for positive behavior. Older children and teenagers may be awarded tokens in the form of points. The child accumulates tokens or points and then exchanges them for rewards or privileges. The child also loses tokens for unacceptable behavior.

To set up the token economy program, you must construct a behavior chart with sections headed Start Behaviors (behaviors you want to encourage), Stop Behaviors (behaviors you want to discourage), Rewards and Privileges, and Tokens Remaining. The chart should be easy to copy or reproduce daily. An easily erasable board might work best.

Step 1. Select Start Behaviors Decide on seven to nine behaviors you want to encourage in your child, and list them in the Start Behaviors section of the chart. (For children ages 6 to 8 years, limit your selection to four or five behaviors.) Be sure to include only observable and specific behaviors you are certain your child is capable of doing if properly motivated. Avoid listing any behavior that is vague, such as "showing good attitude," "being cooperative," "being friendly." Stick with concrete things, such as "putting play clothes away" or "helping with dishes." For Start Behaviors that can occur several times a day, like brushing teeth, or saying " Please" and "Thank you," record in brackets the maximum number of times you will give a reward for that behavior each day.

Next, assign a token value (between 1 and 5 tokens) to each entry in the Start Behaviors section. To be effective, token values should be high enough to encourage your child to display a behavior. Assign the higher token values to behaviors that are more difficult or are more important to you.

Include an additional line in the Start Behaviors section for Extra Credit. Let your child earn extra tokens by displaying a behavior that is not specifically listed as a Start Behavior, but is worth encouraging and rewarding.

Step 2. Select Stop Behaviors Next, select four to six behaviors for the Stop Behaviors section of the chart. (For children ages 6 to 8 years, limit the list to three or four behaviors.) As with the Start Behaviors, include only those behaviors you are certain your child is capable of stopping if properly motivated. Avoid listing behaviors that are annoying but vague, such as "being moody," "being lazy," "acting immature." List only specific behaviors: "yelling at brother" or "cursing."

Next, assign a token value (between 5 and 25 tokens) to each entry in the Stop Behaviors section. To be effective, a fine should be costly enough to deter the child from displaying the behavior. Behaviors you would like to see stopped most urgently should have the highest fine. When a Stop Behavior occurs, immediately record the inappropriate behavior on the chart, but do not argue with the child about the behavior.

Include an additional line for Extra Penalty in the Stop Behavior section. Your child can lose tokens by displaying a behavior that is not specifically listed as a stop behavior but is extremely inappropriate and, therefore, worthy of penalty.

Step 3. Select Rewards and Privileges   Select rewards and privileges that are appropriate and will motivate your child. Because children differ widely in the activities they enjoy, it is important to involve your child in the selection of rewards and privileges.

List at least seven to ten rewards and privileges on the behavior chart. Several of them will be activities that your child may previously have been allowed to do, but will now have to earn, such as television time, staying up past a certain hour, use of the telephone, and so on.

As a general rule, the list should contain rewards and privileges that the child can exchange for tokens fairly often, perhaps one or more times per day. Avoid listing too many privileges that can be used only once a week or once a month. For example, it might be better to offer a reward such as "½ hour of television time," which can be given one or more times a day, rather than "a trip to the movies on Saturday afternoon." When deciding which rewards and privileges to list, consider their practicality based on time, expense, and overall well-being of your child.

Next, assign a token value to each of the items in the Rewards and Privileges section. Determining the value of each item can be tricky. Costs should be low enough to give your child an opportunity to earn one or more rewards and privileges each day. Don't be reluctant to allow frequent opportunities to exchange tokens for rewards and privileges. If your child is earning a lot of tokens, it is not a sign that you have made the terms too easy. Rather, it is usually a sign that the program is working well.

Step 4. Explain the Program to Your Child   Introduce the token economy program to your child in a positive manner. Read through the Start Behaviors and Stop Behaviors you have selected, explain each one, and briefly discuss why you put it on the list. Then explain each behavior's reward value (or fine) in tokens. If you need to, modify the list to reflect your child's ideas as to what will motivate more positive behavior.

Set up a convenient time each day to review the child's performance for that day and to tabulate the tokens earned, lost, spent, and remaining. Record the final payment or penalty.

Older children and teens will understand the concept quickly. Some may object at first to the idea of having to earn tokens for privileges, but most will agree to try out the program. Encourage your child to cooperate; avoid any threatening or arguing about the merits of the program. Simply explain the features of the chart in a firm and positive way.

Some children, particularly those with attentional or impulsivity problems, do best when they are started out with a supply of tokens that they try to retain and add to. This type of system is referred to as a response cost program. You might want to start these children out with enough tokens to trade in for some small but desirable reward, to give an incentive to keep trying.

Anxiety Disorders

Anxiety is a mix of fear, dread, apprehension, and worry that arises in response to a perceived danger. When we feel threatened, our whole body responds, which accounts for the racing heart, "butterflies" in the stomach, pounding headache, and queasy bowels that can accompany anxiety. Anxiety is a vestige of the biological "fight or flight" response that kept our primitive ancestors alert to such dangers as fire and animal attack. It is healthy when it prompts an appropriate response to a threatening situation, but it is a problem when it interferes with such a response.

Anxiety disorders are the most prevalent form of psychiatric illness in both children and adults. Children with serious anxiety problems typically have more than the usual number of physical complaints, are self-conscious, have an almost bottomless need for reassurance, and constantly

THE SIGNS OF SERIOUS BEHAVIORAL PROBLEMS IN CHILDREN

When it comes to your child's behavior, trust your judgment. If your gut tells you that major trouble is ahead, do not be dissuaded from seeking help and setting up a long-term plan to keep the trouble from happening. If your child is under the age of 10 years and experiences significant difficulty with conduct—for instance, displaying serious aggressiveness, bullying or intimidating peers, being deliberately cruel to animals, stealing or lying repeatedly, setting fires, habitually and seriously violating rules, playing truant, running away, or staying out all night—seek professional help. Your pediatrician or school counselor should be able to provide referrals to competent and experienced mental health professionals.

feel tense or unable to relax. School may be only one area of worry. They may also worry about themselves, their family, their friends, and the future. Many of these children demonstrate signs of anxiety well before their school careers begin. The stress of school may exacerbate this disorder.

Anxiety disorders can take many forms—tension, worry, fear, and apprehension—and can affect school performance. *However, problems with anxiety in childhood are usually not the result of school failure.* Researchers suspect that some people are born with a vulnerability to anxiety, and some children seem to be "born worriers."

In children, anxiety disorders are generally one of four types: (a) separation anxiety, (b) generalized anxiety, (c) phobia, and (d) obsessive-compulsive disorder. We will discuss these disorders briefly and then offer some strategies for dealing with them.

Separation Anxiety Disorder

Separation anxiety—fearfulness at being separated from a person, place, or object that represents safety—is the most common anxiety disorder. Children with separation anxiety often experience intense feelings of tension, fear, and apprehension when they are about to be separated from the person with whom they are most closely attached—usually a parent, and particularly the mother. Fear of separation from parents occurs as a normal part of development in babies between the ages of 8 and 15 months. These young children are expected to protest separation with tears and other signs of distress. Some children, however, seem to never outgrow this normal developmental stage.

Children who suffer from separation anxiety may not have to be actually separated from a parent to become anxious. Afraid of being left alone even at home, some children shadow their parents from room to room. Jamie's behavior is typical of children with separation anxiety. As a toddler, she almost literally would not let her mother out of her sight. She insisted that her mother accompany her to the bathroom and refused to leave her to play with other children. Although Jamie is now of kindergarten age, her parents still permit her to sleep in their bed at night, to avoid late-night tears. Her parents, especially her mother, admit that they feel suffocated, but they don't know how to help Jamie become more independent and are worried about her reaction to starting school.

They are right to be concerned. Though children can and do display separation anxiety about visiting friends or relatives, or going to camp, the most common problem is refusal to go to school. In some children, this problem reaches epic proportions; they cry, scream, and throw long tantrums at the prospect of separation, and they become tense and fearful if they are actually forced to leave their parents. They may even refuse to get on—or off—the school bus. They often worry that something may befall their parents in their absence. Most children overcome problems related to separation anxiety by first grade.

In many of the children who suffer this disorder acutely, separation anxiety seems to reflect a biologically based vulnerability that increases the risk of later childhood anxiety problems. For others, however, separation anxiety seems to be the consequence of an acute, major life change such as a move, a death in the family, an ill or absent parent, or a physical illness.

For children whose separation anxiety seems to have been triggered by such sudden life changes, the solution is often extra reassurance and time spent with loving, familiar adults. In cases of longer-term separation anxiety, it's important for parents to recognize that actions such as refusing to attend school are not signs of willful misbehavior but are caused by a child's fears. Parents need to educate themselves about anxiety and to model effective behavior for dealing with anxiety themselves so that their children can learn how to cope. Children who suffer with separation anxiety may end up with low self-esteem, feeling that they are letting their parents down. Chapter Five offers many suggestions for helping children learn to feel confident and competent in this regard.

Generalized Anxiety Disorder

Children with generalized anxiety disorder are born worriers. They worry about anything and everything, harboring feelings of guilt about past events and anticipating problems about future events. To parents, children with generalized anxiety appear tense and anxious. They fidget nervously and often complain of physical ailments that have no demonstrable physical cause—stomachaches, headaches, and shortness of breath. Teachers often describe these children as inattentive, though a discussion with the children often reveals that the problem is anxiety. An anxious child begins looking around the classroom; starts to worry that everyone else is doing better, more acceptable work; becomes obsessed with worry; and then loses track of the task at hand and thus appears inattentive. As with separation anxiety, there appears to be an underlying biological risk for this problem.

Phobic Disorders

A phobia is a variety of fear. However, phobias differ from normal fears in that they are more intense and more distressing, and they often persist over long periods of time. Phobias are the most common anxiety problem in the general community. Fears of heights, closed spaces, air travel, and certain animals and insects are the most common.

As a normal part of development, children often experience a variety of short-lived fears—of animals, the dark, and imaginary creatures such as ghosts and monsters. They usually outgrow these as time goes on. Older children report more realistic fears, such as physical dangers, school failure, or loss of a family member.

When fear becomes phobia, however, the problem can become quite disabling, especially when the feared object or situation cannot be avoided. Fortunately, problem-focused therapy, which is designed to reduce the anxiety caused by the feared object, is very effective with phobias. This kind of therapy may involve systematic desensitization, in which the child gradually learns how to tolerate what is feared. In most cases, the problem can be solved in a fairly short period of time by working with a mental health professional.

Obsessive/Compulsive Disorder

Most of us have had the annoying experience of having a particular musical phrase or a jingle from a television or radio commercial repeat itself over and over in our minds. Magnify this many times, add a distressing or unpleasant quality, and you have an *obsession*—a persistent thought, image, or idea that seems to be beyond the sufferer's ability to control. The most common obsessions are: repeated thoughts about becoming ill, doubts about not having completed certain tasks, and concerns about physical harm. People—even children—who suffer from obsessions recognize that the thoughts are products of their minds, and they attempt to suppress them by substituting other thoughts or actions.

Compulsions are repetitive behaviors, such as hand washing, checking, counting, or repeating words silently, which a person feels driven or compelled to perform to reduce the distress that goes along with an obsession. For example, people who obsess about disease may try to reduce their anxiety by scrubbing their hands and continuing to do so until their skin is raw or bleeding.

Children who suffer from obsessive/compulsive disorder often spend a significant part of their day either obsessing or engaging in compulsive behavior to reduce obsessions. These behaviors are habitual and self-reinforcing: the more a child does them, the more he or she *has* to do them in order to obtain the same level of relief. It is not uncommon for children with obsessive/compulsive disorder to spend many hours getting ready for school in the morning, or preparing for bed at night. Each behavior follows a certain ritual. If the ritual is broken, the pattern must be repeated again from the very first step. For example, a girl who has a ritual of brushing her hair 200 strokes each evening before bed will begin counting again from 1, if interrupted or distracted while brushing.

Obsessive/compulsive disorder is a relatively rare disorder in childhood, but it becomes somewhat more common during the adolescent years. Over the past ten years, a number of medications, as well as a form of psychotherapy involving self-control training, have proven to be very effective in the treatment of the disorder.

Help for Your Anxious Child

Many children become anxious about school performance at one time or another. Often, the solution is simply to help them improve their skills in the areas where they feel weak. (In fact, one of the reasons to intervene when a child has a school problem is to deal with the problem before fear of failure makes the child too anxious to perform well.) To help overly anxious children, however, mental health professionals consistently suggest cognitive treatments, which involve learning how to think differently and thus manage their behavior differently. These treatments also involve teaching children how to relax, speak positively to themselves, recognize the signs of anxiety, and modify their thoughts. Parents are often asked to learn these techniques as well, so that they can help their children—largely by demonstrating the use of the techniques themselves. Usually, this training is accomplished in individual treatments that extend over a two- or three-month period.

A large number of children who refuse to attend school, or who do so only under daily intense protest, are likely to be suffering from separation anxiety. These children, too, respond to learning how to manage their behavior more effectively and to programs that seek to boost their self-esteem. In some cases of extreme anxiety, a consultation with a physician about the use of antianxiety medicine may be helpful.

Depression

Many parents whose children have school problems observe that their children seem gloomy, sad, and often angry. This is not surprising; a good number of them progress from feeling incapable to actually experiencing strong feelings of helplessness and hopelessness—two of the characteristics of outright depression. Depression, however, involves more than these dark feelings. Like anxiety, it has been described as a whole-body illness, involving changes not only in mood but in almost every area of a child's life.

Depressed children often complain of minor physical ailments such as stomachaches or headaches, and may experience sudden changes in patterns of sleep, appetite, energy, and overall health. Their sadness interferes with concentration, which can in itself lead to a decline in school performance. Moodiness, anger, and emotional changes put a strain on family relationships. Friendships suffer as the depressed child becomes increasingly withdrawn, isolated, aggressive, or argumentative.

Children suffering a major depressive episode exhibit a change in functioning over at least a two- to three-week period. If this happens to your child, you may see either a marked increase in sad or angry moods or a loss of interest or pleasure in activities that were previously enjoyed. Sometimes, however, it is difficult to recognize a child's depression because of the complicated interactions among learning problems, mood, and temperament.

Let's consider two different children, both of whom suffered from depression.

Marguerite, a third-grade student, had always bounced back from sadness or disappointments relatively well—until she suffered the sudden losses of her beloved grandmother and her dog within a few months' time. Because her parents hadn't wanted to overwhelm their daughter with worries about her grandmother's health, they hadn't told Marguerite that her grandmother had a serious heart condition, and so the girl was unprepared for the grandmother's death. In the weeks following, sometimes she looked sad; at other times, she was irritable and "spacey." After her dog Max was run over, Marguerite had difficulty concentrating in school. Her grades, which had always been fine, took a nosedive. At the same time, she seemed to stop enjoying many of her favorite activities, such as riding bikes with her friends. She said she just "didn't feel like it" or was bored. Although her parents offered to get the family a new dog, Marguerite wasn't interested. Fortunately, her parents noted that their daughter wasn't herself and consulted her pediatrician, who was able to recommend a counselor who specialized in helping young children deal with grief. The counselor helped Marguerite—and her entire family, who were still reeling from the loss of the grandmother—acknowledge the deep sadness she was feeling. The counselor also suggested approaching Marguerite's teacher for her help in getting the girl through this difficult time. After several months of counseling, and sympathetic support from her teacher and parents, Marguerite was back to her old self. She was once again able to enjoy herself, and her grades began to recover.

Marguerite's case of depression was fairly straightforward. Alex's was complicated by a number of elements, including the fact that his problems were longstanding. His parents had long sought to identify the cause of his irritability, poor self-esteem, moodiness, and social and academic difficulties.

Alex's problems began when he was quite young. As he grew out of toddlerhood, he was impulsive and couldn't sit still. In first grade, he had difficulty concentrating and learning to read, and was placed in a special education program. A psychological evaluation during second grade suggested that his problems stemmed from attention deficit/hyperactivity disorder (ADHD), and stimulant medication was prescribed. Although Alex complained that the medicine was not helping, and his teachers reported only minimal improvement, medication was continued over the course of a year. By third grade, despite academic assistance, he continued to struggle with his schoolwork; at the same time, he often complained that he was bored. Meanwhile, his temper outbursts had become commonplace at home and school. As a result, Alex was ostracized by his classmates and had few friends.

In fifth grade, after his parents completed the evaluation on the building blocks of learning, Alex was seen by yet another mental health professional. By this time, he was thoroughly demoralized and felt helpless, worthless, and unhappy. He was disruptive in class, frequently angry, and, when frustrated, suggested the world would be better off if he were not here. Alex's parents were worn out and increasingly doubtful that any professional could be of assistance.

The new doctor spent a great deal of time reviewing the records and reports of everyone who had worked with Alex. With these observations and findings in mind, he interviewed the family and identified a history of depression in a number of Alex's relatives. The doctor concluded that, although it was likely that Alex experienced ADHD and had a learning disability, it was also clear that he had a history of depressive symptoms and was currently suffering an episode of depression. Treatment was begun to teach Alex how to cope more effectively with his negative thoughts and feelings and to build more success into his life.

The clue that Alex had several depressed relatives was important. Depression, like diabetes and other disorders that seem to run in families, may have a genetic component. More often than not, a depressed child will have at least one parent who also suffers from depression. If a parent has a depressive disorder, a youngster has about a one-in-four chance of having a similar disorder. Thus, it appears that some children are inherently more vulnerable to becoming depressed. However, a genetic predisposition does not guarantee that they will become depressed; rather, it increases the likelihood that they will develop depression when faced with other life stresses.

It's important to remember that children, like adults, have their ups and downs. Some days go well, others not as well. Also, childhood is a time in which emotions are intense but fleeting. Parents have the difficult job of distinguishing between a youngster who is responding normally to stressful life circumstances, such as school difficulties, and one who may be depressed and in need of professional help. For this reason, it is important for parents to educate themselves about depression and to spend time thinking about whether changes in mood and behavior are interfering with their child's life.

Help for Your Child Who Seems Depressed or Unhappy

If you suspect that your child is depressed or dysthymic—if you recognize in your child some of the descriptions we have provided—it is critical for you to seek professional help. Antidepressant medications thus far have not proven as helpful in treating depressed children as in treating adults, but in some cases they can be an extremely important component of the treatment plan. To learn more about the use of medication to treat depression, consult *Lonely, Sad and Angry: A Parent's Guide to Depression in Children and Adolescents* by Barbara Ingersoll PhD and Sam Goldstein PhD.[5]

Depression appears to have biological roots, but it also represents a powerfully dysfunctional way of thinking. And once children begin to think in negative ways and to experience depressive feelings, the pattern frequently recurs, often continuing into adulthood. If your child appears depressed or chronically unhappy, in addition to seeking professional help, it is important to do the following:

- *Be prepared and educated.* Recognize the key symptoms of depression, the course it takes in children, and the significant impact it has on children's daily functioning. Being prepared and educated allows you to make decisions as problems arise, rather than after they reach a crisis stage.

- *Approach, don't withdraw.* Remember that depressed children may often act in angry, defiant ways that tend to drive other people away. If you suspect your child is depressed, continue approaching, regardless of the negative attitude or behavior.

CHRONIC UNHAPPINESS

Not all children who experience temper tantrums or complain that no one likes them suffer from clinical depression. But some children—with or without school problems—do appear to be always unhappy. They may not be depressed, but they have low self-esteem, are irritable, do poorly with friends and family and at school, and may have problems with sleep and appetite or with low energy levels. Most days for these children are "down" days, and this pattern typically goes on for years. Nonetheless, they continue to participate in pleasurable activities and do not experience suicidal thoughts. Mental health professionals describe these children as chronically unhappy or *dysthymic*. Although less serious than depression, dysthymia should be taken seriously. It clearly affects school performance, and mental health professionals consider it a gateway to depression because the majority of children who are diagnosed as dysthymic eventually experience a major depressive episode. If your child tends to be on the gloomy side and you notice an acute mood change involving irritability, anger, sadness, or a decline in schoolwork or self-esteem, a professional evaluation is in order.

- *Reframe, don't blame.* Children who are depressed often feel guilty and worry excessively. In your efforts to help your child develop responsibility for his or her behavior, you may inadvertently fuel this pattern of depressive thinking. When problems occur, try not to become angry; instead, help your child recognize that mistakes do not necessarily represent failure but are experiences from which to learn. Think about the ways you describe your child's behavior. A child's approach to doing homework can be described as "slow," which is blaming, or reframed as "careful," which is accepting.

- *Emphasize strengths, not weaknesses.* Depressed children need to be repeatedly confronted with their successes, no matter how minor. Your child must believe that some special, unique talents make him or her a person worthy of respect. We discuss this at greater length in Chapter Five.

- *Never quit.* No matter how discouraging things may appear, you must remain your child's coach and most optimistic friend. With help, depressive patterns do shift, though it often takes time.

- *Take care of yourself.* Many children who receive a diagnosis of depression have at least one parent who is also suffering from depression. If you recognize these signs in yourself, getting help for yourself will benefit your entire family.

Getting Professional Help

If, upon reviewing the ten characteristics on page 62 and completing this chapter, you feel your child is behaving oppositionally or is showing symptoms of conduct disorder, anxiety, or depression, it is important for you to seek professional help. Ask your child's pediatrician or school psychologist for referrals to knowledgeable mental health professionals in your community. Once you locate a knowledgeable professional, be sure that he or she is a good "match" for your child and your family. Use your common sense and trust your judgment as you seek help.

As a first step, you'll need a comprehensive evaluation, in order to develop an understanding of your child's emotional development, behavior, and academic skills. In most cases, the professional who conducts this evaluation will also be available to provide help, though some professionals choose to focus their practice on evaluation and offer referrals to other professionals for help.

WHO'S THE RIGHT PERSON TO HELP MY CHILD?

Parents frequently ask who is best qualified to treat children's emotional and behavioral problems. We believe the letters after the person's name—MD, PhD, or LCSW—are not as important as his or her knowledge, personality, and, most importantly, willingness to take the time necessary to understand your concerns and problems. For anyone getting help with emotional difficulties, the "fit" between patient and therapist is important. This is especially true for children, who need to trust and feel comfortable with someone in order to benefit from any offer of help.

Once you find the right person to help your child, don't be surprised if there are some ups and downs as treatment begins. However, you can reasonably expect certain things. First, you have the right to expect a thorough assessment that helps you better understand the reason or reasons for your child's current problems. Second, you have the right to expect a treatment plan that makes sense: a clear set of goals, an explanation of the methods that will be used to achieve those goals, and a time line for success. Finally, you have the right to expect that the mental health professional working with you and your child will be available to take your calls, respond to your questions, interact with your child's teachers, and, most importantly, keep you informed of treatment progress.

Remember, even if your child has strengths in the other nine building blocks of learning, unaddressed weaknesses in the block of emotions and behavior will significantly compromise any chances of school success. And unaddressed problems here will make dealing with any other weaknesses that much more difficult.

Chapter 5

Self-Esteem

Helping Your Child Become a Confident, Resilient, and Persistent Learner

With Robert Brooks, PhD

Self-esteem encompasses children's feelings and beliefs about their competence and worth—their talents, their ability to make a difference in the world, to confront and master challenges, to learn from their failures as well as their successes, and to treat themselves and others with respect.[1] Your child's self-esteem is shaped by happenings throughout childhood—on the playground, in interactions with the family, during work on a self-designed project, and, of course, in the classroom.

Although they may not use the term *self-esteem,* children's comments about their accomplishments—or lack of them—quickly let us know how they feel about themselves. Consider the following statements made by underachieving students, who believe that their school problems mean that they will never succeed:

- "Everyone in class is smarter than me."
- "I'm really dumb."
- "I just can't do math."
- "The teacher doesn't like me."
- "School is too hard. I'm going to take the easiest classes I can."

Contrast them with statements made by confident children:

- "I'm smart."
- "I can get 100 on my math test."
- "The teacher likes me."
- "School is easy."
- "When I work hard, I earn good grades."

Skills within the building block of self-esteem guide and motivate the actions of adults and children alike. The outcome of their actions in turn affects self-esteem, so that an ongoing process is always operating,[2] which is why low self-esteem can lead to despair and ultimately to avoidance of life's challenges. High self-esteem brings with it a sense of hope and efficacy and ultimately the ability to confront and learn from challenges.

Evaluating Your Child's Self-Esteem

A review of the following ten characteristics will help you evaluate your child's self-esteem.

If you checked "Yes" for several of these traits, it is likely that your child's self-esteem is low. It will continue to be low unless you make efforts

Self-Esteem	Yes	No
1. Seems uninterested in academic tasks	———	———
2. Complains about not being smart	———	———
3. Complains that academic tasks are too difficult	———	———
4. Worries excessively about school performance	———	———
5. Complains about not being liked	———	———
6. Has trouble succeeding on many tasks	———	———
7. Gives up easily on tasks and assignments	———	———
8. Seems overly sensitive to criticism	———	———
9. Seems unhappy	———	———
10. Seems to feel successful only rarely	———	———

to understand the feelings and forces that have shaped them, and begin to take steps to counteract your child's negative self-image.

The Roots of Self-Esteem

Studies have shown that some children are very vulnerable to stress in their lives; they react to every setback as though it were a major failing. Other children are more resilient; they bounce back quickly from adversity. The work of Dr. Martin Seligman, a pioneering psychologist and researcher, demonstrates that children who have a negative mind-set—a significant feature of low self-esteem—are less resilient and thus more vulnerable to depression. If your child believes that school problems reflect unchangeable inadequacies, he or she will be less resilient and more prone to developing emotional problems such as depression later in life.

Most likely, a child's level of self-esteem reflects an interaction of temperament—the unique and distinctive inborn psychological characteristics—and life experiences. It is important to keep in mind, however, that the term *interaction* means a two-way activity. Not all children who have "difficult" temperaments, such as those with ADHD, are destined to have low self-esteem. Instead, their level of self-esteem depends on the sum *total* of their experiences—their temperament plus the way others respond to them time after time. The responses of others are very important. For instance, some adults regard the restless, annoying behavior of children with ADHD as evidence of their energy, creativity, and diversity, and they respond positively to it; other adults view the same behavior as an unacceptable reflection of a decision to misbehave or ignore rules, and these adults respond negatively. The former reaction enhances a child's self-esteem. In the latter case, the child's self-esteem is chipped away. There is a third possible response: An adult may dislike the *behavior* of a child with ADHD and tell the child so, especially when the behavior is disruptive, but may make it clear that the child is considered to be an energetic, creative, and interesting person. Wise parents make certain to reinforce those qualities and that belief.

Parents' expectations and temperamental styles—the patterns of behavior that result from their own temperamental qualities—also influence their reactions to their child. Consider how well or poorly your child's temperament meshes with your own. If you tend to be active and outgoing, you may become more frustrated and tense dealing with a child who tends to be cautious and quiet than you would be with one whose approach to the world is more like your own. Similarly, achievement-oriented parents often have difficulty in dealing with a child who has problems with school performance. They may scold their child for being lazy and unmotivated, when in reality the child is trying hard but is struggling because of weak skills in the thinking or processing blocks.

Mismatches between your temperament and expectations and your child's temperament and learning style are likely to result in anger and disappointment. If you become irritable because your child responds differently than you would, your child may believe that he or she has let you down and is a failure. Low self-esteem is common when there are temperamental and expectational mismatches between parent and child.

It is critically important for you to accept your child and to communicate that acceptance. Accepting your child does not mean you approve of every behavior or action but rather that you can see and accept your child "as is," and your expectations do not cloud your acceptance.[3] Your ability to view the world through your child's eyes is critical to bolstering his or her self-esteem. It is also important for you to be aware of the way your own personality style, likes and dislikes, or expectations affect your day-in, day-out parent–child interactions and so either promote or chip away at your child's self-esteem. Remember that what looks like "plodding" behavior to you may be "cautious" behavior to someone else. A child whom you might label hyperactive can also be described as one who is "full of energy."

Dealing with Failure and Success

Negative Feedback

A child who has school and learning problems receives significantly more negative feedback than the average child without these problems. To return to the example we used above, it is not uncommon for a child with attention deficit/hyperactivity disorder (ADHD) to hear one or more of the following statements during the course of a school day:

- "Why can't you behave?"
- "Everyone else can sit still. Why can't you?"
- "Pay attention!"
- "This work is so sloppy!"
- "I don't think you're really trying. You'd do fine if you'd just apply yourself."

How does hearing a constant stream of negative comments affect a child's development? Some people believe that adversity encourages the development of strong character, and that overcoming difficult experiences makes children tougher and healthier. We doubt that this is true for most children with learning or behavioral difficulties.

How a child responds to failure depends partly on the child's temperament; a big part of the response is shaped by life experience and the messages received about self and self-generated actions. Think about the messages your child receives when a failure occurs. Do those messages lead your child to believe that he or she is stupid and a disappointment to you and to teachers? Has your child begun to conclude that "I can't really do anything right"?

If people continually describe someone as lazy, stupid, or deliberately disobedient, that person is likely to begin to believe them, even if what they say is untrue—especially if that person is a child and many of the people doing the describing are parents and teachers. Thus, some children decide that the negative comments they hear when they fail are correct, and they begin viewing themselves negatively. This negative self-view then influences their efforts and motivation when they must attempt difficult tasks. They come to assume that their efforts on schoolwork do not matter and that the best way to avoid feeling bad is to avoid trying at all. Other children respond to negative feedback by trying to divert the attention of whoever is doing the criticizing. They may go out of their way to seek adult approval, becoming increasingly dependent on the opinions and comments of parents, teachers, and other authority figures, and less and less certain of their own opinions and capabilities.

Each child is unique, and how each responds to failure has a good deal to do with the messages received about self and actions. Consider John and Tom, two equally capable fifth-graders. Both did badly on a math test because they did not prepare well for it. John's life experiences lead him to take the poor grade as a sign that he must study more. He does so, and improves his score on the next test. Tom's life experiences, by contrast, have taught him that failure is a sign of weakness, for which he will be punished. He has vowed that he will pretend to be sick when it is time for the next math test, so as to avoid the problem altogether. What makes the difference in their responses to the same situation? Self-esteem.

Attribution Theory and Success and Failure

Attribution refers to the way people think about the causes of events, and attribution theory is one way of understanding your child's self-esteem. In the example of the two boys taking a math test, John attributed his failure on the test to something internal but not stable; that is, *he felt he was responsible, but he knew he could do something different* to be more successful the next time. Tom attributed his failure to something internal but fixed, unable to be changed. His life experiences led him to believe that there was not much he could do about failing and that avoidance was his best strategy for coping with future math tests. In his view, *he was "weak" and could do nothing to change the situation.*

Locus of Control

Children who believe that their lives are controlled by external forces or by inner forces they cannot change, such as lack of intelligence, are said to have an *external locus of control.* They see themselves as being destined to fail, and even when they have opportunities to take control of their lives and make a difference, they make only minimal efforts because they believe their actions will not affect the outcome. In contrast, children with an *internal locus of control* believe that they have control over their lives. They accept responsibility for their behavior, and they recognize that their actions, feelings, and thoughts have consequences. In other words, they possess a realistic belief that they are important forces in controlling their destinies—a major component of healthy self-esteem.

Children encounter many challenges as they grow; some result in failure, others bring success. However, because they experience a high ratio of failure to success, children with school problems often develop an external locus of control. They don't believe that their achievements depend on the efforts they make; instead, they see them as hinging on luck, chance, fate, or favoritism. Because these factors are outside of their control, they lose confidence that they will be able to succeed in the future, and their sense of self-esteem drops.

Children with repeated school problems and poor self-esteem are quick to dismiss a good test performance with comments such as "The teacher made the test easy" or "I was lucky." Developmental pediatrician and learning disabilities expert Dr. Melvin Levine has described these children as suffering from "chronic success deprivation" because they rarely experience success in school.[4] Because of the weight of their past history of failure, the children do not believe that their efforts play a role in achieving success, even when confronted with evidence to the contrary. In contrast, children with high self-esteem view their successes as determined by their own efforts, resources, and abilities. They take credit for their accomplishments and feel a sense of control over what transpires in their lives. Although many people believe that success breeds more success, this occurs only when a child has an internal locus of control and believes that the success is a result of personal abilities or efforts, rather than of luck.

Children's locus of control also affects how they interpret the mistakes they make and the failures they experience. Think back to John and Tom. Leaving class after the first test, John reminded himself that he could do better, that he had to study more, and that he needed to ask for extra help. He has an internal locus of control; he feels he can learn from his mistakes and is hopeful of future success. In contrast, Tom, who has an external locus of control, left the classroom telling himself that he was stupid. He was convinced that he couldn't learn, and he decided that there was no point in studying—that, instead, he should just try to avoid the next test.

As we will see, there are parenting strategies that you can adopt to help your child develop an internal locus of control.

How Children with Low Self-Esteem Cope

It is important to be aware of and sensitive to the behavior that children with low self-esteem typically exhibit as they try to cope with their negative experiences and feelings. Some children are very direct; they often describe themselves disparagingly, saying that they are stupid or dumb.

For instance, 7-year-old Wendy has a history of attentional problems, underachievement, and difficulty completing work. When invited to write a story about how it feels to have trouble paying attention and learning, Wendy described herself through the main character, a dog named "Hyper," who had difficulty concentrating. The issue of low self-esteem was immediately evident in Wendy's story: "Hyper told herself that she would get over this problem someday, but she wondered if she really would. She was worried that when she grew up and her own puppies asked her something, she would not know the answer and they would wonder why their mother was not very smart." Wendy not only has a profile of low self-esteem but also has expressed a fear common to many children with school problems—that things will never get better.

Coping Strategies

Some children express their sense of low self-esteem directly; others do not. Instead, they demonstrate counterproductive behaviors or coping strategies that have the unfortunate effect of actually lowering their self-esteem still further. The behaviors that follow are frequently used by children with low self-esteem to cope with the reality or the perceived possibility of failure.

Quitting When frustrated because they cannot master a task after repeated attempts, some children simply quit trying, often offering excuses, such as that the task is too boring to perform.

Avoiding Avoiding is related to quitting, but instead of quitting after repeated attempts and failures, children who avoid often refuse even to try. Rather than have anyone believe they are incapable or stupid, these children prefer to have the adults around them focus on their unwillingness to comply.

Cheating Some children are so certain that they cannot win at a game or pass a test that they begin to alter the rules or copy answers. When questioned, they often rationalize this behavior, offering what they believe are valid explanations for their cheating.

Rationalizing Children who do not believe they are capable of succeeding frequently offer excuses for failure rather than accept responsibility. Sometimes, these children blame everyone else for their difficulties; at other times, they blame themselves but explain that some inner inadequacy has stopped them from performing well.

Clowning and Regressing Some children who lack confidence consistently act silly, clown around, pretend that everything is funny, or act much younger than their age. They behave this way to minimize the importance of failure in a given situation, but the strategy often backfires, leading to ridicule from their peers or disciplinary actions from their parents or teacher.

Controlling Many children with low self-esteem believe that they have little control over their own lives, which often leads to a sense of helplessness. Paradoxically, they often try to avoid these uncomfortable feelings by telling others what to do. On the playground, they may attempt to dictate what games should be played and who should play them; when doing homework, they may resist all help, insisting on doing things their own way.

Aggressiveness and Bullying Teasing, belittling, and striking out at others are very common counterproductive ways of dealing with frustration and low self-esteem. Children who use aggression in this way are desperately trying to hide their own feelings of inadequacy.

Passive/Aggressive Behavior   Some children with low-self esteem try to exert control by promising to meet certain responsibilities but conveniently "forgetting" to do so. They are engaging in what psychologists call passive/aggressive behavior. For example, when Joannie was angry that she had to miss play time in order to complete a social studies assignment, she repeatedly told her parents that she was starting to work but instead continued playing in her room. As we describe in Chapter 4, a child who engages in passive/aggressive behavior runs the risk of being labeled oppositional and progressing from having low self-esteem toward having an outright conduct disorder.

Denying   Children with poor self-esteem commonly use denial as a way of dealing with the pain that might result if they were to acknowledge their limitations and vulnerabilities. They may deny that they are worried about a school assignment, that they care about how things are going in the classroom, or that they are having trouble completing their homework.

Complaining of Boredom   When frustrated, children may complain that the tasks they are being asked to complete are boring or uninteresting. They may yawn or put their head down on the desk to show the teacher exactly how uninvolved they are, when, in reality, they feel that the task is beyond them.

Rushing   Children with low self-esteem often rush through tasks as a means of contending with their difficulties. Although some children rush because they are impulsive or inattentive, children with low self-esteem often try to finish a challenging task as quickly as possible, strictly for the sake of finishing it. For these children, completion is more important than accuracy and success.

Excessive Seeking of Adult Approval   Some children with low self-esteem go out of their way to be overly charming to adults, in an attempt to divert attention from the fact that they feel they are unable to do what is requested.

If you have seen these behaviors in your child, it is important to recognize that they are relied on to avoid feeling defeated, worthless, or stupid—and to hide the real problems.

Strategies for Building Self-Esteem

Beyond helping to build specific learning skills that can lead to greater school success, you can improve your child's self-esteem by creating an environment that encourages a sense of control, ownership, and responsibility for one's life. The importance of children's having at least one adult who believes in them and is consistently there for them has been heralded by many researchers, including the late Dr. Julius Segal. In his review of factors that help children overcome adversity, Dr. Segal wrote:

> From studies conducted around the world, researchers have distilled a number of factors that enable . . . children of misfortune to beat the heavy odds against them. One factor turns out to be the presence in their lives of the charismatic adult—a person with whom they identify and from whom they gather strength. (p. 1)[5]

As a parent, *you* are in the best position to be that positive, charismatic adult for your child. Following are a dozen strategies to help increase your child's self-esteem. Although these strategies are effective for all children, they are especially needed for those whose learning problems contribute to a steady chipping away of their self-esteem and self-image.

1. *Help your child to develop responsibility and make contributions.* One of the best ways to help children develop healthy self-esteem is to provide them with opportunities for assuming responsibilities, especially by making contributions to their home, school, or community. Making a positive difference in the lives of others builds self-respect and hopefulness and serves as a powerful antidote to feelings of helplessness and despair. Here are a few suggestions to help get you started. The stories are drawn from real life.

- *Help your child learn to help children who are younger.* Beth, a sixth-grade student, masked her low self-esteem by oppositional behavior and attempts to control her peers. Because Beth enjoyed interacting with younger children, Beth's teacher asked her to tutor first- and second-graders at school and suggested that Beth should also try baby-sitting in the neighborhood. These experiences bolstered Beth's self-esteem, which helped her to become more comfortable with her peers. As her self-confidence grew, the confrontational behavior diminished.

- *Encourage your child to get involved in doing charitable work.* With parents serving as role models, advisers, and cheerleaders, even young children can hold fund-raising fairs or join walkathons to raise money to feed the hungry or further research for AIDS or other diseases. In this concrete way, children can see that what they do can make a difference in their lives, their community, and the broader world.

- *Encourage your child to help out at home and at school.* When they do so, children not only learn a sense of responsibility, but also develop a sense of themselves as essential, competent, and even expert components of their world. One teacher we know asked David, a boy with learning problems who disliked school but loved animals, to become the school's "pet monitor." This position required that David take care of various pets in the school, write a brief manual about pet care for the school library, and deliver a short lecture on the subject to each class. Until the teacher suggested he write the manual, David usually avoided writing tasks, but with her encouragement, he completed the booklet. He felt that his words were having a positive impact and soon began to write other things as well. He also became an expert on the care of goldfish, hamsters, guinea pigs, and snakes.

2. *Provide opportunities for your child to make choices and decisions and to solve problems.* When they have opportunities to learn how to make decisions and solve problems, and to apply these skills in their everyday lives, children begin to believe that they have some control over what is transpiring in their lives, that they are the masters of their own destiny.

This is especially important to children who need to develop an internal locus of control. Here are some ways to involve them in making decisions and solving problems.

- *Engage children in solving family problems.* Let the "fussy eater" choose the food for the family's dinner, or ask the offenders how they can avoid fights over where to sit in the car or which television program to watch. When children arrive at solutions to family or personal problems themselves, the plans are often more creative and successful than those imposed by adults. A teenage boy, whom we counseled, frequently got into morning screaming bouts with his parents when he forgot to take his medication. When asked what his parents should do to remind him, without nagging, Luis thought for a few moments and then said, "Let them hold up a sign." Although he offered this solution in a half-joking fashion, it solved the problem. Whenever he forgot to take his medication by 7:25 A.M. (Luis himself proposed the exact time), one of his parents held up a sign. Because the idea had been Luis's, he followed through and the morning fights stopped.

- *Offer more choices to children, whether about household chores, school-work, or homework.* A teacher of our acquaintance assigns eight math problems for homework each night, but tells her students that they are required to do only six of the eight problems and they can choose which ones to do. She and other teachers who have tried this experiment report getting more *completed* home-work assignments from students who have a choice of which prob-lems to do. They note that building such choices into the lesson plan helps students take more responsibility for completing homework. Similarly, the family of one of our clients lets the chil-dren choose which household chores they will do, encouraging them to negotiate among themselves when they don't agree on their choices.

3. *Give encouragement and positive feedback.* Parents who are frustrated or angry usually find it easier to give their children negative feedback than to make positive or encouraging remarks. Yet, *all* children need to feel special and appreciated, especially those with learning problems and low self-esteem, who often have difficulty accepting the positive feedback they do receive. Therefore, the adults in their lives must persevere with comments of positive encouragement. Even small gestures of apprecia-tion have the power to generate long-lasting, positive effects. Let's look at some illustrations:

- *Schedule uninterrupted private time with your child each day.* Make it a time for telling each other what has gone on that day. Some par-ents use this time to teach their children to give themselves credit for working hard, even when the work's outcome is not as suc-cessful as planned. "Private time" can be particularly important when things are not going well. Michael, a 7-year-old boy with a difficult temperament, believed—correctly—that his father was disappointed and angry with him. When his father shared his frus-tration about Michael in therapy, the counselor encouraged him to find a way of helping his son feel special. Once a week, he scheduled breakfast at a local donut shop with Michael before school. Michael was very enthusiastic about having private time with his father, and these early morning breakfasts served as a catalyst for a significant improvement in their relationship.

- *Arrange family schedules so that you can attend everyday events in your child's life as often as possible.* Research shows that although they may not acknowledge it at the time, children are very much aware of their parents' attendance at events such as soccer games or musical recitals. From their parents' presence, they learn that they are valued and their efforts are appreciated, even when they make mistakes.

- *Acknowledge your child's accomplishments, both academic and nonacademic.* Just as schools set up assemblies to acknowledge students' achievements, parents can make a point of recognizing—in one-on-one conversation and in family meetings—each child's special achievements and contributions to the family.

4. *Discipline in ways that promote self-control.* As you discipline your child, try to strike a balance between rigidity and permissiveness, keep your expectations realistic, and offer well-defined regulations with logical and natural consequences. After all, the goals of discipline are to teach children and to encourage self-discipline and self-control, not to ridicule, intimidate, or humiliate them.

When children develop a comfortable sense of self-discipline, they are able to reflect on their behavior, judge its impact on others, and change it when necessary. We use the word *comfortable* because we believe that self-discipline is most effective when children are not laden with feelings of guilt or overburdened by pressure.

To develop self-discipline, children need to contribute solutions to their problems. Here are some examples of effective forms of discipline that help to foster self-control.

- *With your child's input, set logical consequences for behavior.* After Matt rode his bicycle on a dangerous street that he knew was off-limits, he was forbidden by his parents to ride his bike for a few days—a logical consequence. He and his parents then discussed dangers related to bicycle riding, and Matt was asked to put together a list of places he could and could not ride his bicycle. He also provided suggestions for rewards and punishments for following and not following these guidelines.

- *Encourage children to identify a problem and propose a solution.* Jeannie was having difficulty getting to sleep and fought bedtime constantly. Her parents often found themselves yelling at her, which intensified the problem and led to tantrums. When the family consulted a therapist, Jeannie revealed that she had been having terrible nightmares and was afraid to sleep alone. Her parents' sympathy and understanding, plus Jeannie's ideas of using a night-light and placing a photo of her parents next to her bed, solved the problem.

- *Institute family meetings.* At these meetings, children can help create household rules, review the reasons for them, discuss strategies for remembering them and abiding by them, and determine the appropriate consequences when they are broken. Teachers can use a similar approach in school. When children participate in such discussions, they are less likely to consider the rules arbitrary.

5. *Teach your child to feel OK about mistakes.* All children make mistakes, but not enough of them are taught that errors are part of everyday life and are important steps in the natural process of learning. As a result, many children grow up believing that making mistakes is proof of failure with a capital F, or the result of internal imperfections that cannot be changed.

A child who views mistakes as proof of failure is likely to feel defensive, criticized, and judged—and resistant to efforts of assistance. After learning to view mistakes as an acceptable and inevitable part of learning, that same child will be happier to play an active role in the instructional activities we describe elsewhere in this book. We are not suggesting that failure is always beneficial, or that all blows should be softened; however, neither should failure be considered a tragedy.

Children with learning difficulties make more mistakes than others; perhaps as a result, they are typically more fearful than their peers of making mistakes and looking foolish. To avoid what they experience as near-constant criticism and humiliation, they often spend more energy in attempting to avoid tasks that they believe will result in failure than in seeking solutions. Therefore, they need both protection from the dangerous effects of too much criticism, and help in experiencing success. They need to learn that mistakes are a part of learning rather than merely discouraging experiences.

Help your child become comfortable with sharing and discussing school mistakes with you. When you offer corrections or help, don't state how your child should feel or what your child should do; instead, listen to his or her fears. Keep repeating the message that mistakes are valuable, educational, integral parts of the learning process. Here are some ways you can help your child learn to deal more effectively with mistakes.

- *Model acceptance when you make mistakes.* Remember, children learn more from what we do than from what we say. If your child sees you yelling or putting yourself down or blaming others or giving up, the lesson may be that these are the main ways to deal with mistakes. After a mistake, make a point of letting your child hear you say, "What can I do differently the next time?"

- *Keep your expectations realistic, and avoid overreacting to your child's mistakes.* It's natural to become frustrated with the behavior of your child occasionally, but keep reminding yourself that mistakes are part of learning, and learning is your child's job. Avoid comments like "I told you it wouldn't work!" or "If you would only use your brain!"

- *Recognize that all children are frightened of making mistakes.* On the first day of school, one teacher we know makes a point of asking, "Who feels they will make a mistake and not understand something in class this year?" Before any of the students can respond, she raises her own hand to let them know that making mistakes is something everyone does.

- *Take a lesson from the Slingerland multisensory phonics method,* which we discuss briefly in Chapter 8. When writing first drafts, children are encouraged to use pencils without erasers. If they make a mistake or want to get rid of something they've written, they are told to just put those words in brackets. In this way, children learn that mistakes are part of the process of learning.

- *Don't lecture or preach when you offer lessons from your own childhood.* Most children are genuinely interested in the childhood stories of the significant adults in their lives—as long as the stories are told with sincerity.

- *Keep the focus positive.* Emphasize what your child knows and *can* do, rather than the opposite. When you review homework, start with what has been done right, before offering corrections.

6. *Use errors as teachable moments.* Errors have been described as "food for teachers," because they allow a teacher to determine exactly what a child knows and what is still confusing. Armed with this information, the teacher can then determine what material to reteach or review. You can do the same thing at home. Review your child's work, locate the errors, attempt to determine why they were made, and then show how to

correct them. If you are unable to determine why your child made the mistakes, talk through and solve a similar problem together.

- Jason, a fourth-grade student, brought home a math paper on which he did not do very well. On the first section, he was to choose the "greater than" or "less than" sign when comparing two numbers. All of the signs were written going in the wrong direction. As feedback, his teacher wrote: "All of these are mixed up. You must read the numbers at the left first." On the second section of the paper, Jason's task was to translate into standard notation a number that was written in words. From his answers, it was clear that Jason did not understand how to do the task. For example, for five thousand six hundred and forty-two, Jason had written: 5000, 600, 42.

Fortunately, Jason's father noted and reviewed the errors, then sat down with his son. For the first part of the assignment, he taught Jason a simple strategy for remembering which way to turn the comparison sign: He drew a profile of a face with a mouth shaped like the "greater than" sign. He then told Jason, "This is a very hungry creature who always likes to eat the bigger number. When you do these problems, make sure that the mouth will eat the bigger number." Then they practiced writing standard notation, first reviewing the concept of place value: the 1s, 10s, 100s, and 1000s. They began writing two-digit numbers, gradually progressing to larger numbers. Because his dad took advantage of Jason's errors to teach, Jason successfully dealt with problems of both types on the unit review. Furthermore, Jason was able to see that there were ways to learn from his errors.

Remember that your child *will not learn from mistakes that go uncorrected.* Feedback, clarification, and understanding are needed. (See Chapters 10 and 11 for more advice on teaching math.)

7. *Enforce realistic expectations for your child, in the classroom and on homework assignments.* To learn and to remain motivated to continue to learn, your child needs to be in a classroom where it is possible to succeed—where the curriculum's standards and goals are not beyond his or her present performance level. Homework assignments should also be within your child's capabilities. Otherwise, you will spend excessive time doing homework. Following are some tips for dealing with the problem of unrealistic school expectations.

- *Be alert to papers with too many errors.* If the concepts your child is being taught, or the assignments given, are too difficult, your child will become frustrated and begin to develop a self-image of a failure. One clue that the work is too advanced is too many corrections on the papers your child brings home. If many school assignments are unsuccessful, negotiate adjustments and/or an individualized curriculum.

- *Be alert to papers with a lot of negative comments.* When teachers comment, they should point out errors while offering encouragement and motivation. Their comments should never belittle or denigrate. If your child is receiving too many negative comments, it may indicate a need for adjustments to the assignments.

- *Intervene when you discover problems.* As a parent, you want to reinforce your child for persisting even under difficult circumstances. But reinforcing persistence does not mean merely imploring your child to try harder, but rather ensuring that there is appropriate assistance for any learning problems. When she realized that Pam needed more than two hours to read the assigned chapter in her social studies book, her mother consulted a neighbor, who reported that her fifth-grader was completing a chapter in about half an hour. Pam's mother then shared her concerns with the classroom teacher, who agreed to make adjustments. Pam was allowed to read the chapter in four sections, across four days, to compensate for her slow reading rate. Similarly, because Kevin was having trouble finishing assignments in class, he was bringing home twice the average amount of schoolwork each night—the day's classroom assignments as well as the evening's homework. Even with assistance, he was rarely able to complete all of the work. Kevin's parents brought up the problem at a conference with his teacher, who decided that she would either reduce the amount of work she gave in class or give Kevin extra time to complete assignments. In this way, Kevin would not end up with an unreasonable amount of homework.

You need to ensure that your children's assignments are within their present levels of competence. Otherwise, they will fail through no fault of their own. When children face repeated failures in school, they give up; they expect to fail and they do. To stop this vicious cycle, you must make sure that the work your child's teacher assigns is challenging, but not too difficult. When your child is actively receiving instruction in the classroom, the work should be only slightly beyond what he or she already knows and can do. Homework, on the other hand, should provide practice with and review of information that your child has already learned. If your

"I Can't" Versus "I Won't"

It's important to recognize the difference between problems that result from noncompliance ("I won't") and those that result from incompetence ("I can't"). Some children fail to do assigned work that they are capable of doing because they are fatigued, forgetful, unmotivated, or uninterested. Other children do not do assigned work because it is beyond their current functioning range or performance level—they do not understand the concepts of the assignment. In the first case, the problems often stem from weaknesses in the foundational blocks. In the second case, the problems tend to arise from weaknesses in the processing or thinking blocks. As a parent, you will want to differentiate between these problems and react accordingly.

child often brings home papers with many corrections or has homework assignments about which he or she is unclear, something needs to change.

8. *Praise the process rather than the product.* Children with learning problems often become very sensitive about the quality of their performance and the appearance of their product—their homework, reports, and tests. They know that what they produce suffers in comparison to the work of other students and often try to keep their work hidden. When faced with a paper full of crossed out words or numbers, it's tempting to say, "Can't you just be neater?" But that is counterproductive. Instead, emphasize the effort made, and help your child develop pride in his or her accomplishments by praising the process of learning.

- *Praise effort.* After Chris worked hard on an assignment, his mother said, "You should feel good about how hard you worked on that," adding, "You really spent a lot of time on that."
- *Praise perseverance.* After Barb had completed all of her math homework, her dad commented, "I'm proud of the way you worked through all of those problems—you should be, too."

By emphasizing the *process* of learning, we can help our children—even those with less confidence—become more resilient and learn to persist, even with difficult school assignments.

9. *Help your child become a polite self-advocate.* An important key to success in school—and in life—is the ability to be one's own advocate. This ability is particularly important for children who have weaknesses within the skills of the thinking and processing blocks. With proper coaching, they can learn to intervene before problems in a particular class or subject become insurmountable.

To become a self-advocate, your child needs to develop a sense of which types of tasks are completed easily and which types are more difficult—and why. It's not enough to know that math = a hard time. Your child needs to understand that math facts are hard to learn because of problems with memorizing, and that these difficulties can be circumvented by using a calculator. Following are several examples of how children acted effectively on their own behalf.

- Andy, a fourth-grade student, has strengths in the thinking blocks but weaknesses in the auditory processing blocks. If a teacher speaks too rapidly, he has difficulty following. On several occasions, he discovered that he had written down the homework incorrectly. After explaining the problem to his teacher, Andy asked her to write assignments on the blackboard so that he could be sure that he had recorded them correctly. His teacher agreed and Andy's problem was solved.

- Patricia, an eighth-grade student, was falling behind in her class reading assignments because her reading rate was slow. When she spoke to her teacher about her concern, the teacher provided her with a taped version of the text to listen to as she followed along. In this way, Patricia was able to keep up with the class and to work on building her reading speed as well.

- Sam, a seventh-grade student, informed his English teacher, during the first week of class, that he had trouble with spelling. He told the teacher that he would be happy to edit his work, but even with a spell-checker, he would need help finding and correcting the spelling errors. His teacher thanked Sam for letting him know of his difficulties and told him that he would not penalize him for misspelled words on class assignments, but he expected Sam to get help before turning in final drafts. Sam agreed that this was fair.

10. *Make the task interesting and the payoff valuable.* We teach our children that conscientious effort leads to success and, ultimately, to self-satisfaction. But if your child has to put forth great effort to master simple

TRAINING FOR SELF-ADVOCACY

Self-advocacy is very important, but, like many other aspects of education, it is a skill that must be learned. It's natural for a child to be a bit nervous when approaching a teacher concerning a problem. To help an anxious child feel more comfortable with the process and to give parents an idea of what the child will say, parent and child can role-play the conversation until they are both satisfied that the child can handle the meeting with the teacher.

In spite of such training, however, your child may at some time encounter a teacher who does not understand or accept the difficulties or who resists efforts at self-advocacy. We believe quite strongly that if this happens, the teacher becomes a part of the problem rather than a facilitator of a solution. If your child reports that a teacher is resistant, you should step in and work with the teacher. If this fails, request that the school's principal participate in a parent–teacher meeting on the subject. Most principals will stand behind their teachers, but will also be willing to help mediate a problem by assisting in brokering a workable compromise and acting as a resource.

tasks that do not pose any significant challenge for most children, the investment of time, effort, and energy may far outweigh the satisfaction received in return. To keep your child motivated, make tasks that require engagement for long periods of time interesting. Thus, if the study time for spelling words is twice or three times as long as for other children, select two or three different ways to go about presenting and studying those words. (Many specific strategies for learning spelling are presented in Chapter 9.)

In addition, consider balancing pay-offs, or offering extra incentives. A number of examples follow:

- Because she had difficulties with memorization, Susan had to study long hours to learn the multiplication tables. Recognizing her efforts, her parents helped her make up rhymes to learn the math facts. They also set up rewards along the way: Susan loved miniature golf and they agreed that when Susan had mastered an entire "family" of facts—all of the 4's, for instance—she and her parents would spend the next Saturday afternoon playing miniature golf.

- Mr. Cohen realized that his son Allen, a fifth-grade student, was sacrificing a significant amount of play time in order to prepare for tests. He offered Allen added incentives for studying. For every additional minute of study beyond the minimum they had agreed to, Allen earned a point. Allen collected the points in a "savings bank," and he could trade them in for a variety of activity rewards.

11. *Help your child to develop a sense of balance and self-confidence.* As you teach your child to complete assignments, be careful to develop an accompanying sense of achievement. Otherwise, if your child studies hard and doesn't do as well as had been hoped, there may be a fear of being simply incapable of success. Your child may say, "I know I am responsible for my grades, and I studied and prepared. Since I did poorly, I must be awfully dumb." To resist discouragement and keep motivation high, your child needs to become optimistically realistic. For instance, though she studied very hard, Mary received a B rather than an A on a science test. She was disappointed, but when her parents asked her about it, she told them that the teacher had said the material was very difficult and no one in the class had received an A. Mary was able to put the test in perspective—she had spent a sufficient amount of time studying for the exam and was proud of her achievement. She informed her parents that she might start studying for the next test a few days earlier, in an effort to earn an even higher grade.

12. *Help your child build islands of competence.*[6] For good emotional health, we all require islands of competence—areas in which we do well, and things that we enjoy. Unfortunately, children who struggle with learning and behavior have a fewer-than-average number of islands of competence. And if they view themselves as academically incapable, their negative thoughts and feelings may eventually come to affect their performance in areas outside school.

One of the most important ways that you can help your child build self-esteem is to ensure some islands of competence. Children need to become good at something and then have people tell them that they are good at it. In other words, they need to develop a specialty. We believe it is important for children to spend as much time engaged in activities they enjoy and are good at as in doing things they don't enjoy and may not be good at—a half hour playing or being involved in a pleasurable activity, for every half hour they spend studying.

The choices are endless, and what interests one child may not be of interest to another. Activities such as cooking, singing, stamp collecting, playing hockey, or roller blading could be activities your child uses to build an island of competence—but so could dancing, painting, computer games, or taking care of animals. Don't be discouraged if it takes your child quite a while to find something he or she really likes and is good at; the point is to be as persistent about this diversion as you are about schoolwork.

And don't make the mistake of treating the activities your child likes as only reinforcers, to be enjoyed only when less appealing activities have been completed. This strategy can easily backfire, and your child will be deprived of activities that he or she truly loves. Instead, consider the activities to be potential islands of competence—enjoyed independent of academic achievement. Though the basic activities are not privileges to be earned, you might want to offer additional opportunities to participate, based on completion of other less attractive activities. The key word here is *additional*. Following are some examples of how parents helped their children build islands of competence.

- Jack and his father spend at least an hour and a half riding dirt bikes in the hills behind their home each weekend. Depending on Jack's effort at school during the previous week—completing homework or doing well on a test—their riding time on a given weekend might be longer. On some weekends, it might even involve traveling to ride in a new location. For Jack, riding dirt bikes with his father gives him an island of competence *and* an incentive to keep working in spite of his school struggles.

- Lance struggled to learn to read and write, but he has strengths within the motor block. To give him an island of competence and boost his self-esteem, his parents enrolled him in soccer and signed him up for tennis lessons. By the end of the year, Lance was a star on his soccer team and a competitor in community tennis tournaments. His reading and writing skills were also improving, but his real islands of competence were athletics.

- David was not athletic. Although his grades were good and he was generally successful in school, he was unhappy and felt socially isolated from his classmates and the other kids in the neighborhood. Because David had strengths in the thinking block of images, his father got him interested in chess. He soon joined the school's chess club and made some new friends. He began competing in weekend matches and enjoyed the challenges. David's success in chess, an island of competence, helped to improve his self-esteem.

It's helpful to recall that, in school, children are asked to focus on a relatively small group of tasks. Later in life, however, they will be allowed to choose from a broader spectrum of activities. Children who struggle in school often find their successes in other areas. Sam became the classroom expert on dinosaurs. Mary learned to play the violin. Blanche became a whiz at card tricks and magic, even developing a small business of performing at children's birthday parties.

What are your child's particular strengths? Which activities require these strengths? Before you hone in on weaknesses, encourage and help your child to develop particular islands of competence based on strengths, learning style, and interests. Remember also that those interests are likely to change over time. For instance, Mary, the star violin player, gradually became much more interested in playing soccer. And some children "bloom" slowly, finding their islands of competence only after years of searching. The child who can't find an interest at age 8 years may have six different interests by age 11 years—if constantly exposed to different kinds of activities.

Self-Esteem and You, the Parent

As we have suggested, your own self-esteem is likely to have a significant impact on how you cope with and respond to your child's problems. The quality of these interactions, in turn, will significantly impact your child's self-esteem.

There are two important rules for every parent: the "Three C" rule and the "Three P" rule.

The Three C rule stresses *commitment, challenges, and control.* Recognize the importance of what you do as a parent, and give yourself credit for remaining *committed*—sticking with your role even in the face of struggles. Learn to view difficult situations as *challenges,* or opportunities to learn, rather than as stresses to avoid. Finally, recognize what you can change and what you can't, and keep your focus on what you have *control* over rather than on what you do not.

The Three P rule is simple: Be *proud* of your child despite the struggles, and convey your belief in him or her. Be *patient.* Recognize that although it may take your child longer to master a task, time and practice will bring success. And be *persistent:* develop a set of goals, and keep focusing on accomplishing these goals and on helping others, including your child's teachers, to help your child meet these goals.

Teach these rules to your child. Being committed, learning to recognize difficult situations as challenges, and recognizing that in every situation each of us has some control will help your child build, nurture, and foster self-esteem. It will protect against being wounded by unthinking adults or other children. Likewise, learning to be proud, patient, and persistent will develop extra resources for facing unexpected life events.

Chapter 6

The Learning Environment at School and at Home

School Issues: The Right Classroom and Teacher, and the Necessary Special Services; Home Issues: Emotional Support, Self-Discipline, and a Cease-Fire in the Homework Battle

Children learn best in environments that are comfortable, reassuring, efficient, and appropriate, whether at home or at school. We know that children who come from chaotic home environments, and whose parents do not read to them, discuss school projects, or help them with homework, are at high risk for school failure. A home environment that is supportive of education instills in a child the motivation to meet the demands of school and to succeed, regardless of any learning problems or the family's income level. The school environment is equally important. A classroom that is poorly structured, a teacher who does not recognize differences in students' learning styles, or a school system that does not make appropriate adjustments to students' genuine educational needs can derail children's progress, especially if they have weaknesses in any of the other building blocks of learning.

Because you are not a learning specialist, you might feel that you don't have the tools to discover whether problems in your child's school or home environment are contributing to below-average school performance. However, clues to such problems can often be found in the answers to a few simple questions: How does your child feel about school? Do you get complaints about having to go to school every morning? Is your child able to complete schoolwork at home? Your review of the following ten characteristics will offer you a more detailed understanding of how your child's learning environments affect school success.

If you answered "Yes" to a number of these characteristics, it is likely that factors within your child's daily school or home life are contributing to school problems.

The School Environment

If you often hear how your child hates school or the teacher, there may be a good reason for the protests. The classroom environment and the teacher's abilities to understand children's learning styles and manage the classroom effectively are key factors in success at school. Matthew's story emphasizes this point.

In kindergarten, Matthew's teacher complained that he spent a lot of time wandering about the room, and the year did not go well. By contrast, his first-grade teacher felt he was creative and had a lot to offer.

Environment: Home and School	Yes	No
1. Resists suggestions from parents to complete school tasks	____	____
2. Spends little time on homework	____	____
3. Has trouble keeping a consistent schedule for homework	____	____
4. Has trouble completing homework without assistance	____	____
5. Has siblings with school performance problems	____	____
6. Complains about attending school	____	____
7. Frequently reports feeling ill at school	____	____
8. Seems to have difficulty getting along with peers	____	____
9. Seems to have difficulty getting along with teachers	____	____
10. Has trouble following rules in home or school	____	____

Second grade started out well for Matthew, but problems developed and worsened over time. By May, he was spending more time in the time-out zone than in class getting instruction. Third grade started out poorly, but, at the year's end, Matthew was nominated as the most improved student behaviorally and academically. In fourth grade, things started out well and then again his work and behavior slowly deteriorated.

In successful years, Matthew had teachers who understood his learning style. Unsuccessful years started with a carryover from the prior year's positive experiences, then slowly deteriorated as the teacher's negative, often punitive methods of reinforcement resulted in Matthew's behavior getting worse instead of better. In other words, Matthew's successes or failures were linked directly to the personalities and instructional styles of his classroom teachers.

The Right Teacher and the Right Classroom

As a parent, you are entitled to participate actively in making recommendations for the selection of your child's teachers. The following guidelines will help you identify the right teacher and the right classroom environment for your child. The guidelines are based on a combination of scientific research, professional judgment, and common sense, and they are absolutely critical for children with severe building block weaknesses. (If your child suffers from attention deficit/hyperactivity disorder, see Chapter 3 for additional thoughts on this subject.) Some of the issues can be addressed by speaking directly with prospective teachers. Others may require talking to parents whose children have worked with a particular teacher; or, you may want to do an evaluation by observing the classroom directly.

The right teacher for your child:

- Is knowledgeable about learning problems and willing to acknowledge that these problems have a significant impact on your child's responses in the classroom.
- Understands the difference between problems that result from incompetence ("I can't") and problems that result from noncompliance ("I won't").
- Knows how and when to use a variety of reinforcers to maintain discipline, and avoids negative reinforcement or punishment.
- Communicates in positive ways—for example, "Please walk" rather than "Don't run."

- Provides positive comments to children throughout the day.

- Distributes small, consistent, and frequent social and material rewards, and involves students in selecting their own rewards.

- Is able to anticipate problems, and plans ahead to avoid them.

- Demands and follows through with specific requirements for behavior.

- Provides academic work at each child's level of ability, and shortens homework assignments into manageable parts when needed.

- Offers specific and brief instructions and is willing to repeat directions or present them in a variety of ways.

- Emphasizes the processes of learning (understanding a concept) rather than focusing solely on the final product (e.g., completing fifty subtraction problems).

- Uses a logical, problem-solving approach to helping children learn to deal with problems in the classroom and among themselves.

- Is comfortable communicating with parents and is willing to send home frequent notes if required.

- Teaches organizational skills and planning through the use of assignment books for recording both daily and long-term assignments.

- Values cultural and ethnic differences, and treats each student with respect.

- Is able to maintain control over an entire classroom. A visitor to such a classroom should be impressed by the organization and efficiency of classroom management.

Just as the selection of the right teacher is important, so too is making sure your child is in the right kind of classroom. The organization and structure of the classroom will have a significant impact on your child's academic adjustment. Depending on each child's learning style, different combinations of flexibility and structure may be necessary.

The right classroom for most children:

- Is a closed area—with four walls and a door—that is uncluttered and organized in an orderly fashion, with desks in small clusters, a semicircle, or rows.

- Has a clear and consistent set of class rules, which is posted for all students to learn.
- Runs on a predictable schedule with regular breaks.
- Has a low pupil-to-teacher ratio—ideally, no more than 20 pupils per teacher.

If you feel that the classroom setting is not conducive to your child's learning or social adjustment, share your concerns with the teacher. If that conversation does not yield results, consult the school's principal.

School–Parent Partnerships and Communication

Remember, no matter how tough a time your child is having, school personnel are your allies, not your adversaries. You will need to work closely with them in order to provide your child with optimum experiences. When acting on your child's behalf, strive to be realistic and to recognize when you are evaluating the teacher through your child's eyes. Children may not always interpret events accurately, so it is important to seek clarification of any issue before taking action or becoming angry.

Be aware that you are likely to bring some baggage of your own to any meeting with your child's teacher. For instance, your recollections of your own school history—the less fortunate as well as the good experiences—can affect your relationships with your child's teachers. If you are confused by your child's problems, you may worry that the teacher is judging you harshly or think that you are not doing enough to help. You may be concerned, too, that if the teacher does not understand your child, the negative judgments will affect his or her self-esteem. Finally, because you may not always understand school decisions, you may feel reluctant to ask questions or assert your opinions.

For all of these reasons, it's important to remember that school personnel are your allies. Most teachers are sincere, caring individuals who entered the profession because they love children. Despite the difficulties they encounter, they continue to try to meet your child's needs in the best ways they know. Most of your knowledge of a teacher comes from your child's reports; the teacher, in turn, learns most about you from the same source. Children who experience school problems often feel angry, frustrated, even hopeless. These negative feelings may be expressed in inconsistent or inaccurate reports about school and home experiences. When you deal with your child's teachers, remember that you're all working together. Remember, too, that teachers, like all of us, respond to and benefit from feedback, especially praise.

Parent–Teacher Conferences

Good communication between parents and educational professionals is key to planning a successful program. Besides notes and phone calls, the primary contact between parents and teachers is through conferences. They are often your only opportunity for face-to-face discussions with your child's teachers, so it's important that they go well. To make the most of parent–teacher conferences:

- Be on time and respect time limits. Typically, each meeting is scheduled for about 20 minutes.

- Be prepared. Inquire beforehand whether the principal, school counselor, or special education professional should participate in the meeting. Collect your thoughts before the conference, and write down your questions. Take along any samples of your child's work that you would like to discuss.

- Don't bring your child to the meeting unless specifically requested.

- Begin the conference with a positive comment—something your child likes about the educational experience this year. Show an appreciation for the teacher's efforts in some part of the educational experience.

- Be a good listener. Make sure you understand what's being said. Do not be afraid to ask questions.

- Be honest. Open communication creates an alliance. If you are struggling, say so; the teacher may be struggling with your child as much as you are. Even if you feel defensive, remember that you are an advocate for your child, not an excuse-maker.

- Keep the focus on issues and concerns about your child's performance rather than on the teacher's performance. Ask for specific suggestions. Mention particular resources you have explored independently that might be helpful.

- When you have assessed your child's building block strengths and weaknesses, share your insights with the teachers. Seek their opinion and feedback. Reinforce the idea that you are all a team working together to help your child.

- Most importantly, keep in mind that everyone wants what is best for your child.

Special Educational Services and Your Child

All children with school problems need some kind of help, but not all school problems merit a child's receiving special educational services. Your child's need for such services depends not on receiving one failing grade or performing poorly on one homework assignment, but rather on exhibiting repeated difficulties—a *pattern of underachievement.* If such a pattern is demonstrated, your child may be eligible for some type of special help at school.

A major theme of this book is that you must become an advocate for your child. If your child is identified as having an educational disability, you need to understand the specific legal protections and educational services to which he or she is entitled. The school will provide you with some information, but you must take it upon yourself to become knowledgeable—not only about your child's legal rights, but about what to expect at meetings and how to make mandated conferences successful and productive.

Special Education Services and the Law

Fifty years ago, children who underachieved or failed in school were written off as lazy, unmotivated, or unintelligent. These children were often forced to repeat grades, but because there was often no clear understanding of why they had failed the first time around, this was seldom a good solution. Most of these children eventually dropped out of school and drifted into low-paying jobs.

As time went on and we learned more about the needs of children who underachieved, changes were made. Congress passed several federal laws, among them the Education of All Handicapped Children Act (Public Law 94–142), the Rehabilitation Act of 1973, and the Americans with Disabilities Act (ADA; Public Law 101–336); together, they provide the framework for nondiscriminatory education for all children and the delivery of special educational services in school.

Laws with Accompanying Federal Funding   The Education of All Handicapped Children Act, passed in 1975, and the reenactments, the Individuals with Disabilities Education Acts of 1990 and 1997 (Public Law 101–476 and 105-17, commonly referred to as IDEA), transferred the

SPECIFIC DISABILITIES COVERED UNDER THE IDEA

Autism, deaf-blindness, deafness, hearing impairment, mental retardation, multiple disabilities, orthopedic impairment, other health impairment, serious emotional disturbance, specific learning disability, speech or language impairment, traumatic brain injury, and visual impairment are the relevant conditions.

responsibility for a child's failure to learn, once solely the family's, and placed it squarely on the public school system. These laws state that all children, regardless of severity of disability, are entitled to an education that is free and "appropriate."

Under the IDEA, this appropriate education is mandated for American children between the ages of 3 and 21 years, regardless of any disabilities they may have. The IDEA identifies 13 categories of disabilities and provides a detailed set of eligibility standards for each condition. It also describes the general procedures for identifying and evaluating children suspected of having a disability.

After a child has been identified by a multidisciplinary team—which often includes parents, educators, psychologists or other mental health professionals, a pediatrician, a speech therapist or other physical health specialist, and possibly others—as having a disability, the local educational system must provide all necessary educational services to increase the child's success in learning, as well as related services such as speech therapy, occupational therapy, and transportation. The services for each disabled child must be fully detailed in a written document known as the Individualized Education Plan (IEP). The IEP must include:

- A description of the child's current level of achievement and behavior.
- A description of annual goals and short-term objectives to meet those goals.
- A description of the specific education-related services that will be used to achieve these goals, including the number of hours per day, or days per week, when the services will be provided, along with the expected duration of each service.

- A description of the process by which the program will be monitored and the interventions will be evaluated.

The IEP must be reviewed by the team annually, or more often if a teacher or parent requests it. You must be given proper notice of each IEP meeting, and the meeting must take place at a mutually convenient time and place.

Over half the children identified as needing special services are classified as having learning disabilities. Many of the other areas of disability—blindness and deafness, for example—are clearly defined, but the guidelines for learning disabilities vary from school district to school district. Your child may be identified as having learning disabilities by the team in one school, and then be declared ineligible for services by a new team if you move and your child attends a new school.

Regardless of the circumstances, common sense is important. The real issue to consider is whether your child is struggling relative to his or her own potential or to the achievements of other students in the classroom. Keep in mind that if your child does not qualify for special services under IDEA guidelines, protections under Section 504 of the Rehabilitation Act, which we will discuss shortly, may be available. Regulations aside, it is helpful to create a working alliance with your child's teachers. Focus on helping them recognize and acknowledge that your child is not performing up to potential.

The IDEA requires that services be provided in a least restrictive environment. Children with learning or related problems should not be segregated from other students any more than is necessary, and any placement plan must take into account the distance and amount of time involved if the child must travel to receive services. A policy known as "inclusion" has resulted in increasing numbers of children with disabilities receiving services within the general education classroom. Depending on the nature and severity of your child's problems, this may or may not be what is needed. A child who functions several years below grade level may be better served in smaller groups or in a resource setting.

Typically, in resource settings, your child is removed from the classroom for a certain amount of time to get specific help. Some children prefer going to a resource room; they would be too embarrassed by the special education teacher coming into their classroom to help them. Others feel embarrassed to be singled out for extra instruction outside of their classroom. Fortunately, public school systems are required to provide a continuum of alternative placements for children with disabilities. As a parent, you need to think about where your child's needs at this point in time can be best met.

DEFINING LEARNING DISABILITIES

The term *learning disabilities* has been in use since the early 1960s, but there is disagreement about exactly what the term means. The most broadly used definition is the federal government's, which is incorporated in the Individuals with Disabilities Education Act (IDEA) and is the basis of many states' definitions of the term.

There are two parts to the federal definition. The first comes from a report to Congress by the National Advisory Committee on the Handicapped:

> The term "specific learning disability" means those children who have a disorder in one or more of the basic psychological processes involved in understanding or in using language, spoken or written, which disorder may manifest itself in imperfect ability to listen, think, speak, read, write, spell or to do mathematical calculations. The term includes such conditions as perceptual handicaps, brain injury, minimal brain dysfunction, dyslexia, and developmental aphasia. The term does not include a learning problem which is primarily the result of visual, hearing, or motor handicaps, of mental retardation, of emotional disturbance, or of environmental, cultural, or economic disadvantage.

The second part of the federal definition comes from a separate set of regulations for children with learning disabilities, drawn up by the U.S. Office of Education. It states that a student has a specific learning disability if the student (a) does not achieve at the proper age and ability levels in one or more of several specific special areas when provided with appropriate learning experiences and (b) has a severe discrepancy between achievement and intellectual ability in one or more of seven areas: oral expression, listening comprehension, basic reading skill, reading comprehension, written expression, mathematics calculation, and mathematics reasoning.

Another definition comes from the National Joint Committee on Learning Disabilities (NJCLD),* an organization of representatives from several professional disciplines and professional

(continued)

DEFINING LEARNING DISABILITIES (CONTINUED)

organizations involved with learning disabilities. The NJCLD definition considers that learning disabilities can be varied in their presentation, that they are due to factors within the person rather than to external factors such as environment, that there is a biological basis to the problems, and that they may occur along with other disabilities, such as emotional disorders.

The reasons for differences in the definitions have to do with the fact that learning disabilities are being studied and described by a variety of disciplines, professionals, and organizations; that learning disabilities are varied and often complex; and that different definitions serve different purposes, from identification to description, assessment, instruction, and research. The learning specialist you consult about your child's problem may use a different definition of learning disabilities than does the classroom teacher, whose definition, in turn, may not be the same as those used by a researcher or a government administrator.

For more information on the complex subject of learning disabilities, we recommend *Learning Disabilities, A to Z: A Parent's Complete Guide to Learning Disabilities from Preschool to Adulthood*, by Corinne Smith, and Lisa Strick, (Free Press), and *Attention Deficit Disorder and Learning Disabilities: Myths, Realities, and Controversial Treatments*, by Barbara D. Ingersol and Sam Goldstein (Doubleday).

---

*References: National Joint Commission on Learning Disabilities: The needs of adults with learning disabilities. Washington, DC: U.S. Government Printing Office.

The IDEA provides for parents' participation in all aspects of a child's education. You must give written permission for your child to be evaluated, and you have an absolute right to review all records. The IDEA amendments of 1977 specify that parents are to be members of their child's eligibility, IEP, and placement teams. In fact, special services cannot be provided until your child's IEP has been written and signed. In addition, you have the right to request an IEP meeting any time you have concerns about your child's performance. A child who attends a private or parochial school still has the right to receive special education services from a public school. If your child attends a private school and needs speech therapy, this service must be made available at no cost to you, through your public school system.

MAKING THE IEP PROCESS WORK FOR YOUR CHILD

If your child is eligible for special educational services, the annual IEP meeting is crucial for your child and for you. Beforehand, you'll want to make preparations. Consider collecting your child's schoolwork and school records, notes from teachers, your own observations and those of other family members, and the results of your building blocks assessment. Make prioritized lists of your goals for your child, both long- and short-term, as well as your expectations regarding progress reports and frequency of home–school communication. List any questions you might have, and rehearse what you'll do if you feel that your concerns are not being addressed or if the conversation lapses into professional jargon. On the day of the IEP:

- Introduce yourself.
- Make sure you get the name of the person who is officially representing the school district.
- Ask questions and share your concerns as the meeting unfolds; request time to present your prepared information if it hasn't already been scheduled.
- Take notes or use a tape recorder.
- Ask for clarification of anything you don't understand, and don't sign anything until you understand it thoroughly.
- If you disagree with any part of the findings or plan, make sure your disagreements go into the official minutes of the meeting.
- If the scheduled meeting time runs out before all of your concerns have been addressed, request another meeting.
- Stay calm, cool, and cooperative.

Keep in mind that the school's assessment often focuses on the quantitative aspects of performance—that is, determining whether your child is sufficiently delayed in a specific area of academic achievement to qualify for placement in a special program under IDEA guidelines. Often this assessment is focused not on understanding *why* a child is struggling, but rather on determining the extent of the struggle as compared to grade peers. Getting this information is important, but it is only a critical first step. Next, you must combine it with the information from your building block skills assessment, which provides a pattern of your child's strengths and weaknesses. Using the two sets of information in combination will allow you to monitor your child's progress and to focus on strengthening the skills that are essential for academic achievement and emotional adjustment.

Laws That Offer Protection But No Federal Funding   Called the "civil rights acts for individuals with disabilities," Section 504 of the Rehabilitation Act of 1973 and the Americans with Disabilities Act of 1990 (ADA) have

---

WHAT IF YOU AND THE IEP COMMITTEE DON'T AGREE

If you don't agree with the recommendations or decisions made by the IEP team for your child, you have the right to request an independent evaluation at the school's expense. You and the school jointly choose a professional from the community who will then evaluate your child, speak with you and the school personnel, and provide recommendations regarding the problem in question. If there is still disagreement, you can request an independent hearing with a trained hearing officer to whom both you and the school present information and opinions. The hearing officer then weighs all the data and issues recommendations, which, although not binding, usually are followed. But if a disagreement continues, you have a right to pursue your child's case through a state review, and eventually through the courts. All states and local education agencies must have a mediation process. Although this process is voluntary, we encourage you to try and resolve your concerns through the mediation system rather than the legal system. Fighting your cause with attorneys can become both costly and stressful to all parties involved.

a broader definition of disability than is found in the IDEA. Unlike the IDEA, these laws do not define specific disabilities. A child can qualify for services under these laws if he or she has a physical or mental impairment that substantially limits a major life activity such as learning. This means that if a child has a disability but has been deemed ineligible for school services under IDEA, that child is entitled to protections under Section 504. For example, many children with ADHD and similar problems do not qualify for school services but do receive accommodations, ranging from untimed tests to shorter assignments, under Section 504.

Unlike the determination of a student's eligibility for help under the IDEA—which brings with it some federal funding for the school district, to aid in providing adequate and appropriate services—qualification for help under Section 504 brings no additional funding. Instead, Section 504 promotes awareness of the wide range of individual abilities and disabilities, and, recognizing that identical treatment may be a source of discrimination, mandates equal opportunity for educational benefits. The protections of Section 504 extend to private institutions that have 15 or

KEEPING A SCHOOL FILE ON YOUR CHILD

If your child is being considered for special services, it is critical that you have accessible, accurate records. Although creating a file system may seem time-consuming initially, it will save you time in the long run.

Organize materials in a file cabinet or in a large three-ring notebook. Date all documents in the upper right-hand corner so that they can be filed in chronological order. Keep copies of: any testing results, including those from psychological and educational tests, and group achievement tests done in the school; any relevant medical records; report cards and notes from teachers; copies of the IEP or Section 504 Accommodation Plan; written summaries of any school meetings and any important telephone calls; and representative samples of your child's classroom work. Write questions or explanations of your own on separate sheets of paper. If you have to be an advocate for services for your child at some time, you will find the collected information invaluable. In addition, other helping professionals may request to see these documents at a later date.

more employees. Private schools that are independent and self-supporting, with the exception of those directly affiliated with religious organizations, are now responsible for providing accommodations for students with disabilities.

What this means in practice is that Section 504 "accommodation" plans are written for these children. Any modifications and curricular adjustments are usually provided within the general education classroom. These might include using behavior management techniques, modifying the child's workload, adjusting the child's schedule, or providing alternative means of evaluation.

It's important to realize that, although professional evaluations of your child are usually helpful, you're the person who knows your child best. If your child is very bright and is doing only "average" work, or if teachers dismiss your concerns about poor performance because the scores achieved on standardized tests are on the low side of average—that is, if your child is underachieving relative to personal potential or to peers—you may have to press hard to get the needed help.

The Home Environment

You are reading this book because you are concerned about your child and interested in helping toward better learning. You try to be active in promoting success at school, and you may worry that you have only limited control there. The good news is that you can do plenty of things *at home* to help your child—and you are probably already doing many of them.

Emphasizing the Importance of Learning

Your child is probably already aware that you consider learning to be important, because you've said so. But beyond just saying so, you can demonstrate actively your regard for and your enjoyment in learning new things. Talk about how you learn in the course of the day: interacting with employees and bosses at your worksite; following the news on television, radio, and the Internet; reading books and magazines; trying new recipes; attending to family investment strategies; learning new computer skills. Discuss what's involved in following or participating in the arts, or taking up a new sport or exercise program. Demonstrate that you enjoy reading, and read aloud to your child. By calling your child's attention to these activities, you reinforce the fact that learning isn't just something that is done in school or to pass tests; it is an active, enjoyable, and practical part of one's everyday life.

In addition, you can provide your child with a rich environment for active learning. Make your home a place where it's taken for granted that asking questions and seeking answers are important, whether the topic is sports, music, art, mathematics, cooking, model-building, camping, or anything else. Providing a learning-rich environment needn't be costly: enrichment programs are available through many schools, churches, and temples and at local Ys, community organizations, and colleges. When done consciously, nearly all of the things that you normally do with your children—performing chores around the house, visiting with relatives and neighbors, pursuing hobbies, attending religious services, volunteering in the community—can enrich their environment, build self-esteem, and provide opportunities for learning. Everything you do should encourage your child to be involved actively in life. Parents are children's most important teachers, the persons they look to first for guidance.

On the Emotional Front

As a parent, you want to provide emotional support to your child, but being able to do this requires you to pay some attention to your own emotional state. When your child has school problems, your emotions pull you in two different directions. Sometimes you see yourself as a normal parent with an abnormal child; at other times, you feel that your child is normal but you are a poor or inadequate parent. Both thought patterns are counterproductive. The first leads to anger and resentment; the second encourages guilt and overpermissiveness on your part, which can result in a lack of self-control in your child.

Parental Misconceptions

Parents of children with problems are exposed to a variety of misconceptions, often fueled by comments from other people who have gathered random bits of information from sources they have read. School personnel may lead parents to believe that repeating a year of school will "solve" the child's problems, or a pediatrician may inform them that their child will outgrow a particular condition. Or, in response to the criticisms of neighbors or relatives who believe they have been either too permissive or overly demanding, they may come to believe that their own bad parenting is the cause of the problem.

Some parents feel guilty when their child misbehaves in school. If your child is frequently in trouble, you may even feel, at a school function, that you are being stared at by teachers, children, and other parents, or that you have to apologize for who your child is. Guilt leads to self-blame, doubt, and feelings of inadequacy, and then to a cycle wherein parents feel hopeless, helpless, angry, and resentful.

Other parents get angry, believing that their child simply does not want to learn or listen. This is one of the most seductive misconceptions that parents can form, because it assumes that a child is fully responsible for any problems with school. In reality, this is a form of blaming the victim, and it packs a double whammy for children whose behavior is inconsistent because of impulsivity or inattentiveness. Their problems often appear to be purely a matter of the children's choosing to behave badly.

Let's look at how the opinion that a child is lazy or just doesn't want to learn affected one student. When discussing the performance of his son, Chris, a fifth-grader, at a parent–teacher conference, the father commented that his son's main problem was laziness. He had observed that Chris seemed to do many things easily, and therefore attributed his son's school difficulties to a lack of effort. Chris could do the work, his father was sure, if he would just try.

The teacher, however, knew that Chris was not lazy. She understood learning difficulties and differences and knew that, for Chris, studying for hours was no guarantee of success. She explained that Chris had excellent reasoning and problem-solving skills; when the class focused on such activities, he was often the first student to propose a workable solution. In contrast, he had difficulty with tasks involving memorization, such as problems whose solutions required recalling memorized math facts. When tasks of this nature came up, Chris became frustrated and often gave up. But this apparent lack of motivation—or laziness, as described by his father—really stemmed from weaknesses in the processing blocks. When the teacher explained Chris's learning style to his father, it was as though a light came on. The father found that the explanation made perfect sense. His final comment at the end of the conference was: "Chris is just like me." As a result of the knowledge gained at the parent–teacher conference, his father stopped saying things like, "Come on, you can do it if you really try. Why don't you just apply yourself?" He was able to help Chris with exercises and interventions designed to build on his strengths in the reasoning blocks and to shore up his weaknesses in the processing blocks.

Years of experience have shown that children with learning and attentional problems have marked inconsistencies in day-to-day performance.

On some days, they can perform well; on other days, they cannot. This misconception about a child's supposed lack of effort leads to increasingly punitive and negative interventions—often with an escalation in family conflict—but little improvement in the deficient behavior or skills. Some parents, concluding that their child is on the road to delinquency, throw their hands up in despair.

Alternatively, some parents come to believe that someone else is the source of their child's problems. They often become so caught up in blaming the supposed inadequacies of the child's teacher, principal, coach, scout leader, friends, or others, that they become immobilized. Not only are they unable to understand and accept their child's problems, but they do nothing constructive about solving them.

These ideas, thoughts, and feelings are very human, but when your child has school problems, it's important to recognize and rid yourself of these misconceptions. The most effective remedy is to understand your child's learning style, follow the "Three P" rule we discussed in Chapter 5 (be proud, patient, and persistent), and develop a set of strategies that will lead to school and home success.

Assertive and Supportive Emotional Care

During the elementary school years, most children behave in predictable ways. They frequently test ideas and values, ask questions, practice and learn skills. As they enter adolescence, they begin challenging their parents' values. During these years, they learn to reason about their wants and needs and begin experiencing the consequences of success and failure. Slowly, they develop an internal set of controls and a sense of responsibility to themselves, their family, and the community. They learn the capacity to cooperate and work with others successfully, and they develop both self-discipline and self-confidence. Not surprisingly, when children struggle at school, this developmental process is often interrupted. Researchers have demonstrated repeatedly that the self-esteem and life accomplishments of adults with histories of school problems are less than those of others who did not experience school problems.

All children require nurture and structure. They need parents to be supportive, accepting, and tolerant of their individual strengths and weaknesses. They need a careful balance of discipline that both assures them that they are loved and lovable, and requires them to accept limits, learn skills, and embrace standards. Most importantly, they need to hear, day in and day out, that their parents believe in them and that they will be able to accomplish the tasks required in their lives because they are worthy

ELEVEN STEPS TO PROVIDING A
SUPPORTIVE EMOTIONAL ENVIRONMENT

1. Try to see the world through the eyes of your child. All is not always as it appears to you. Make an effort to understand how your child thinks, feels, and then behaves. You must be able to see the world from your child's perspective—a task that will take time, patience, persistence, and effort on your part.

2. Be reliable and available. When possible, schedule private time with your child each day.

3. Continue to offer love, safety, and security, regardless of any problems. Make certain you express your care and concern even when your child disagrees with you.

4. Reinforce effort, even if he or she is not successful. Provide lots of love—hugs, kisses, and pats on the back.

5. Consistently foster self-esteem. School success is not a matter of your child's succeeding at all costs; instead, feeling good about successes is the goal. Do not spend so much time on academic performance that you neglect other strengths and talents; instead, help to find activities that promote those natural talents. (Other specific suggestions for building self-esteem are presented in Chapter 5.)

6. Build responsibility. Allow your child the opportunity to do things independently and to learn from experience, while keeping in mind that, for some children, responsible behavior develops in very small steps.

7. Start with the end in mind, and set goals that can be accomplished. Whether the goal is developing math, reading, or behavioral skills, know where you want to go and review this information with your child. Be specific about what "behaving better" entails, and set small, attainable objectives along the way.

8. Use a problem-solving model. It is critically important that you offer your child a good example of how to deal with life's problems day in and day out. Demonstrate that you believe

ELEVEN STEPS TO PROVIDING A
SUPPORTIVE EMOTIONAL ENVIRONMENT (CONTINUED)

failure is something to learn from and that an understanding of today's failure can lay the foundation for tomorrow's successes.

9. Make certain that there is a balance in your child's life. Children with school problems often spend an inordinate amount of time completing schoolwork, and they end up feeling that they do little beyond trying to deliver a satisfactory finished product in an area that doesn't matter to them. They often don't spend much time in activities that they enjoy. When after-school time is limited, make sure that your child spends some of it in activities that are enjoyable and reinforcing.

10. Take care of your relationship with your child. Among the best predictors of children's success in adult life is the quality of the relationship they have with their parents—independent of school success or failure. Your relationship with your child may become strained because of repeated problems, so take extra time to keep the scales balanced and the overall relationship positive. No matter how things are going at school, find a way to spend enjoyable, nonstressful time with your child at least a number of times each week. It doesn't matter whether you play cards, go out for pizza, or toss a ball back and forth—what's important is having a regular activity that is enjoyable for both of you.

11. Remember that your goal is to be a safety net, not a savior. Not surprisingly, children with school difficulties often seek gratification in other areas. That's why it's so important for you to provide structure, support, and successful experiences in the home, which your child can then transfer to mastery of the world outside. You must walk a fine line of encouraging your child, supporting his or her endeavors, and acting as a safety net rather than a keeper.

and capable of success. This need is especially intense when children have school problems.

When problems arise, your child requires *assertive care,* to meet needs directly by finding solutions to problems, whether they involve learning the multiplication tables or negotiating with the school system, and *supportive care:* sympathy, a hug, a pat on the back, to make it clear that you understand his or her pain.

Celebrating Your Child's Strengths

One of the most important things you can do to make your home environment emotionally supportive and conducive to your child's success is to help your child find islands of competence among extracurricular activities at home and at school. Does your child feel appreciated for the individual strengths evidenced at home? Build on those strengths and look for activities that your child enjoys and is good at. For instance, the parents of Marilyn, a sixth-grader, knew that she had marked strengths and weaknesses that were affecting her school performance. Because of weaknesses in the auditory processing block, she was struggling with spelling and with trying to learn Spanish. In contrast, Marilyn had strengths in the thinking block of images. She had a strong interest in engineering and excelled in activities that allowed her to apply her visual skills. Because Marilyn's parents understood her strengths and weaknesses, they were able to help her pursue areas of interest where she would excel. When she entered high school, she enrolled in a program for learning sign language, several computer courses, and an elective in visual arts. This all helped to build her self-esteem, in spite of her specific learning problems. (See Chapter 5 for more suggestions on building your child's self-esteem.)

Check Your Perspective

Keep in mind that the ways you think about your child and his or her behavior are critical determinants of your actions. Different perspectives yield different perceptions. As noted in Chapter 3, you might describe your child as "careful" (meaning working with great diligence), whereas the teacher's description may be "too slow." The same behaviors in a child might be viewed as "stubborn"/"persistent," as "overly sensitive"/"concerned," as "annoying"/"curious," as "easily frustrated"/"eager to succeed," or as "highly energetic"/"hyperactive." Keep in mind that what one person views as a negative behavior may be a positive attribute that ultimately contributes to your child's life success.

On the Disciplinary Front

It is often difficult to decide and summon the appropriate response when children misbehave. Many parents' automatic response is punishment, but we all need to remember that punishment and discipline are not necessarily the same thing. Punishment is a penalty for wrongdoing; discipline's goal is to educate a child about how to succeed in school and get along in life. Punishment may be part of discipline, but discipline itself is what we are after.

Unfortunately, as we try to provide discipline, we sometimes talk to children as if they were rational adults. We try to point out and discuss problem behaviors, and we assume that the children will immediately rectify the situation. Although one of the major jobs of parenting is to provide a consistent framework of values and morals, keep in mind that lengthy lectures based on morals and values are often a waste of time. It's important to communicate with children in a way that they can understand—in brief, firm, and age-appropriate discussions of behavior and attitudes. If the issue at hand is finishing homework, stick to that point rather than getting into a full-blown discussion of school and family responsibilities.

Teaching Discipline Through Consequences   In disciplining their children and responding to misbehavior, most parents employ *consequences*. Consequences fall into four general types: natural, logical, practical, and random. Depending on the situation, any of the first three might be appropriate. We believe that the fourth type, random, rarely works.

Let's examine these four types within the context of a specific problem: Your son comes home late for dinner, with no acceptable reason and without apology. A *natural* consequence would involve the rest of the family starting dinner at the prescribed time, with your son's meal put on a plate and left out to get cold until he arrives home. Or, if he misses dinnertime altogether, you may decide to let him go hungry for the evening. In most instances, more is gained by allowing your child to face the natural consequences of a behavior, rather than engaging in destructive fights and arguments.

For a *logical* consequence, your response is in some way directly related to the infraction and usually involves a loss of privileges. Thus, a logical consequence for your son's coming home late to dinner might involve keeping track of how late he is, doubling that amount of time, and requiring him to come in from playing that much earlier on the following day.

A *practical* consequence involves restriction of another unrelated but enjoyable activity—in this case, perhaps not allowing your son to watch television later in the evening, when he arrives home late for dinner.

A *random* consequence is one that is not prearranged, not well connected to the behavior, and not consistently followed, such as yelling at or reprimanding the child one time for being late, but saying nothing the next time and then not allowing him to ride his bike for a week. Often, this kind of consequence is based on frustration or anger, and usually leads to hurt feelings but not to changes in behavior.

Try to form an alliance or partnership to help your child solve behavioral problems and learn self-discipline. Being strict without being punitive allows maintaining dignity. Natural consequences are often the best teacher. When natural consequences are impossible or inappropriate, it's up to you to think of logical consequences that are somehow related to the offense. Let's say your daughter throws a tantrum in the bank because you will not give her money for the candy machine. It will not help to tell her that she cannot have pizza for dinner on Sunday. Instead, you need to create a meaningful connection between what happened and the consequence. You may choose to forbid candy for the day (or longer) or tell her that she cannot accompany you on your next trip to the bank.

Remember, too, that one of the best ways to avoid discipline problems is to focus on preventing misbehavior from occurring in the first place. This means, for example, that if your child is temperamentally difficult or impulsive and tends to have tantrums if forced to wait, it may be better to avoid restaurants in which a wait is required—at least until better self-control is developed.

If your child's behaviors are frequently problematic, you need to restructure your home environment so that: (a) expectations about behavior are clearly spelled out, (b) you provide support to encourage meeting such expectations, and (c) a system is in place for tracking behavior and providing appropriate rewards, privileges, and consequences. Two such systems are the establishment of a token economy and the use of contracts. See Chapter 4 for descriptions of these interventions.

Handling Homework

Even under the best of circumstances, homework is one of the hottest of parent–child crisis buttons. In households with children who have school

WHEN PUNISHMENT IS NECESSARY

Punishment is an effective means of discipline only when your child has the capacity to choose an alternative behavior but does not do so. For punishment to be effective, children need to possess the capacity to change and to be given the opportunity to behave more appropriately. When punishment becomes necessary, *don't:*

- Engage in lengthy discussion or arguments before or during the punishment.
- Offer punishment that is reinforcing, such as sending the child to a room filled with enjoyable diversions.
- Punish your child while you are very angry; a punishment given after you cool off is guaranteed to be more thoughtful, more appropriate, and more effective.
- Use punishment as a threat or fear tactic.
- Provide punishments that are too short, too long, inconsistently applied, or enforced too long after the offending behavior.

See Lynn Clark's *S.O.S. Help for Parents* for help on deciding on punishments that are rational but not aggressive or emotionally abusive.*

* L. Clark, *S.O.S.: Help for Parents* (Bowling Green, KY: Parents Press, 1996).

problems, it is not uncommon for these children to come home with classwork that they have not been able to complete during the regular school day, as well as the standard homework assigned to all students. The prospect is for hours and hours of schoolwork at home. Not surprisingly, children rebel, and parents, who feel the pressure of meeting their child's school demands, feel they are under the gun—which leads to conflicts. One mother told us: "In the last five years, our family life has been entirely dominated by conflicts about homework."

Compared to their peers, students with learning differences tend to experience significantly more difficulties completing homework. These children are more likely to forget their assignments, lose their homework, require assistance in doing their homework, and make mistakes when completing it. The problems may be caused by the child's being easily distracted, overly dependent on others for assistance, poorly organized, or limited in motivation. In other instances, the assigned homework is too difficult for the child to do independently. Punishment is ineffective for these types of problems, and some consequences will just hurt the child. What's needed instead is a real plan to help children learn to manage their daily assignments. Below is a comment written by Warren, a fifth-grade student. He acknowledges his difficulties with memory.

> *If I could change anything I would my memory I always forget*

Strategies for Homework Success

Remember that different kinds of problems require different kinds of solutions. If you and your daughter are struggling each evening to complete the assigned homework, it is likely that she will require some adjustments or adaptations. Many teachers provide students with adaptations when they discover that the assigned homework is too difficult or is inappropriate for a specific child. As one option, the teacher might give shorter, more frequent assignments. Other options include giving fewer or different assignments than for other students in the class. If your child is consistently overwhelmed, speak to the teacher about making adjustments in the homework load. When Ms. Owen called Ms. Clark about the quality of her son's homework, they agreed that Sam should spend a half hour per evening on the homework. Ms. Owen could then sign the incompleted work to verify that Sam had worked this long.

If your child cannot do homework independently, a different solution is called for. The problem may be the result of learning weaknesses combined with a feeling of helplessness relative to academics. Suppose your daughter can complete some tasks, but feels that she cannot. Her primary goal in completing homework may be to earn "freedom" from supervision, rather than mastery of the tasks at hand. A solution may be to ask her teacher for an initial reduction in the amount of homework and a simplification of the tasks involved, to a level where your daughter is clearly capable of completing them. Slowly, her confidence will increase and, in time, she will be able to complete her homework independently.

STRATEGY If your son never seems to know exactly what the assignment is, he is likely to benefit from the use of a daily assignment notebook or calendar. A sample page appears on page 134.[2] Considerable research has supported the effectiveness of school–home note programs, which teach responsibility and self-reliance without punishment. At the start, the note system should be on a daily basis. A weekly basis can begin once the desired behavior is well established. Ask your son's teacher to check the calendar or assignment notebook on every day that homework is assigned, and to initial it if your son has recorded the homework assignment correctly. After he completes the homework in the evening, initial the notebook yourself to document completion. You might have your child carry a small tape recorder for recording the nightly homework. The teacher would record the assignment. When your child has completed the assignment, you can record a short message as confirmation of your supervision. At the beginning, either system requires a lot of structure and follow-through from both the teacher and the parents. Gradually, your child will get into the homework habit and assume more responsibility for keeping track of the homework assignments. This system also works well for children who have difficulty remembering which book to bring home. If your child has problems with remembering, organizing, or bringing home the right material for homework assignments because of attentional problems, try some of the suggestions at the end of the chapter.

STRATEGY If your child has problems keeping track of longer-term assignments, apprise the teacher of the problem and ask for a copy of the semester lesson plan or a list of tests, quizzes, papers, and project-due dates for the semester. Many teachers provide these to students as a matter of course. Post the dates on the family activities calendar. It should then become a matter of habit for your child to check when an important assignment is due. If your child works slowly or finds larger tasks overwhelming, try breaking the assignment or study sessions into smaller, more manageable time segments. Agree mutually about interim accomplishments, and post those dates on the calendar.

Creating a Homework Alliance with Your Child

Homework tends to cause battles in many homes, especially when a child has a learning problem, because homework brings a child's school

HOMEWORK ASSIGNMENTS

NAME _____   DATE _____

SUBJECT	ASSIGNMENT	DATE DUE
Language Arts	_____	
Math	_____	
Reading	_____	
Social Sciences	_____	
Spelling	_____	
Science	_____	
Other	_____	
Other	_____	

Important to take home:

1. _____
2. _____
3. _____
4. _____

Remember to bring to school:

1. _____
2. _____
3. _____
4. _____

_____   _____
Teacher's signature   Parent's signature

Reprinted with permission of Wadsworth Publishing.

problems home. Children with learning problems often consider homework another opportunity to fail, and so they resist it. Just as you need to form an alliance with your child's teacher when it comes to your child's school experience, you need to create an alliance with your child regarding homework. Your role requires you to help your child get started, make sure there is an understanding of what needs to be done, and then get him or her to work independently. It's better for your child to do half of an assignment well than to do all of it poorly—and you should not do it yourself, to "help out."

Don't feel that you have to help your child with homework. Ask about it, but don't force the issue if your help is not wanted. Doing so will only result in conflict and reduced motivation. You can provide incentives (more about that below) and offer assistance, but do not insist that you be allowed to help. Remember, learning to deal with homework independently and responsibly is as important a goal as completing the homework. If your child does want help, agree in advance who will assist. One parent may work better with a particular child, or you may wish to hire a tutor.

As your child's ally in getting homework done, you have several important tasks:

- *Help your child find a place to work.* Experiment with a variety of locations and noise levels, to figure out what works best for your child: silence or soft music, a table or the floor, bright or muted light.

- *Help your child set up a routine and a schedule.* Consistency is an important part of learning. If the family rule is that homework is done right after playtime and a snack—and before TV—make sure that happens every day. Homework time should not be late in the evening or when your child is fatigued. A number of shorter homework periods in the early afternoon, interspersed with reinforcement time, are often preferable.

SAMPLE SCHEDULE

4:00	Snack	6:30	Social Studies
4:30	Math	7:00	Video game
5:00	TV show	8:00	Science
5:30	English	8:30	TV show
6:00	Dinner	9:00	Reading for upcoming book report

- *Help your child establish the purpose of a homework assignment.* If knowledge rather than skill is emphasized, do not allow a child's skill weaknesses to interfere with gaining knowledge. For instance, a history homework assignment can quickly become a remedial reading lesson. This is nonproductive and will not only lead to a dislike for reading but for other subjects as well. If your child has a problem with reading or reading speed, read the material to or with him. The section on reading fluency in Chapter 8 provides several suggestions for helping your child with reading material that is too difficult.

- *Help your child learn to plan ahead.* Show your child how to set up a systematic schedule for the month that breaks bigger projects into more manageable parts and keeps track of upcoming tests, quizzes, and reports.

- *Help your child develop study skills.* Show her how to take notes, skim text, and summarize what she has read in her own words. See Chapter 9 for strategies on mastering material.

- *Keep your comments and directions clear and task-oriented.* Emphasize the task at hand, not your values—"You need to get through problems 1–7 tonight," rather than, "You're being rather lazy about this math, and I won't tolerate that." Such comments only heighten anxiety and rarely lead to greater productivity. Your comments should provide your child with direction for accomplishing the task based on his or her skills.

- *Accept all of your child's responses as genuine.* The solution to a problem may be apparent—to you. If your child makes a mistake, help correct it in a nonpunitive way. Your child should see that you are there to provide information, not criticism. Involve your child in self-evaluation.

- *Avoid offering excessive corrections.* Instead, look for similarities in mistakes, and point them out as a group. Excessive corrections increase the risk of reduced motivation, as well as feelings of low self-worth and incompetence. Be honest but sensitive when providing feedback. For every correction, try to provide at least three compliments.

- *Speak up on your child's behalf if you believe that the assigned homework is excessively repetitive, too difficult, or just too much.* The purpose of homework is to practice skills that have been already learned, not to teach new information. Children with school problems, especially those experiencing foundational and processing skill weaknesses, do not perform well on repetitive, rote assignments. If this is the only kind of homework your child is getting, a change is needed.

Homework Survival Strategies

To avoid stress and encourage your child to manage homework more efficiently, help with mastery of some basic homework survival strategies. The list that follows has been developed for use with parents, but is by no means complete. Talk with your child's teacher and with other parents, to learn their secrets for turning homework struggles into school success.

- Save time by having your child keep all homework materials—papers, pencils, pens, scissors, notebooks, rulers, markers, dictionary—stored in one convenient location. If all the materials can't be stored in the same place, try putting them all in a bright plastic bin.

- Teach your child to set reasonable goals and priorities. Ask which tasks are manageable and which ones might require assistance. Make a nightly homework plan that takes into account the next day's demands: daily assignments, weekly quizzes, and longer-term projects such as reports.

- If your child has attentional or impulsivity problems, plan short homework sessions. If your child has difficulty with tasks and becomes easily bored with repetitive homework, try "racing the clock" games, using a timer or alarm clock to stay on the time track. Rewards may be very helpful here.

- Have your child start out with and complete the easiest tasks first, to establish success and a pattern of reinforcement.

- Be prepared to provide rewards to get your child to finish homework. Try the token economy system or the homework contract, discussed in Chapter 4. Extra TV time, snacks, time alone with a parent, renting a video, going to a movie, or purchasing a new toy or cassette tape are some rewards to consider. Depending on your child's incentive level, you may want to reward daily behavior—all homework finished by 9 P.M., for example—or weekly behavior—a certain grade on a weekly quiz, for example. Work out rewards and incentives with your child. See Chapter 5 for more ideas.

- If a homework routine is not working, be flexible. For example, if one of your child's islands of competence is sports and the teams meet right after school, adjust the homework routine to a time after supper.

- Eliminate Sunday-night arguments about homework by agreeing on a schedule for tackling weekend assignments in advance or no later than Saturday.

- Build "free" time into your child's schedule, especially after he or she has completed a large project, or finished studying for and taking an important test.

- Use a homework "buddy" approach, wherein your child may call a buddy to check homework assignments.
- Use assignment folders or notebooks. Create one pocket for work to be completed, the other for work that is ready to be handed in.

Strive to be patient, fair, and flexible. Remember, homework can play an important role in instilling confidence, helping your child to acquire a positive attitude toward school, and developing academic self-esteem. Listen carefully to what your child has to say about homework and study habits, and be sensitive to the feelings and frustration that are expressed.

Being a "Fair" Parent

Children who have problems with learning require a great amount of time, especially from their parents. If you have several children, don't feel guilty about treating them differently, according to their needs. Rick Lavoie, a national educational consultant, notes that "fairness" is too often defined as meaning "equal." In other words, if Sam gets a candy bar, it's only fair for Danny to have one. If Martha gets to stay up late, it's only fair that Tim does too. "Fairness" does not mean that everyone is treated equally, but rather that everyone gets what he or she needs.

Each child needs something different from the family environment. Children with attentional and behavioral difficulties require exceptional parents because parenting these children is more demanding and challenging than parenting children who do not have these problems.. The fairest thing that you can do as a parent is: respond to and attempt to meet the individual needs of your children. When children grow up in warm, supportive homes and participate in classrooms where expectations are realistic, they are far less likely to develop other weaknesses in the foundational blocks of emotions and self-esteem.

Being a conscientious parent is not an easy job. Remember to pat yourself on the back occasionally, and keep your sense of humor. Make a contract with your child to watch a sunset together, or promise a reward for the absolutely best story made up as a reason for being late for dinner. You and your child will have your share of bad as well as good days, but be assured that your patience, persistence, and efforts *will* pay off.

◄ Part III ►

THE BUILDING BLOCKS
OF LEARNING

Now that you have an understanding of the importance of the foundational blocks, which affect your child's ability to learn, we will turn to the skills of the processing and thinking blocks. With the exception of the skills in the motor block, which are discussed in Chapter 7, the information in the rest of the book's chapters does not correspond directly to specific building blocks of learning. Instead, Chapters 8 and 9 focus on the development of literacy skills and will help you understand how to help your child improve in reading, spelling, and writing. Chapters 10 and 11 address the development of numeracy skills and tell you how to help your child improve in math performance.

Successful academic performance requires skills from both the processing and the thinking blocks. All elementary education depends on a child's ability to read with comprehension, to express ideas clearly in words, and to understand mathematical concepts and solve math problems. Mastering these activities requires different combinations of skills from the processing and thinking blocks. We arranged the topics according to the combination of skills needed to perform the learning activities. For instance, the skills involved in cracking the alphabet code to recognize and pronounce words are exactly the same skills that are required to spell words accurately. Chapter 8 discusses both reading and spelling. As you help your child increase reading skills, you will also be working toward improved spelling skills. Likewise, as you help your child develop the ability to understand ideas, you may also be improving the ability to organize and express thoughts verbally and on paper. Chapter 9 discusses reading comprehension and written expression. Although mathematical facts and concepts differ from reading in that they must be mastered in a particular order, once your child has done so, he or she can combine the concepts in a variety of ways, as part of thinking about, understanding, and solving problems. Chapters 10 and 11 address performance in math calculation and math problem solving, respectively.

Reading, Writing, and Comprehension

To read, a child needs both the processing skills involved with decoding—the ability to pronounce and identify words rapidly—and the thinking skills involved with reading comprehension, which allow an understanding of what is being read. In the course of learning to read, difficulties may arise in one or both of these areas. These difficulties will be directly related to the child's strengths and weaknesses in the building blocks of learning. For example, a child who has weaknesses within the processing blocks will have difficulty with word identification, whereas one who has weaknesses in the thinking blocks will experience difficulty understanding what has been read. As suggested by the arrow in the figure, problems with pronouncing and recognizing words will also affect a child's ability to derive meaning from the words. Children who have difficulty with both

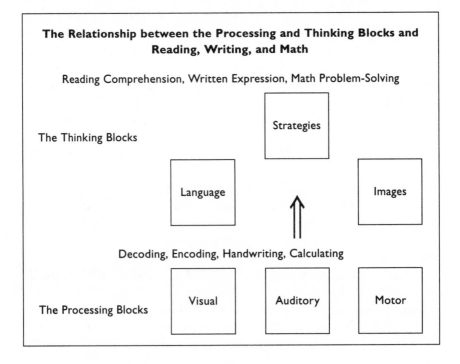

The Relationship between the Processing and Thinking Blocks and Reading, Writing, and Math

processing tasks and thinking tasks will struggle with all aspects of reading. In contrast, children with strengths in the processing and thinking blocks develop reading skills easily and naturally.

Like reading, writing requires a child to use both the processing (or "secretarial") skills needed for spelling, punctuation, and capitalization, and the thinking skills necessary for written expression, which requires an ability to express ideas clearly and coherently. The motor skills for producing handwriting—whether printing, script, or words typed on a computer keyboard—are also needed. When learning to write, a child may experience difficulties in any or all of these areas, depending on the strengths and weaknesses that are present in the building blocks.

A child who has weaknesses in the auditory or visual processing blocks will experience problems with basic skills, particularly spelling or encoding; weaknesses in the motor processing blocks will show up in handwriting that is illegible or very slowly produced. A child with weaknesses in the thinking blocks will experience difficulty in organizing thoughts, expressing ideas, and using strategies for planning and monitoring performance. To return to the ideas expressed in the figure on page 140, problems with spelling or encoding affect and limit a child's ability to express ideas in writing, as do motor problems. Such a child may find writing uncomfortable and will use only words that he or she knows how to spell. As is the case with reading, children who have strengths within the processing and thinking blocks develop writing skills easily and naturally. Children who have weaknesses within both the processing and thinking blocks experience difficulty with several aspects of writing.

Mathematics and Problem Solving

Mastery of mathematics requires the processing skills used to perform basic math calculations—adding, subtracting, multiplying, and dividing—and the thinking skills necessary to understand mathematical concepts and solve problems. In learning mathematical concepts, a child may experience difficulties in any or all of these areas.

A child who has difficulties in the processing blocks will experience problems with basic skills, particularly memorizing basic math facts and producing legibly written calculations. A child who experiences difficulty in the thinking blocks may have trouble understanding problems, organizing information, or using strategies for planning and monitoring performance. As noted by the arrow in the figure on page 140, problems with calculating in the processing block may also affect or limit a child's ability to solve problems. Some children have weaknesses within both the processing and the thinking blocks; thus, they experience difficulty with many aspects of mathematics. Children who struggle with either word recognition or reading comprehension will encounter difficulties with mathematics because story problems place great demands on those skills.

From our clinical experience, we recognize three groups among children with learning problems: those who struggle only with basic skills, those who struggle only with understanding and expressing ideas, or applying the skills, and those who struggle with both skills and the application of skills. Completing in-depth assessments of the specific skills related to the processing and thinking blocks will help you to create a comprehensive profile of your child's present strengths and weaknesses and thus to develop a better understanding of why certain aspects of school performance are causing trouble. Once you know which group your child is in, you will be able to select appropriately helpful interventions.

Assessing Your Child's Processing Skills

If your child has weaknesses in the processing blocks related to visual, auditory, or motor abilities, some difficulty has probably been experienced in one or more aspects of learning and mastering basic reading and math skills. Some children have weaknesses throughout the processing blocks; others have weaknesses within only one block.

Interestingly, we often find that a child's writing can serve as a mirror to the underlying difficulties. The handwriting of a child with visual problems reveals frequent letter reversals as well as an overreliance on sounds to spell. Children with auditory problems confuse similar-sounding letters, such as m with n or b with p. Children with motor skill problems write so poorly that the letters are very difficult to read.

Although you may not be able to arrive at a definitive diagnosis by analyzing your child's writing, a careful analysis of the types of errors he or she is making will give you insights into the strengths and weaknesses within the processing blocks. On pages 143–144 are lists of the characteristics associated with visual, auditory, and motor skills. Pinpointing your child's strengths and weaknesses will allow you to focus on the specific techniques and strategies that bring improvement in those skills. If your child is older than age 8 years, indicate whether these difficulties were experienced to a greater extent than for other children when your child was younger.

Visual Skills	Yes	No
1. Forgets how letters look	————	————
2. Confuses letters with similar appearance (e.g., **n** for **h**)	————	————
3. Misreads little words (e.g., **A** for **I**)	————	————
4. Reverses letters when writing (e.g., **b** for **d**)	————	————
5. Transposes letters when reading or writing (e.g., **on** or **no**)	————	————
6. Has trouble remembering how words look	————	————
7. Has trouble copying from a book or from a chalkboard onto paper	————	————
8. Spells the same word in different ways	————	————
9. Spells words as they sound	————	————
10. Reads at a slow rate	————	————

Auditory Skills	Yes	No
1. Has trouble rhyming words	————	————
2. Has difficulty pronouncing sounds	————	————
3. Has trouble learning letter–sound associations	————	————
4. Has difficulty learning the days of the week and months of the year in sequence	————	————
5. Has difficulty recalling information	————	————
6. Has trouble distinguishing letters with similar sounds, in speech or spelling (e.g., /b/ and /p/, /f/ and /v/	————	————
7. Has trouble sounding out unfamiliar words when reading	————	————
8. Has trouble ordering sounds in the correct sequence when spelling	————	————
9. Has trouble pronouncing multisyllabic words in speaking and reading	————	————
10. Reads at a slow rate	————	————

Motor Skills	Yes	No
1. Has difficulty learning physical activities and seems not to enjoy them	———	———
2. Walks and or runs with an awkward gait	———	———
3. Has difficulty handling small objects and using tools	———	———
4. Seems uninterested in drawing or learning to write	———	———
5. Has difficulty holding a crayon, pencil, or pen correctly	———	———
6. Forms letters in odd ways (for instance, starts from the bottom rather than from the top)	———	———
7. Forgets how to form letters	———	———
8. Has poor or sloppy handwriting	———	———
9. Has trouble learning cursive writing	———	———
10. Writes at a slow rate of speed	———	———

The motor processing block consists of two major kinds of skills: gross motor skills, which involve whole-body movements such as those needed for swimming, jumping, and climbing, and fine motor skills, which involve isolated small-muscle movements such as those needed for cutting with scissors or for drawing or writing the letters of the alphabet. Gross motor skills usually develop early; fine motor skills appear more slowly but increase in importance as children enter school. When you review the ten characteristics for the motor processing block, you may observe that your child only has difficulty with gross motor skills or with fine motor skills.

If your child seems to have the most difficulties with the skills of the motor block, be sure to read Chapter 7. If your child has more difficulties with skills in the visual and auditory blocks, you may wish to skip Chapter 7 and read the other chapters in Part III.

Assessing Your Child's Thinking Skills

When children experience problems with the thinking blocks of language, images, or strategies, they often have trouble applying the basic skills that they have mastered. As they progress into the higher elementary grades, their frustration with school tasks grows. When you review the

Language	Yes	No
1. Developed language slowly	————	————
2. Has trouble understanding directions	————	————
3. Has trouble sustaining conversations	————	————
4. Has trouble generating ideas	————	————
5. Has trouble organizing thoughts and ideas	————	————
6. Often forgets what has been read	————	————
7. Has trouble remembering concepts	————	————
8. Has trouble summarizing facts or drawing conclusions	————	————
9. Has trouble answering questions	————	————
10. Seems to dislike tasks involving reading or writing	————	————

characteristics related to the thinking blocks (pages 145–146), keep in mind that skills in all three of these areas are required for effective reading comprehension, for learning advanced academic subjects, for expressing ideas in writing, and for solving math problems. Pinpointing particular strengths and weaknesses in each of these three blocks will help you first to understand your child and then to choose the most helpful strategies and techniques.

Many of the skills of the thinking blocks are life skills as well as study or learning skills. By helping your child build up a repertory of means to

Images	Yes	No
1. Has trouble putting puzzles together	————	————
2. Dislikes playing with construction toys	————	————
3. Struggles with telling time	————	————
4. Has trouble distinguishing between left and right	————	————
5. Has difficulty understanding math concepts	————	————
6. Has trouble making a mental picture of information	————	————
7. Has trouble with tasks involving spatial reasoning	————	————
8. Has trouble using maps	————	————
9. Has trouble understanding diagrams or graphs	————	————
10. Has trouble with tasks involving geography	————	————

Strategies	Yes	No
1. Seems unaware of a need to plan	___	___
2. Has trouble identifying the steps of a task	___	___
3. Has trouble developing a plan to complete tasks	___	___
4. Has trouble formulating and revising a plan	___	___
5. Has trouble identifying the most relevant aspects of a task	___	___
6. Has trouble generating alternative plans	___	___
7. Has trouble evaluating a completed performance	___	___
8. Has trouble selecting and using techniques for memorization	___	___
9. Has trouble selecting and using techniques for studying	___	___
10. Has trouble generalizing (for instance, taking what is learned in one situation and using it successfully in another)	___	___

study and solve problems, you will be making an important contribution to his or her future success.

Now that you have a greater sense of your child's strengths and weaknesses within the processing and thinking blocks, you should have a better idea of why there are struggles—and what remedies will help. As you read through the chapters in Part III, note the interventions that are likely to work best for your child's particular combination of strengths and weaknesses.

▼

Chapter

7

Your Child's Motor Skills

Helping Your Child to Physical Mastery and Legible Handwriting

Even in these days of word processing, your child needs to be able to move comfortably through the world and communicate by writing. Children who won't join in games and other physical activities because of a "klutz" label, or who write so slowly that they cannot finish class assignments, or so illegibly that their homework cannot be read, will do poor schoolwork and will suffer damage to their self-esteem.

Delayed development in either gross (large muscle) or fine (small muscle) motor skills can affect your child's school performance; however, weaknesses in fine motor skills, sometimes referred to as visual-motor skills, are a greater barrier to academic success. For this reason, although the chapter begins with a discussion of gross motor problems, the major focus is on helping your child develop fine motor skills.

Overall Motor Development

Andrew and Angie both struggle with fine motor but not gross motor skills. Though he is the captain of his soccer team, which requires gross motor coordination, Andrew has fine motor weakness; his handwriting is virtually unreadable and he is not good at using tools or building toy models. Angie, a whiz on a set of jungle bars, is struggling to learn to write letters. Other children have trouble with gross motor skills, but not fine

147

motor skills. Lily, for instance, has difficulty skipping rope and bouncing a basketball, but no problem writing letters or numbers. Sam can assemble models of complicated machines using a Lego™ set, but he has little luck hitting a tennis ball despite a year of lessons.

Still other children, like Danny, have difficulty with both fine and gross motor tasks—difficulties that affect major parts of Danny's life. His parents are both concerned and perplexed because Danny's motor development has been so different from that of Mark, his older brother.

At the age of 5 years, Mark was able to catch and throw a ball with ease. Even at 6 years of age, when someone threw him a ball, Danny would close his eyes and stick out his hands—and invariably, the ball would bounce off some part of his body. During hopscotch games at summer camp, Danny didn't have much success; he stumbled and fell forward when he tried to jump, and he couldn't hop on one leg.

Mark had started playing soccer in kindergarten. Danny was not interested, even though all his friends were on soccer teams. When he did finally join a soccer team and was out on the field, he was more interested in the snack than in the game.

Danny's fine motor skills were also late in developing. By the age of 5 years, Mark had been able to write his name and had begun to form other words. In contrast, even when Danny had completed kindergarten, he could not write his name legibly. He didn't like to draw or use coloring books; when he tried—which was only when pressured by his parents and teacher—his efforts consisted of scribbles and a few straight lines drawn through the pictures.

In contrast to his motor skills, Danny's oral language skills were well developed. He loved looking at books, was eager to learn to read, and had a remarkable vocabulary. At one point, when his mother was reading to him from a book that featured a purple tree, she asked, "Have you ever seen a purple tree?" Danny replied, "No, but I think that one is magenta." His strength within the thinking block of language was as readily apparent as his weaknesses within the motor block.

His parents wondered whether Danny's motor delays would affect his success in school. Should he repeat kindergarten? Would he catch up if held back? From our experiences with children like Danny, we are firmly convinced that being held back ("retention") is not advisable unless a child is socially immature and has trouble relating to children of the same age group. We believe that these children should be promoted, but with emphasis on building on their other strengths and getting help with their motor difficulties. Because Danny has strengths in the thinking block of language, he will be able to keep up with his peers in certain activities;

however, he will struggle with other types of academic and recreational activities. He will need to work on building his gross motor skills for major physical activities, and his fine motor skills to learn to write, draw, and use scissors.

If your child, like Danny, has severe motor problems or delayed motor development, consult your child's teacher or your pediatrician. Your child may need to have an occupational or physical therapist evaluate both gross motor skills, including muscle control and body coordination, and fine motor skills. Most likely, the therapist will prescribe a series of exercises and activities designed to enhance development. Ways that you can assist your child with motor development are provided in the following sections. If you are concerned about poor motor development, you may wish to consult with a specialist for additional ideas.

Gross Motor Development

The figure on page 150, provides a brief overview of gross motor development between the ages of 2½ to 6 years. The black band shows the age range during which most children master certain basic skills. These skills usually develop naturally because most children love to run, climb, slide, and throw and catch balls.

The figure shows that different children may develop at different rates, even within a family. One child may catch a bounced ball several times, before age 4 years; an older brother may be unable to catch the same bounced ball until he is nearly 5½ years old.

Motor coordination improves with age. However, delayed gross motor development often persists throughout the school years, which can affect a child's self-esteem and interactions with peers. Children with weaknesses in gross motor skills encounter problems in daily physical activities. They are often insecure with movement and slow to develop the skills needed to succeed in physical activities. Arms and legs may not work as essential parts of a well coordinated system. These children may have trouble telling left from right and judging spatial relations; they are often chosen last for team sports and they try to avoid physical education classes. They may unintentionally bump into desks or jostle classmates, inviting laughter and ridicule from their peers.

Even when strengths in the thinking blocks help a child compensate, poor physical coordination can contribute to feelings of low self-esteem. This is especially true in an environment that places a high value on success in sports and views athletic success as a measure of competence.

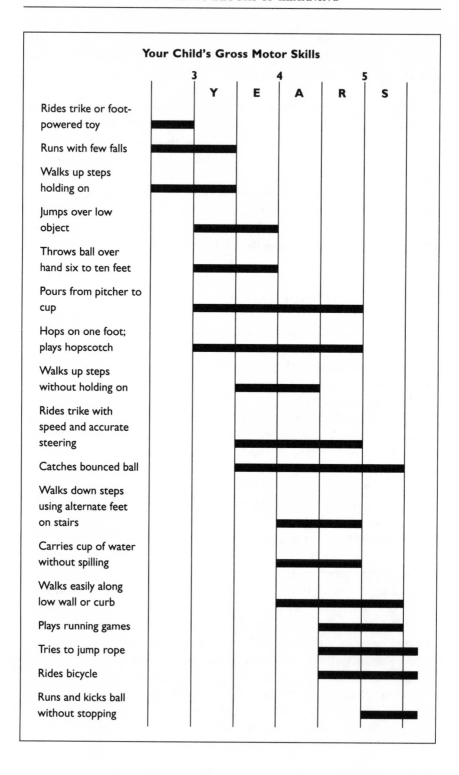

Your Child's Gross Motor Skills

Many parents encourage their children to engage in athletic activities as a way of increasing their gross motor skills. They teach their children to swim, take them to parks to run and slide, patiently toss balls back and forth. They set aside short periods of time each day to focus on activities designed to improve body coordination. When Danny's parents realized how difficult it was for him to lift both feet off the ground when jumping, they decided to help him improve his skill by holding his hands and encouraging him to practice jumping up and down. As Danny's confidence increased, his father held on to him with only one hand. Once Danny had mastered jumping, his parents helped him practice activities that required weighting the body on one foot. They began by holding both of his hands for support. Gradually, Danny became more proficient in both jumping and hopping.

Becoming skilled and successful in motor activities will help build your child's self-confidence, and will strengthen the building block of self-esteem. As we discussed in Chapter 5, the loss of self-esteem because of poor academic performance can be minimized by success within other domains. This same kind of compensation holds true for children who have poor physical performance; if your child is weak in motor skills, there are almost certainly other areas of strengths. Even so, all children need to feel physically competent. If your child has problems performing one kind of physical activity, identify others in which participation is successful. Because Danny did not like soccer, his parents enrolled him in swimming lessons—a way to increase his physical strength and coordination while performing an activity he found enjoyable. Don't be dismayed if your child tries out many sports and activities before finding one that is liked well enough to stick with.

Encourage your child to help with tasks in the home that promote the development of gross motor skills and coordination: set the table for dinner, pour a beverage into glasses, or clear the dishes after the meal. Provide opportunities for using simple tools, such as hammers and screwdrivers, in recreation projects.

It was once thought that learning problems occurred when a child skipped a physical developmental stage, and that learning to crawl "properly" would help a person learn to read better. Few people today would advocate this type of therapy to improve reading ability, but we do know that activities such as jumping, stretching, throwing, and running can increase a child's endurance and contribute to a positive body image and thus to higher self-esteem. For all of these reasons, engaging in physical play with your child is time well spent, during the early as well as the later childhood years.

Fine Motor Development

"Your child has the worst handwriting I've ever seen," Alex's third-grade teacher announced to his parents at their first parent–teacher conference. Though his mother quipped, "That's OK—he'll probably grow up to be a doctor," she and his father were both startled by the teacher's negative pronouncement. Was handwriting really that important? they wondered. The teacher explained that Alex's poor handwriting could signal a serious ongoing problem.

Alex practiced painstakingly each day, but his writing was not improving and his embarrassment was increasing. At school, he often sat at his desk with his arms shielding his work so that no one could see his writing. Indeed, his handwriting difficulties were beginning to affect the foundational blocks of emotions and behavior, as well as the block self-esteem.

Even indecipherable handwriting will not cause your child to fail in school, but it can be a contributing factor. Alex's school performance was clearly hurt because he could not write legibly. It is important for parents and teachers to understand that a child's difficulties in this area stem from a severe weakness in the motor processing block, not a poor attitude or lack of effort.

Preschool children engage in many fine motor activities as they learn to use a spoon, to draw, and to turn the pages in a book. The figure on page 153, provides a brief overview of fine motor development for children between the ages of 2½ to 6 years. The black band shows the range in which most children master particular skills. These skills usually develop naturally because young children are inveterate artists who like to color, paint, cut, draw, and write.

The major way that a weakness in fine motor skills will affect your child's school performance is in handwriting, rather than in drawing. There may be trouble with drawing, but poor artists can be highly successful in school. Failure to develop a legible writing style, however, is problematic to a child (and the teacher) in any grade. If another person cannot read a written message, communication does not occur. A frustrated third-grade teacher wrote, at the top of one child's illegibly written paper, "I can't read your paper (although I would like to . . .)."

Writing-Readiness Activities

Some children begin exploring the possibilities of print as early as age 3 years. They enjoy activities that involve small-muscle control, whether

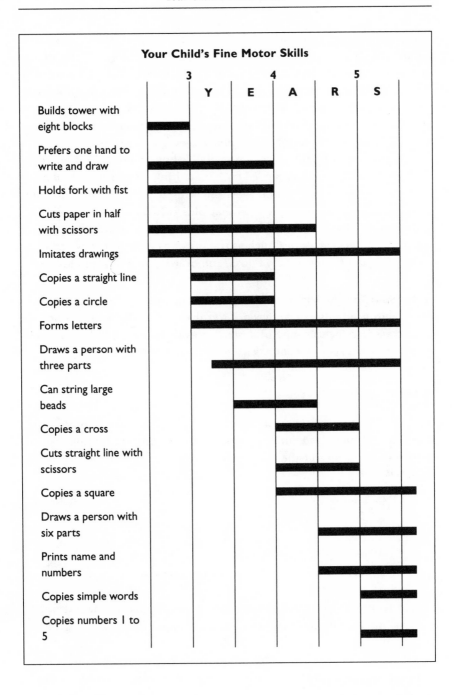

Your Child's Fine Motor Skills

Y E A R S (3, 4, 5)

- Builds tower with eight blocks
- Prefers one hand to write and draw
- Holds fork with fist
- Cuts paper in half with scissors
- Imitates drawings
- Copies a straight line
- Copies a circle
- Forms letters
- Draws a person with three parts
- Can string large beads
- Copies a cross
- Cuts straight line with scissors
- Copies a square
- Draws a person with six parts
- Prints name and numbers
- Copies simple words
- Copies numbers 1 to 5

drawing, writing, or using a computer. They may begin copying print from books or magazines, or writing "stories" that consist of long strings of random letters to accompany their pictures, even before they start reading. Other children are slow to develop the fine motor coordination that writing requires. In fact, by first grade, some children will not have mastered the fine motor coordination required to form letters.

As soon as a child can hold a pencil, marker, or crayon—drawing or even scribbling—should be encouraged. Scribbling will help prepare for the fine motor movements needed for handwriting. Provide different mediums, such as finger paints or crayons, and offer different activities to pique interest. Suggest drawing pictures that illustrate the stories you read together, or the stories your child tells you. As skill increases, help with more specific readiness activities, such as tracing and copying shapes and lines, completing dot-to-dot activity books, and drawing lines and circles.

STRATEGY: Many children have trouble writing with the large pencils sometimes used in schools; they are too thick for small hands. Do not use these large pencils at home. Instead, provide your child with regular pencils or markers when practicing drawing and forming letters.

Prewriting Activities

To learn how to form letters and numbers, your child needs to be able to draw circles, lines, and curves. Besides encouraging scribbling, you can help your child master these prewriting activities by instruction in how to draw:

- Horizontal lines.
- Circles.
- Crosses, squares, and rectangles.
- Lines that slant to the left and lines that slant to the right.

Encourage your child to use these lines and shapes when drawing. For example, ask for drawings of a winding road, a long fence, a group of balls, some valleys and mountains, a curvy snake. You may not be an artist or a calligrapher, but make sure that your child sees your writing skills— in preparing shopping lists, writing letters, addressing envelopes, or writing checks when paying bills.

Should you be concerned if your kindergarten-age child is not yet beginning to experiment with writing or appears uninterested in learning to

---

WHEN THE HANDWRITING'S ON THE WALL . . .

Most parents have had firsthand experience of their children's drawings and scribbling, on walls and in books. It may be tempting to forbid the use of pens, pencils, paints, crayons, and markers at home, but it's not a good idea. Their prohibition may ensure that your home stays tidy, but you will be squelching young children's inborn enthusiasm for drawing, writing, and reading. A much better solution is to keep stacks of blank paper on hand for their efforts. You needn't spend a lot of money on artists' drawing pads or fancy notebooks. Newspapers, the paper in junk mail, the cardboard in shirt boxes sent from the laundry, or discarded computer printouts can all be supplies for your budding artists and writers.

---

write? No. This child may just need extra enticing. Rajeesh showed no interest in writing when he entered first grade. In fact, he refused to write in class. He did, however, like to draw. In the first few weeks of school, his teacher encouraged him to draw pictures during writing time, and his parents did the same at home, asking him to draw pictures of scenes from books they'd been reading and movies they'd seen together. Soon, Rajeesh started putting titles on his pictures or writing a few words to describe each scene. As his desire to write increased, his teacher and parents gave him more help with letter formation and spelling.

Fundamentals for Handwriting

A few children need assistance in establishing hand preference or "handedness." If your child has not become a confirmed righty or lefty by kindergarten, watch some attempts at writing, and try to determine which hand appears more coordinated and is used more often. Which hand is used to hold the telephone, eat with a spoon, comb the hair, or bounce a ball? Although there may be some switching back and forth, one hand will usually be used more than the other. Through careful observations, the natural hand preference will become apparent.

Some children seem to be ambidextrous, using both hands equally well. Denise tended to use her left hand for most activities, but when she was using a pencil, she would pass it from her left to her right hand, depending on which side of the paper she was drawing on. Denise found it uncomfortable to cross the midline of her body, so her simple solution was to pass the pencil from one hand to the other. Her parents, noticing that her overall preference was for her left hand, decided that Denise would use that hand for writing. However, she could not remember which was her left hand. For a few weeks, she wore a ring on her left hand as a reminder. As time went on, her preference became well established and she no longer needed the prompt.

STRATEGY   Beyond establishing a hand preference, some children have further small motor difficulties when learning how to write. A sizable number of children have ineffective pencil grips. Most people hold a pencil between the thumb and index finger, with the pencil resting on the middle finger. Some children cannot get comfortable this way; after writing for a few minutes, they complain of fatigue in their writing hands. These children often benefit from using triangular pencil grips, available at most teaching supply stores. This type of rubber grip helps position the fingers around the pencil. One parent told us that she "modeled" using these pencil grips so her children wouldn't feel "different" when using them in school. Other children can be helped to establish a proper pencil grip by winding a rubber band around the pencil at the point where the middle finger rests on it.

When writing, a child should be able to move the writing arm smoothly and easily across the paper. For printing, the writing paper is usually positioned straight up and down in front of the body. For writing in script or using a manu-cursive style (see page 158), a right-handed person typically slants the paper to the left, and a left-handed person slants it to the right. Some children have trouble keeping the writing paper positioned correctly on a table or desk. They find it easier to write when their papers are attached to a clipboard.

Handwritten Communication

Even though many children have trouble developing legible handwriting, instruction in handwriting has tended to fall by the wayside in recent years. All too few children have practice sessions on how to form letters. Handwriting may not be emphasized in your child's school curriculum, so spend some time at home developing a legible writing style so that others can easily decipher your child's written ideas.

Sloppy handwriting affects how readers, especially teachers, respond to a paper. To a teacher, a neatly written paper implies thoughtful effort, whereas a sloppy-looking paper appears to reflect a hurried, anything-goes attitude and will likely receive a lower grade. Stress legibility with your child, not perfection. A few people in each generation take up the fine art of calligraphy; the rest of us are concerned only that our writing can be read with relative ease.

Most children require some guidance as they are beginning to learn how to form letters. Initially, you may physically guide your child's hand as you say the letter's name. Teach how to form letters beginning at the top of the stroke. The first independent attempts at letter formation will appear awkward, but most children, with practice, learn to form letters easily from memory.

While your child is learning, do not worry about the size of the letters or their appearance. Some may turn out to be facing in the wrong direction. This is not unusual or dyslexic. Do not worry about reversals until your child has been exposed to the alphabet systematically for at least one year. The direction a letter faces is arbitrary, and it takes children time and practice to learn the letters correctly. If your child persists in reversing letters past the age of 7 years, this suggests weaknesses in the visual or auditory processing blocks. Activities for reducing reversals are presented near the end of this chapter.

Before you start helping your child with handwriting, find out what type of writing style is being taught in the school, and get a copy of the alphabet, illustrating how the letters are formed. Three different types of writing styles exist: (a) manuscript or printing, (b) cursive or script, and (c) manu-cursive, a combined approach. Most schools adopt a certain approach to teaching handwriting. In some programs, handwriting instruction begins with printing letters and then progresses to cursive handwriting instruction in about third grade. In other programs, children begin learning a manu-cursive alphabet, which naturally progresses into cursive writing. In a few programs, students begin with cursive writing. A brief description of the three writing styles follows.

1. *Manuscript/printing.* In a traditional manuscript instructional program, children are taught that letter forms are composed of simple sticks and circles. They then learn how various combinations of circles and sticks form the individual letters of the alphabet.

2. *Cursive/script.* In cursive writing or writing in script, all letters are formed with a continuous motion, and words are written as

units. Most schools introduce cursive writing in second or third grade.

3. *Manu-Cursive/D'Nealian.* The manu-cursive writing style combines manuscript and cursive letter formation. The most widely used manu-cursive writing style is D'Nealian.[1] In this method, the majority of letters are formed with a continuous motion, thus providing a natural progression from manuscript to cursive letter formation. Joining strokes connect the letters. In addition, D'Nealian offers visual, auditory, and tactile-kinesthetic clues to help children remember how the letters should be formed. Appendix B presents D'Nealian manuscript and cursive letters, along with the suggested oral instructions when teaching the letters. You may want to teach your child this writing style at home.

Learning a new writing style is often difficult for children with fine motor weaknesses. Not surprisingly, when the new writing style is introduced, other aspects of writing performance often deteriorate, leading to more spelling errors or greater problems in word spacing, for instance. When this happens, talk to your child's teacher about making some accommodation so that all writing isn't derailed. Often, teachers will agree that every first draft can be printed so that the children can devote their attention to expressing their ideas. When the paper has been edited and the spelling errors have been corrected, they can then write the final draft in cursive.

Letter Formation

The major goal of handwriting instruction is to help children learn and maintain a consistent and legible writing style. Start by having your child practice writing individual letters in isolation, rather than whole words or sentences. After the basic forms of the letters are mastered, progress to practicing letters within words and then words within sentences. The following activities will help your child establish reliably legible writing.

Tracing   Tracing exercises are critical for children who have severe weaknesses in fine motor skills. Have your child practice tracing letters until the motor movement becomes easy and automatic. Tracing will help boost speed and ease in forming letters.

STRATEGY   Younger children can be encouraged to trace plastic magnetic letters or letters made from sandpaper or felt. Or, make letters or numbers

CHOOSING A HANDWRITING STYLE

Some educational professionals contend that young children should learn to write using manuscript or printing because printed letters seem easier to form than cursive letters and are similar to the print that children see in books. They also note that cursive writing, which requires fine motor coordination to sustain a rhythmic motion and make the required continuous strokes, can pose problems for some children with motor weaknesses.

Other educators believe that children with fine motor weaknesses should begin with manu-cursive or cursive styles. They prefer these approaches for several reasons. First, when using these writing styles, children make fewer reversals because the letters are formed differently and are easier to discriminate—b's from d's, for instance. Second, children need not learn two different methods for writing (first manuscript and then cursive). Third, the continuous motion and rhythm needed for manu-cursive and cursive can help children develop skills with spacing and speed.

Depending on your child's fine motor skills, one writing style may be easier to learn and use than another. Some children learn to print easily but struggle to learn cursive letters; others have tremendous difficulty learning to print and then experience similar difficulties in learning to write in cursive. Don't fall into the trap of spending so much time on developing an alternate writing style that other learning suffers. Remember that the major goal of handwriting instruction is legibility, not proficiency or mastery of a certain style. Some flexibility should be allowed in your child's school program. For many children, mastery of one handwriting system makes more sense than automatic progression to a second one.

with a raised surface: write the letters on index cards in different colors, then layer the outline of the letter with Elmer's® glue. After the glue dries, the raised surface of the letter can be used for tracing. Guide your child's index finger over the letter. After repeated finger-tracings of the letter, begin attempts to write the letter with a marking pen.

Older children can use tracing paper or go over letters with a crayon or marking pen. Take advantage of your child's motor memory by encouraging repetitive tracing.. This awareness of and emphasis on muscle movement will help memorization of the letter forms.

Oral Descriptions Some children who experience problems with letter formation have trouble getting a mental picture of a letter. If this is your child's problem, enlist the skills in the thinking blocks of language and images to shore up the weaknesses in the motor or visual processing blocks. During a session of tracing a letter or number, describe the movement needed to form the symbol correctly. For example, when forming the printed lowercase letter *b,* say: "Start up at the top, go down, and then swing around to the right in a circle." This verbal description will prompt memory of the sequence of movements. Gradually, encourage your child to say the verbal prompts aloud.

When they learn to write, some children find it helpful to visualize a clock face with all of the numbers written in, or a human head with ears, nose, and chin. Typical instructions are:

- Using a clock as a guide to teach formation of the letter *c,* say: "Start at 2:00 and drive back, all the way around, to 4:00." Using a head image, say: "Start at the right ear, swing over the top, and come all the way around to the end of the chin."
- Using a clock to teach the letter *d,* say: "Start at 4:00 swing all the way back to 2:00, and then draw a straight line up and then down." Using a head image, say: "Start at the right ear, swing all the way around, back to that same ear, and then make a line up to the top of the face and down."

If you are teaching your child a manu-cursive writing style, use the oral descriptions provided with the D'Nealian letters in Appendix B. Gradually, encourage recital of the movements while writing the letters. Encourage verbalizing the process as the letters are formed. For example, when printing the letter *n,* your child may say: "Move down and then back up. Make one hump."

Persistent Reversals

A few children continue to reverse letters and numbers past the age of 7 years. These children usually have weaknesses in the visual processing block and have trouble getting a mental image of a letter. Thus, they find

DIANA'S ALPHABET

When she entered first grade, Diana was unable to copy, trace, or draw a straight line. She had severe weaknesses in the visual and motor processing blocks, but strengths in the auditory processing block and the thinking block of language. Though she couldn't write, she had learned the sounds of the letters easily the previous year and was now reading short books on her own.

When Diana's mother understood the need for practice and reinforcement with motor skills, she devised some strategies to help her daughter learn to form letters. Her mother showed her that the letter O was similar in shape to a ball and that the letter l was a stick. Together they spent time using balls and sticks to draw snowmen and houses. Using these two initial shapes, Diana began to see that she could make drawings that other people could recognize.

Then her mother showed Diana how to talk herself through letter formation. Together they created stories or language links to help Diana remember how to form each letter. Following are the descriptions they developed for each letter:

A build a tepee, add a stick for support

a make a ball and then come down on the side so it won't roll away

B draw a stick, add a face and belly

b draw a stick with a belly

C half moon

c smaller half moon

D stick with half a ball

d stick with a bottom

E stick with three floors: top, middle, and bottom

e middle floor, up and around the door

F top and middle floor

f make a candy cane, split it in half

(continued)

DIANA'S ALPHABET (CONTINUED)

G half moon, come in for a smile

g floating ball or a bobber with a fishhook

H two sticks touching hands

h chair: make the back and then the seat

I stick with top and bottom

i stick with a fly on top

J fishhook above the water

j fishhook with a fly in the water

K stick with an arm and a leg

k stick with lower arm and leg

L stick with bottom floor

l stick

M mountain: up the mountain, down, up, down

m hill: up the hill, down, up, down

N mountain: up, down, up

n backless chair

O large ball

o small ball

P stick with a face

p face with stick body under water

Q head with a tongue

q bobber: line down into the water

R stick with a face and leg

r stick with a seat

S snake

s baby snake

T stick with a roof

t stick with a falling roof

U large cup with a stick so it doesn't tip

u smaller cup

DIANA'S ALPHABET (CONTINUED)

V in the valley, out of the valley

v little valley, in and out

W down the mountain, up, down, up

w down the small mountain, up, down, up

X two sticks losing their balance

x smaller sticks

Y tilting sticks: tie them to the ground

y tilting stick, anchor it in the water

Z top floor, stairway to the bottom floor, across

z middle floor, stairway to the bottom floor, across

When practicing the letters, Diana and her mother often grouped them by characteristics: the people letters, the underwater letters, the building-and-stick letters, the mountain-and-valley letters, and the ball letters. Using this type of approach, which capitalized on her strengths in language, Diana learned to write all of the letters within a few months.

it difficult to remember which direction each letter should face. A few simple suggestions can help to reduce the frequency of reversed letters:

- Have the child describe aloud the movements for forming a letter. For example, using the image of a clock face, the description for making the letter *d* is: "Begin at 4:00, swing all the way back to 2:00, and then draw a straight line up and then down."

- Have the child associate a problematic letter with another letter that does not cause confusion. A lowercase *b* can be related to an uppercase *B*, or a lowercase *a* can be recalled as the beginning movement for making a lowercase *d*. The child may say: "I start the letter *d* just like the letter *a*."

- Teach a common word, to help remember the problematic letters. For example, if your child reverses the letters *b* and *d*, teach the word *dad* and point out that all three letters face the same way. Encourage thinking of the word *dad* when there is uncertainty as to letter formation. Or, use a cue word that contains the two problematic letters, such as *bed*. Draw a line across the word to show how it looks like a bed. Encourage your child to think of the word *bed* as a clue for which way the letter *b* or *d* faces.

- Encourage the use of cursive, not manuscript style writing. Reversals appear less frequently in cursive writing.

STRATEGY   If your child persists in reversing letters and numbers when writing, make sure that the teacher understands that the reversals are caused by weaknesses in the processing blocks, not because your child cannot think or is not trying. To protect against becoming anxious or losing interest in writing, treat reversals as minor handwriting or spelling mistakes that will be corrected on the final draft. Show your child how to use strengths in the thinking blocks to recall the distinctive features of letters and numbers.

Self-Evaluation

Explain to your child that neat, legible handwriting is a courtesy to the reader, and that observing margins, indenting paragraphs, avoiding cross outs, and spacing words neatly will increase the chances of receiving a favorable grade.

Help your child increase legibility by teaching how to evaluate the quality of his or her own handwriting. For example, as Maria practices printing, on ruled paper with a middle horizontal line between the line guides, she uses the acronym of PRINT to ask herself: Does my work show:

Proper letter formation?

Right amount of spacing between letters and words?

Indented paragraphs?

Neatness?

Tall letters above the middle line, short letters below?

Be creative about finding ways to help your child improve the appearance of papers. Charlotte, a sixth-grade student, had trouble remembering to stop writing when she got to the right margin of the paper. To remind her to stop at the margin, her father placed a piece of clear tape along the margin line. When her pencil came to the tape, Charlotte was reminded to stop writing there and go on to the next line. After a few weeks, the tape prompt was no longer necessary.

If your child tends to make many erasures, encourage using a pencil, or supply an erasable pen so that mistakes are easy to erase and correct.

Word Processing

Although it is important to continue to help them develop legible handwriting, some children who have severe weaknesses in the motor block may find learning to write so frustrating that it makes sense to find handwriting alternatives. Many of them can, in effect, bypass handwriting difficulties by learning to type and using a word processing program.

These days, many children begin using computers very early; some begin hunting and pecking at the keyboard as young as age 2 years. This is a fine introduction, but at some point your child will require formal instruction in keyboarding skills so that both hands are used and the word processing program's capabilities are fully and efficiently utilized. You can introduce keyboarding skills as soon as your child's fingers can fit the keyboard. Most children are ready for formal instruction by the age of 8 years. Several commercial typing tutors and word processing programs have been designed for children; some provide self-paced drills and come in game formats, which may increase your child's interest and motivation. The complexity of these programs varies, so select one that is appropriate for your child's skill level.

This kind of technological assistance is often critical for children with fine motor problems. One child we know had struggled with handwriting for several years. Despite lots of practice in letter formation, his handwriting was difficult to read. In third grade, however, he learned to type and began to complete the majority of his assignments on a laptop computer. He loves the appearance of his printed work: the letters are the same size, the spacing is even, and there are no smudged or crossed-out words. He finally feels proud of the assignments he turns in. And, as his computer skill grew, he began to be recognized as the class's computer expert, which provided an additional boost to his self-esteem.

These days, every child is encouraged to become familiar with a computer. Your child is most likely very comfortable playing games on the computer, but you can also suggest some practice in writing stories on the computer and drawing pictures to illustrate them. The experience of doing this for fun will make it easy to complete schoolwork assignments of this type.

With your guidance and support, the effects of weaknesses in the motor block can be greatly reduced. In addition to practicing

YOUR CHILD AND THE COMPUTER

Word-processing software gives your child the opportunity to correct spelling, delete or add words, or rearrange sentences without having to recopy the entire written assignment by hand. But to use these tools, your child must learn to operate the word-processing program—how to enter, save, edit, print text, and use the special checkers that correct spelling, grammar, and punctuation.

A note of caution: Before attempting to help your child on the computer, get comfortable with using the word-processing system yourself. As any computer user knows, without familiarity with a particular system, even small mistakes can be disastrous. For instance, Ryan's dad was not familiar with the various functions of the word-processing software. While attempting to help Ryan delete some text from the middle of a paragraph, he erased the three pages that his son had already written. As you can imagine, Ryan did not think that having to start his essay over was a positive experience. His dad told him that the modern-day excuse for a missing homework assignment is no longer a hungry dog, but an uncooperative computer. This may be true, but the importance of mastering the word-processing system before proceeding can't be overemphasized.

handwriting, encourage your child to participate in activities that will promote both gross and fine motor development—sports, dancing, computer games, model-building, arts and crafts or playing a musical instrument. As with other areas of school performance, plenty of practice and praise will help improve your child's performance.

Chapter 8

The Mechanics of Reading and Spelling

Recognizing the Best Way for Your Child to Learn to Read and Spell

The ability to identify words—to decode—is an essential reading skill. A child who cannot identify words cannot engage in reading as a meaningful and pleasurable activity. However, once the child learns to decode successfully, all of his or her energies are automatically redirected toward understanding the meaning of what is being read. In other words, a child who learns to read can focus on reading to learn. If there are struggles in the early stages of learning to read, the child will be frustrated in the quest to read to learn, and will face increasing obstacles with all forms of education. Similarly, the ability to spell words—to encode—is a fundamental and essential skill of writing. If there are struggles with spelling, the child will find it difficult to progress to all other forms of written communication, and many future writing assignments will be very frustrating.

The skills that make it possible for a child to both recognize and produce words are found in the processing blocks. This chapter focuses on those skills—first those involved with auditory methods of learning decoding and encoding, then those involved with visual methods. The final section addresses ways to help your child improve in the rate or speed of reading. All the methods in this chapter can be used at home.

The Skills of Decoding and Encoding

Learning to decode words requires a great amount of concentration and energy and the coordination and integration of many skills. Children must learn to follow the print from left to right across the page, recognize words by sight, and identify and pronounce new and unfamiliar words. Initially, the task of making connections between the appearance and sounds of letters is quite arbitrary. Children learn that the letter *b* signifies a certain sound, but, turned the other way, it becomes the letter *d*, and a different sound is required. The initial stages of learning to read make intense demands on the perceptual and memory skills of the processing blocks. While juggling all of these tasks, children must simultaneously attempt to convert the printed symbols into meaningful language.

Learning to spell words—encoding—is even more complicated. Children must learn to translate the spoken sounds of a language into the letters or combination of letters that represent those sounds. They must also retain visual images of words and be able to recall these images as needed. Some children who read well have extreme difficulties remembering how to spell because the process of decoding words is much easier than the process of encoding words. To decode a word, a child just has to recognize it; to encode it, the word has to be produced correctly.

Teaching Reading and Spelling

Your child's success in learning to read and spell will depend partly on the school's choice of teaching method and how well it matches your child's learning style and profile. Some children learn to read and spell easily when shown words to remember; they seem to absorb them from the world around them. Other children need more explicit instruction about the letters and their sounds, and still others need more intensive methods that are multisensory, enlisting visual, auditory, and motor activities to enhance memory and learning.

The visual methods depend primarily on whole-word recognition. Two examples of visual methods are the use of flash cards and the "look–say" approach. In these techniques, the teacher shows the child a word, tells what the word is, and then asks the child to say the word. Success with this method depends on the child's ability to retain a mental picture of words. The approach works best for children who have strong skills in the visual processing block—especially, strong memories.

Other reading methods depend more on auditory skills and the teaching of sound awareness. Instructors teach the letters, and the sounds the letters represent, and then show students how to put the sounds together to form new words. Success with these methods depends on children's ability to work with sounds. The methods work best for children who have skills in the auditory processing block.

Still other methods, designed largely for use with struggling readers, depend primarily on motor skills. Using one of these methods, a teacher, tutor, or parent may show the child a word, have the child trace the word several times with a finger, and then ask the child to write the word from memory. These methods use motor memory to enhance learning and can be used to overcome weaknesses in the auditory and visual processing blocks.

If your child is having difficulty learning to read, the reason may simply be that the reading method used at school is not the right one for your child. Although most teachers are eclectic and balanced in their approaches to reading, two distinct schools of thought exist on how to teach reading to children. Teachers from one school of thought—in educational terms, "code-emphasis" teachers—believe that children should be taught the letters of the alphabet and their corresponding sounds, and should learn how to "sound out" words. These skills will then serve as the foundation for all activities involving reading and writing. In contrast, "whole-language" teachers believe that children will develop basic reading skills naturally if they are exposed to print in a "language-rich, interactive environment." These teachers believe that directing a child's attention to the black squiggles on a page may disrupt a natural learning process and decrease the motivation to become a reader.

Depending on the teacher's orientation, classroom instruction in reading and spelling will be geared toward different learning blocks. A first-grade code-emphasis teacher would spend a good deal of time helping children master the fundamentals of letter–sound relationships. When a child doesn't know a word, the teacher may encourage the child to analyze the sound structure of the word. Initially, a code-emphasis teacher presents activities that will enhance children's skills in the processing blocks, such as having students move around magnetic letters to form and then pronounce new words. The words that children learn this way will then be included in their reading lesson.

A first-grade whole-language emphasis teacher, by contrast, will spend a lot of time on activities designed to promote thinking and interacting with language. For example, she may start a discussion on a particular subject, such as spiders, then read the children a story about a spider as she points to the words, then take dictation as the class composes a story about spiders, recording it for them on the blackboard. The theory is that if children are exposed to print in a meaningful, authentic way, they will develop reading and writing skills naturally. When children don't know a word, teachers encourage them to guess what it might be, because a major goal of this method is to teach children to use context to understand text.

Despite what an individual teacher may say, *there is no single right approach to early reading instruction.* The most effective method for your child depends on his or her characteristics. There are no bad methods, there are just bad matches. Most teachers use a combination approach, although a few adhere strongly to specific beliefs and methodologies, As a parent, you need to recognize the philosophy of your child's school regarding reading instruction and the types of methods the teachers use.

When children are learning to read, they may use one or more kinds of information to help with word recognition: the illustrations in the book; the context of the word or the meaning of the text; word order or the patterns of language; or the sounds of the letters in the words. The goal of reading instruction is to ensure that your child can use *all* types of clues when attempting to identify unfamiliar words. Depending on your child's learning style, different types of instruction will be effective.

Each strategy can be helpful. However, a reader who is weak in dealing with letter–sound clues (skills within the visual and auditory processing blocks) will depend too much on picture and meaning clues (skills within the thinking blocks) to aid with word pronunciation. These young readers often guess when they encounter words they don't know; in some cases, they spend so much energy identifying words that they are unable to devote attention to understanding what they are reading.

Other children with weaknesses in the use of letter–sound clues recognize language inconsistencies when they read, but do not use strategies from the thinking blocks to monitor their performance. For instance, Daniel, a third-grader, read the sentence "Ted and Jack saw the girls" as "Ted and Jack *was* the girls." After reading the sentence, Daniel commented: "That doesn't make any sense." He did not, however, reread the sentence to determine whether he had made a decoding error.

Beginning readers who are weak in thinking with language may not understand the meaning of the text. These readers tend to rely too much on the processing blocks and too little on the thinking blocks. They may identify and pronounce words perfectly but have trouble using word order and meaning clues to predict a word that makes sense in the context. If this is your child's pattern, turn to Chapter 9 for help.

When Your Child Struggles with Reading

STRATEGY   If your child needs an approach different from the one being provided in the classroom, share your concerns with the teacher. More than likely, they will be happy to try alternative techniques. If talking to the teacher does not help, share your concerns with the school's principal. She may be willing to move your child to a classroom where a teacher provides a more appropriate type of reading instruction. If you still feel your child is not getting the type of teaching that is needed, consider the following three options:

1. You can supplement the school instruction by working with your child intensively at home.
2. You can hire a private reading tutor.
3. You can enroll your child in a private school that offers more structured teaching.

Charlie's Story

As we've discussed, matching the method of teaching reading to the child is essential. Consider what happened to Charlie. No one imagined that he would have trouble learning to read. In preschool, he was talkative and curious, and he loved to listen to books read during story hour. Then Charlie began first grade in a school that used a whole-language approach to reading. He was exposed to many books and was encouraged to develop literacy skills. Charlie, however, did not seem able to retain even the simplest of sight words, such as *it* and *the*. By the middle of the year, he had been referred to a special reading program. In this program, Charlie memorized many short, interesting books that he would "read" in school and at home, and his mother and teacher both believed that he was learning to read.

In second grade, Charlie attended a reading support program where he dictated stories, practiced reading them, and then assembled his stories into a book. However, Charlie's second-grade teacher soon became concerned about his lack of reading progress. She noted that, when they appeared elsewhere, such as on the chalkboard, Charlie was not remembering the words that he had identified correctly in his small books. She felt that Charlie required extra practice memorizing words, so she sent home a pack of flash cards of the 100 most common words, and requested that he practice and learn these words at home. Charlie and his mother

TEXTBOOK SERIES THAT TEACH READING

Your child's school may adopt a set of reading textbooks designed to be used throughout all the grades. As with teaching methods, these readers may or may not meet the needs of your child. Some provide authentic literature with no specially controlled vocabulary; others offer a more structured system for introducing new words and reviewing words previously learned. Many children learn quite well from literature-based series, but some children need an instructional series that stresses mastery of words and word families.

A few students, usually those with learning or reading disabilities, need even more systematic early instruction. If they do not receive the needed level of instruction, their reading development is hindered and they become quite frustrated when they move on and encounter assignments that depend on reading ability. Further, their failure in reading will begin to affect the foundational blocks of self-esteem and emotions. Before school starts, find out what kind of series your child's class uses so you can head off expected trouble. Depending on the series selected, you may have to plan for supplementary instruction at home.

If the class will be using a literature-based series and your child has severe weaknesses in the auditory or visual blocks, alert the teacher so that adaptations can be made for your child, and be prepared to do a lot of instruction at home. If the class uses a more structured reading series and your child has strengths in the visual and auditory blocks, all will be well, but plan on lots of extra library visits for books that will keep your child challenged.

complied with the teacher's request. Each evening, they focused on ten of the words and spent a quarter of an hour in review and practice. Charlie objected to the tutoring and it became a nightly struggle to secure his attention and involvement. One night, in a burst of frustration, Charlie grabbed the set of flash cards from his mother, ripped them up, and threw them in her face. He stormed out of the room crying, "I can't learn this way." Although the incident was upsetting to both Charlie and his mother, Charlie's comment was quite perceptive. He recognized that this method for teaching reading, which focused on the skills in the visual processing block, was not what he needed.

By third grade, Charlie was still at a primary or beginning level of reading skill. His teacher referred him for a special educational evaluation. The examining team decided that Charlie had learning disabilities and was eligible for special help with reading. By this time, however, he had acquired negative associations with reading and writing, and was insisting that he could not learn even if someone helped him.

Fortunately, the special reading teacher understood the type of instruction that Charlie needed. Once she had gained his trust and persuaded him to try again, she taught him how to decode and encode words using a structured phonics approach. She provided review and practice so that his success was ensured. As Charlie's skills improved and he began to see that he could learn to read, his attitude toward himself and his schoolwork improved significantly.

To parents, teachers, and reading specialists, Charlie's story is all too familiar: a problem that originated in the processing blocks extended into the foundational blocks of self-esteem and emotions. When children struggle to learn to read, they lose confidence in all their abilities and they may perceive themselves as failures. Children like Charlie often require a different or more intensive approach for reading and spelling instruction.

Beginning Reading and Spelling Development

When children have difficulty learning to read or to spell, the explanation can usually be found within the processing blocks because the abilities to read and spell words successfully are dependent primarily on visual, auditory, and motor skills.

Although they are similar, the processes involved in learning to identify words and learning to spell words do differ (see figure on page 174). When children are first learning to read, they often memorize the visual appearance of words. They may know and recognize words as wholes, but they often know little about the sounds of the individual letters. Then, as they are read to, and as they look at books, they start noting how the visual features or letter combinations in a word represent its auditory features or sounds.

When children are first learning to spell, they often pronounce the word (using auditory block skills) and then attempt to write the sequence

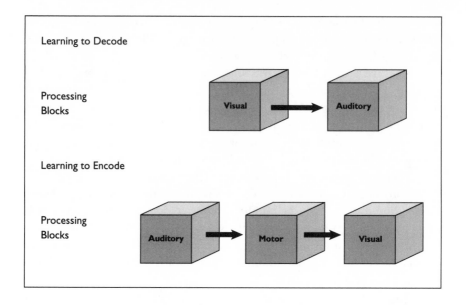

of sounds in order (using auditory block and motor block skills). As their skills increase, they begin to add visual strategies, such as recording memorized combinations of letter sequences (e.g., the *-ing* pattern in the word *sing*). After writing a word, they may analyze it to see whether the sequence of its letters "looks right."

Some children have difficulty with the visual aspects of decoding and encoding; others struggle with the auditory aspects. Some children have difficulties with both, and the processes of learning to read and spell mystify them. For these children, the processing blocks become the stumbling blocks to learning.

The Auditory Processing Block

The auditory processing block contains the skills that help children learn to sound out words and to order the letters in words according to the sequence of their sounds. If you had several "Yes" checks when reviewing the characteristics in the auditory processing block, your child probably has some difficulty with language sounds. Early reading success depends on recognizing words as sequences of letters that are associated with various sounds. Many children learn this concept naturally, but others do not. When Marie was in preschool, for instance, she often

---

KEEPING SENSE ABOUT READING

Learning to read and spell is a bit like learning to play the piano. Every piano teacher encourages the beginning student to practice the scales, to gain rapid finger movement and be able to play more fluently. The really good piano teachers also provide plenty of opportunities for students to play actual music. If only allowed to practice playing scales, students' interest in learning to play the piano will soon diminish. Reading instruction works the same way. To become a real reader, a child must master words, but must also view books as a source of pleasure and information.

Reading and spelling enable children to learn from print and to use print to communicate. Make sure that your child does not lose sight of this goal while practicing various decoding and encoding strategies. Spend time together in reading and writing activities that are both meaningful and pleasurable. Read stories to your child, from books that he or she has selected. Encourage writing as a way to communicate thoughts to others, whether in stories, shopping "wish-lists," or letters to Grandma. Teach your child what you already know: Reading and writing are important parts of life, not just skills for school.

---

mispronounced longer words, saying "aminal" for *animal*, and "psghetti" for *spaghetti*. These types of errors often diminish as children enter kindergarten, but Marie continued to have problems. Her speech difficulties persisted, and similar problems were apparent as she was learning to read.

Sound (Phonological) Awareness

Awareness of sounds—phonological awareness—is the foundation for decoding and encoding skills. In fact, an understanding of the sound structure of language is the strongest single predictor of whether a child will learn to read with ease in the primary grades. The majority of children who struggle with reading do so because they have trouble working with the sounds of language in the auditory processing block. Your child's phonological awareness—or lack of awareness—can be seen in his or her knowledge of rhyming, of matching initial consonant sounds, and of counting the number of syllables in spoken words.

Reading development and success depend on an understanding of what is known as the *alphabetic principle:* Speech sounds (phonemes) can be translated into specific letters or letter combinations (graphemes). In other words, your child needs to be able to relate a letter with its corresponding sound. If a child does not understand this connection, learning to decode is frustrating and nearly impossible.

Most children develop phonological awareness and knowledge of the alphabetic principle naturally and easily, progressing from skill with early rhyming to the ability to hear the individual sounds within words, but a few do not. They do not understand the relationships between spoken and written words and their sounds and letters. Fortunately, when sound–symbol awareness does not come easily to young children, it can be taught directly.

Assessing and Teaching Phonological Awareness

If your child is between the ages of 3 and 8 years, or is older and is still having trouble learning to decode or encode, you must make sure that he or she is developing knowledge of the sound structure of language. To test the present level of knowledge, use the following tasks, presented here in order from easiest to most difficult. If your child does not understand what you are asking, you can use the tasks to teach sound–symbol awareness.

Rhyming Ask your child to think of and say all the words that rhyme with:

1. cat
2. see
3. log
4. shoe
5. pig

Syllable Counting A syllable may be simply defined as one push of breath. Ask your child to clap or tap out the number of syllables in:

1. maybe   (2)
2. turtle   (2)
3. exercise   (3)
4. carpenter   (3)
5. basketball   (3)

If your child has trouble counting the number of syllables, ask him or her to place his or her hand under the chin and then to say the word slowly. Have him or her count the number of times the chin drops. In this way, he or she can feel and count the number of syllables.

Compound Word Deletion   Ask your child to say the word:

1. "cowboy" without the "cow"
2. "cupcake" without the "cup"
3. "birthday" without the "birth"
4. "rainbow" without the "rain"
5. "sunshine" without the "shine"

Phoneme Matching   Ask which of these words starts with a different sound:

1. ball, bat, tree
2. step, dog, star
3. boy, clock, clown
4. milk, man, shoe
5. apple, car, ax

Syllable Blending   Ask your child to tell you the word you are trying to say (as you speak, divide the word into separate but unaccented syllables auditorily):

1. tur . . . tle
2. hap . . . py
3. pen . . . cil
4. com . . . pu . . . ter
5. car . . . pen . . . ter

Sound Blending   Ask your child to tell you the word you are trying to say (use the sounds of the letter units as they are pronounced in the real word, but pause for a second between the units):

1. c . . . at
2. sh . . . oe
3. b . . . ir . . . d

4. t . . . a . . . b . . . le
5. h . . . a . . . m . . . b . . . ur . . . g . . . er

Sound Counting   Ask your child how many sounds he or she hears when you say (start with ordinary speech; repeat more slowly if the sounds are not easily counted):

1. toy (t-oy)   (2)
2. girl (g-ir-l)   (3)
3. box (b-o-k-s)   (4)
4. eight (eigh-t)   (2)
5. rabbit (r-a-bb-i-t) (5)

(Note that the word *box* is composed of three letters, but has four separate phonemes or sounds.)

If your child is not ready to count the number of sounds, have poker chips or spoons available, and have your child push forward a chip or a spoon for each sound heard when you pronounce the word slowly.

Phoneme Deletion   Ask your child what sound is left after the sound of one of the letters is removed from these words (use the sound of the letter, not its "name," as you present each item):

1. "hat" without the /h/ sound—"at"
2. "ran" without the /r/ sound—"an"
3. "sold" without the /s/ sound—"old"
4. "gate" without the /g/ sound—"ate"
5. "cart" without the ending /t/ sound—"car"

Many preschool- and most kindergarten-age children are able to rhyme words. The majority of first-graders can count syllables, delete part of a compound word, and count and blend syllables. By second grade, most children can perform all of these tasks. If your child has trouble with these tasks, spend time on activities that will help him or her to discover the relationships between language sounds and words. These oral language activities will provide a solid foundation for reading and spelling skill development.

STRATEGY   Read nursery rhymes or poems, or sing songs to help increase your child's phonological awareness. Offer activities that involve rhyming words, clapping out and counting the syllables in words, and pronouncing words slowly by syllables. When you read aloud, discuss the rhyming words with your child. Write the words on paper and show how the spellings of rhyming words are similar. For example, after reading the sentence: "He turned off the light and said good night," point out that the words "light" and "night" are spelled with the same pattern of letters.

Most children enjoy playing with the sounds of letters and words, and activities that involve moving around letters to form words are especially beneficial for children who have sound–symbol weaknesses. Use alphabet blocks, Scrabble™ tiles, and/or magnetic letters to help your child increase specific phonological skills.

Invented Spelling   Encourage your child's use of invented or temporary spelling. (Don't worry, you are *not* suggesting that it's OK to simply make up a spelling for a word.) Invented spelling encourages listening carefully to the sounds in a word and then writing the sounds in the correct order. For children who have difficulty picturing the visual appearance of words, producing their own spellings helps to increase their knowledge of sounds. When your child is writing a word, encourage pronouncing it slowly aloud while attempting to write the sounds in the correct order.

Many teachers refer to invented spelling as "temporary spelling." The term reflects the fact that this is only a developmental stage in the process of learning to spell, and that it is important to emphasize correct spelling once a child understands how to sequence sounds in words.

Spelling Instruction

Approaches to teaching correct spelling vary from school to school and from teacher to teacher. Some teachers rely on commercial materials, such as spelling books, as the foundation for spelling instruction. Other teachers use spelling books but supplement them with words the children are using in their writing. Still others develop an individualized program for each child in the room, selecting words from the child's own writing.

Whatever the specific approach, an effective spelling program must be geared to children's present skill level. Unfortunately, some teachers give all the children in the classroom the same list of words to master for the weekly test. The poor spellers may not know any of the words, whereas the good spellers may score 100 percent on the pretest. This type of procedure is ineffective for both groups.

Make sure that your child is being asked to spell words that are in line with his or her present skill level. If the words on a spelling list seem out of line, speak to the teacher about an adjustment. Once you know that the words are appropriate, you need only think about which methods will help your child learn to spell most easily.

We know that simply having children copy or write words a certain number of times is an ineffective procedure. It does not require much attention to copy words, and children are apt to make mistakes or forget the words they've written. It is critical that children with spelling difficulties be provided with more systematic and intensive approaches.

As with reading, spelling requires different approaches for different children. Some benefit from approaches focused on the auditory block; others need a method that emphasizes the visual and motor processing blocks.

Auditory Methods for Teaching Spelling

If your child has difficulty putting the letter sounds of words in their correct order, the remedy is a spelling method that emphasizes listening carefully to the order of sounds in words. This type of spelling program begins with a study of the sounds in words and the letters that represent those sounds. Activities should involve listening to and then arranging or writing the sounds in order. Following are several simple procedures that you can use to help your child improve in phonological skills and spelling ability.

Making Words   "Making Words" is a guided invented-spelling task.[1] The activity takes about 15 minutes and requires a set of magnetic letters, Scrabble tiles, or letters written on cardboard. In this program, the authors provide a group of letters that can be combined and rearranged to form words of increasing length. Each lesson contains a different combination of letters.

1. Give your child six to eight letters, such as *i, t, p, n, s,* and *l.* Be sure to include a vowel.
2. Ask your child to make various two-letter words using the letters, such as *in, is, it.*
3. Ask your child to make three-letter words using the letters (for example, *pit, pin, tin, sip, tip*).
4. Begin a letter pattern and ask your child to form new words that gradually increase in word length by one letter a word. The final

word, a six-, seven-, or eight-letter word, will include all of the letters. For example, ask your child to form the word *it,* then *sit,* then *slit,* then *split,* and then *splint.*

5. As a final step, have your child take the last word apart, a letter at a time, to form new words.

At first, provide your child with several consonants but only one vowel; if you're using letters written on cardboard, you can write the vowel in red. Later, provide two or more vowels. Emphasize how the words change when the letters are moved around or different letters are added to a word. An adaptation of this program, called "Making Big Words," is available for children with more advanced skill.[2] If the making words activity is difficult for your child, begin instruction with forming simple consonant-vowel-consonant words, such as the words hat and cat. Try the changing words procedure described below.

Changing Words   Another way to increase your child's phonological awareness is to make a game of creating new words by changing only one letter. For example, you may write the word *cat.* To form a new word by changing only one letter, your child changes the *c* to an *h* and writes *hat.* You then write the word *hit,* and your child writes *sit.*

You can play simple games like this with your child, using pencil and paper or a set of magnetic letters on a metal plate, a cookie sheet, or the refrigerator. As the letters are moved around to form new and different words, have your child pronounce each word.

Sound Sequencing   The following activity will help your child pay attention to the sequence of sounds when spelling. Again, use a set of magnetic letters or Scrabble tiles, or write letters on small pieces of cardboard.

1. Pronounce a word slowly and have your child try to place the letter tiles in the correct order, from left to right. If necessary, demonstrate how to arrange the tiles before your child attempts to form the word.

2. After the word is formed, scramble the letters and ask your child to say the word and to create the word again, using the tiles as before.

3. Have your child first pronounce the word and then write it on a piece of paper.

4. As your child's skills increase, use individual letter tiles to break words into syllables or to build several new words around a root.

As you break words with several syllables into units, your child will start to see a long word as a series of manageable parts that have their own conventional spellings, rather than as a long string of unrelated letters.

To help with practicing the spelling of longer words, ask your child to:

1. Pronounce the word slowly.
2. Repeat the word, pronouncing the separate sounds of the word individually.
3. Look at the word and note how the letters match the sounds.
4. Tell which sounds go with each letter as you point to the letters in sequence.
5. Write each letter while saying the sounds.
6. Trace the word until it can be written from memory.

When done on a regular basis, these types of activities will help increase your child's understanding of the relationship between letters and their sounds.

Phonics Instruction

If decoding difficulties are pronounced, your child may need specific phonics instruction as well as instruction in phonological awareness. Phonological awareness involves developing sensitivity to the sounds of a language by using oral language activities. Phonics instruction, by contrast, directly teaches the relationship between letters and sounds. A child first learns letter sounds in isolation and then practices blending the letter sounds together to recognize and pronounce words.

Poor word recognition can be a stumbling block for a young reader. Marie—the preschool child with speech difficulties, described earlier in the chapter—was still at a beginning level of reading by third grade. Her third-grade teacher was determined to teach Marie how to read and decided to try a structured phonics approach. Each day, she taught Marie several letters and their corresponding sounds. She then showed her how to analyze the sounds to pronounce new words. At first Marie learned to read words that had regular sound–symbol correspondence. She pronounced the sound for each letter in left-to-right order. The teacher encouraged her to practice and use these new skills in stories. Gradually, as her skill improved, Marie began to recognize more and more words without having to pay specific attention to the letter sounds. After six months of carefully guided instruction, she was on her way to becoming an independent reader.

Phonics Programs   Children like Marie do not understand the connections between letters and their sounds and need a systematic, explicit approach to learn to read. Fortunately, many easy-to-use programs are available. Or, parents may hire private reading tutors who specialize in specific reading methods, or enroll their child in schools that use these methods. Two commonly used phonics methods are: the Orton–Gillingham approach, and an adaptation, the Slingerland approach. These are helpful instructional programs for children who need explicit phonics instruction, but they require a teacher who has taken a year-long course of instruction. If your child has severe difficulties, you may want to investigate public or private schools with teachers who use these methods.

But it isn't essential that you find private instruction to overcome your child's difficulties with phonics. Three other inexpensive methods, described below, can be used at home, with little training. Ordering information for these programs is given in Appendix A.

1. *The Reading Lesson* is a practical, structured program designed for parents to teach young children (ages 4 to 7 years) how to read. The program is divided into 20 easy-to-follow lessons that begin with the most common letters and sounds. Children learn how to combine the sounds to read simple words, and the program gradually progresses to longer words. After completing the last lesson in the series, a child should be reading with ease at the second-grade level.

2. *The Phonic Remedial Reading Lessons,* a step-by-step plan for teaching phonics and reinforcing sound–symbol relationships, is recommended for children older than 7 years. No rules are taught. Instead, the program introduces sounds one at a time, in a variety of words, so that the child develops an automatic response to each sound symbol. As a supplement to the program, the child is asked to write words while carefully pronouncing each sound. Children tend to progress rapidly through this program.

3. *The Spalding Method of Phonics . . .* , which is described in *The Writing Road to Reading* (see Appendix A), is a language arts program that integrates handwriting, spelling, reading, speaking, and writing. Following this program, children learn to recognize and write 70 common phonograms (single letters and two-, three-, or four-letter combinations that

make one sound). The accompanying text includes a complete list of the rules to be taught, and phonogram cards to present the sounds. After children have learned 54 phonograms, they receive instruction in spelling. To help with spelling, children learn to master the 70 phonograms and 29 spelling rules. The authors claim that a child who is armed with the sounds and rules will be able to spell about 80 percent of English words correctly. Their method has been used successfully with first graders, college students, and all in-between ages.

As your child's spelling improves, you can supplement the programs with word games such as Boggle™ and Scrabble, and with elementary crossword puzzles. A wide range of computer software is also available for helping your child develop decoding and encoding skill; check with your child's teacher or a local software retailer for specific suggestions.

Multisyllabic Word Pronunciation

To be a successful reader, your child needs to know how to recognize and pronounce words with several syllables. Unfamiliar words have to be seen as a sequence of recognizable word parts, rather than as a long string of unrelated letters. You can help with developing this important skill by showing and teaching your child the most common *meaning* parts of words (root words, prefixes, and suffixes), as well as the most common *pronunciation* units (common clusters and syllables).

STRATEGY   Before your child begins to read a story or passage, read it through yourself and underline any of the longer words that may cause difficulty. Review these words first, then encourage practice-reading the sentences that contain them.

Activities with Affixes   Many other activities can be done with *affixes*— the beginnings of words, or *prefixes,* and the endings of words, or *suffixes.* These word parts are attached to root words to alter their meaning. For example, the root word *cover* can be changed into the word *uncovered* by adding affixes. The prefix *un-* changes the meaning to "not covered," and the suffix *-ed* makes it clear that the event happened in the past.

To familiarize your child with common affixes, introduce a short list of prefixes and suffixes with their most common meanings. Help with practicing the use of affixes with a variety of root words. You can modify the activity by writing several common prefixes, suffixes, and root words on index cards and then asking your child to build and pronounce both real and nonsense words by rearranging the cards. Extend this process into a spelling activity by having your child write the words one part at a time. Appendix C is a list of commonly used affixes and their meanings.

Glass Analysis Method for Decoding   A simple way to help your child read and pronounce words with more than one syllable is to use the Glass Analysis Method.[3] To begin, write on index cards several multisyllabic words selected from your child's reading material. Show how common letter clusters can be generalized and found in new words. Practice with this technique 10 to 15 minutes daily.

For each word:

1. Identify and pronounce the whole word. For example, present the word *carpenter* on an index card and say: "This word is *carpenter*."

2. Select and pronounce a sound in the word, and ask your child to name the letter or letters that make that sound. Say: "In the word *carpenter*, what letters make the /ar/ sound? What letters make the /pen/ sound?" and so on. For this step, say the letter sounds, rather than the letter names.

3. Ask which sound certain letters or letter combinations make. Say: "What sound do the letters e-r make? What sound do the letters t-e-r make?" For this step, say the letter names, rather than the letter sounds.

4. Remove letters auditorily and ask your child to say the remaining sound. Say: "In the word *carpenter*, if I took off 'car,' how would you pronounce the word? If I took off 'ter,' how would you pronounce the word? If I took off 'penter,' how would you say the word?" Think of as many combinations as you can.

5. Ask your child to say the whole word.

Although the Glass Analysis Method was developed primarily for teaching decoding skills, it can be modified easily to teach spelling or encoding skills. For example, to teach the spelling of the word *consideration*, you could use the following steps:

1. Identify and discuss the visual and auditory clusters in the word.

2. Ask your child to write the letter(s) that make the /con/ sound, then the /sid/ sound, then the /er/ sound, then the /a/ sound, and, finally, the /tion/ sound. Remind your child that every syllable in a word contains a vowel.

3. Have your child write the word *consideration* while pronouncing each part slowly: "con-sid-er-a-tion."

4. Turn the paper over and ask your child to write the word *consideration* from memory, pronouncing each word part as it is written.

5. Repeat the exercise of writing the word from memory two more times.

When you use this adapted method to help your child learn spelling, emphasize putting the sounds of a word in the correct sequence. This is accomplished by practicing the visual and auditory clusters of a word in the order that they appear.

The Visual Processing Block

The visual block is composed of skills that help children learn to recognize letters and words with ease. A child's early reading and spelling performance depends on an ability to memorize the visual appearance of frequently written words. If you had several "Yes" checks when reviewing the characteristics of the visual processing block, your child probably has trouble memorizing words easily. The following interventions can be used to strengthen the skills in the visual processing block.

Language Experience Approach

One easy way to help a child with beginning reading skills learn the relationship between the visual appearance and the sound of words is to use what is known as the language experience approach. As we will see in Chapter Nine, this approach is also very helpful in teaching children to write.

For the language experience approach, use the following steps:

1. Discuss an experience with your child, or make up a simple story.

2. Have your child tell you the story, dictating it as you pronounce and write down each word slowly.

3. Read the story aloud, as dictated by your child.

4. Have your child read the dictated story to you.

5. Repeat the reading until your child can read the dictated story independently with ease.

Children with strengths in the visual processing block are able to memorize the visual appearance of words, using this simple approach of practice and rereading. Other children, primarily those with weaknesses in the visual processing block, will also benefit from this technique but will need more practice and review to master words. This approach has several advantages: it emphasizes interaction between you and your child, and it is more interesting than other methods because the child participates in the writing and reading of a story, and familiarity with it aids in comprehension.

High-Frequency Words

Success in decoding and encoding requires skill in reading and spelling high-frequency words—the words that are most commonly used in writing. Some teachers refer to these words as "sight words" because they are supposed to be recognized instantly, without an analysis of sounds.

The easiest way to work with your child on high-frequency words is to practice with a carefully developed list of words, such as the "1,000 Instant Words" list reproduced in Appendix D.[4] These 1,000 words make up about 90 percent of all words used in written material. The first 300 words represent 60 percent of the words used in all written language.

Mastering this list will help with both decoding and encoding. Ask your child to read (or spell) the words, starting at the beginning of the list. Continue until an error occurs. Begin teaching at the point where your child does not immediately recognize or does not know how to spell a word. Check off the words on the list when your child has learned to read or spell them. Remember that children with weaknesses in the visual or auditory processing blocks require a lot of practice and review for word learning.

STRATEGY   Establish a program to help with mastering unknown words. This program need not be time-consuming; in fact, a word mastery program can be effective when it is conducted only ten minutes each day. Here's how.

Have your child start at the beginning of the list and read as many words as possible within one minute. After the minute, record the number of words read. Review any words that were not recognized instantly. For the next few minutes, practice spelling several new, unfamiliar words. Review these words the following day. Check off each word after your child has learned to read and/or spell it.

STRATEGY   Create a personalized spelling list. Children with spelling difficulties often benefit from keeping an individualized spelling dictionary or
a spell-check list that contains their own frequently misspelled words.
Help your child keep track of the words that seem most problematic,
and encourage consulting the dictionary or spell-check list of words when
it is time to edit written assignments.

Max, a fifth-grade student, has trouble remembering how to spell
the following words: *they, people, many, which, there,* and *said.* On the back
page of his school notebook, he keeps a list of these words, arranged alphabetically. Max knows that he gets particularly confused by homophones—words that sound the same but are spelled differently. To help
him keep these words straight, he consults a short phrase he has written
next to each of the homophones on his list. For example, next to the word
their, he has written "their house." Next to the word *there,* he has written
"over there." Next to the word *they're,* he has written "They're happy."
Max's parents and teacher encourage him to consult this list whenever
necessary.

Multisensory Methods of Teaching

Tracing   Over the past century, many methods involving a number of the
senses have been developed to help struggling readers. These teaching
methods are called multisensory because the child uses the visual, auditory, and motor skills involved in the processing blocks to improve word
recognition and memory. One example would be tracing a word and then
trying to write it from memory. Several procedures for using tracing to
enhance memory follow.

The Fernald Method   One well-known multisensory technique is the Fernald Method,[5] which has been used for more than 50 years to teach children who struggle with learning to read. The Fernald Method provides
instruction aimed at boosting skills simultaneously in the visual, auditory,
and motor processing blocks. It especially helps children increase their
abilities to picture words by building up the skills of the visual processing
block. The method is appropriate for children who have failed to learn to
read with other instructional methods.

To use the Fernald Method, explain to your child that you will be
showing a new way to learn words that has been successful with other children. Have your child select a word—one that your child cannot read but

would like to learn. Discuss the meaning of the word, and then use the following steps to teach the word:

1. Sit beside your child and write the word. Have your child watch and listen while you: (a) say the word, (b) use a crayon to write the word in large letters (in manuscript or script, depending on which writing style is being learned) on an index card, and (c) say the word again as you run your finger underneath it.

2. Show your child how to trace the word. Say: "Watch what I do and listen to what I say." Then: (a) say the word; (b) trace the word using one or two fingers, saying each part of the word as you trace it; (c) say the word again while running your finger underneath it.

3. Have your child practice tracing the word and saying each part of it as it is traced.

4. When your child feels ready, remove the index card and ask your child to write the word from memory and say the word while writing. If at any point an error occurs, stop the writing immediately, cover the error, and repeat the tracing step before proceeding.

5. When your child has written the word correctly three times without the model, file the word alphabetically in a word "bank" (a small file or shoe box). Repeat practicing the words in the file at a later date.

Although a few children continue to need tracing to learn words, most progress through additional stages with this method:

- Your child will no longer need to trace words, but will be able to learn a word by looking at it after you write it, saying the word, and then writing it independently.

- Your child will be able to learn new words directly, without having them written as models. When new words are encountered while reading, help to identify them. Later, when the reading is finished, have your child review and then write the unknown words.

- Your child will begin to notice similarities between unknown and known words and will recognize many new words without needing to be told what they are.

STRATEGY Before reading, encourage your child to glance over the material and underline any unfamiliar words. Pronounce the words and then employ the steps of tracing the words and then writing them from memory.

Tracing words is particularly useful for children who have weaknesses in the visual processing block and therefore have difficulty remembering how to spell. Help your child practice with words from the high-frequency list, or use the words that have been assigned for spelling in school.

Cover-Write Methods

Cover-write methods are useful for children who have trouble remembering how particular words look. Here are three procedures to help your child recall a word:

1. a. Choose a word for your child to learn. Write the word on a card. Show the word and pronounce it clearly and slowly.

   b. Ask your child to look at and pronounce the word.

   c. Have your child look at the word and trace the letters while saying the letter names (or sounds).

   d. Remove or cover up the word and ask your child to pronounce the word while writing it on paper. If the spelling is incorrect, repeat step c.

2. a. Write a word on an index card.

   b. Ask your child to look at and say the word, and to think about the letter sounds; then cover the word.

   c. Ask your child to verbalize the letter sounds while writing the word.

   d. Compare the word as written with the index-card model.

   e. If the word is written incorrectly, repeat steps b through d.

   f. When the word has been written correctly, cover the word and ask your child to repeat the write-and-pronounce step c two or three more times.

3. If saying the letter names is more effective for your child than making the letter sounds, use this procedure:

   a. Ask your child to look at and say the word.

   b. Ask your child to spell the word aloud, using the letter names.

   c. Ask your child to write and say the letter names three times, correctly.

   d. Cover the word and ask your child to spell the word. If an error occurs, repeat steps b and c.

Depending on your child's learning style, different senses or processing blocks should be emphasized when practicing words for spelling. A child with strengths in the visual block can be encouraged to picture the word; one with strengths in the auditory block can be encouraged to pronounce the word slowly; and one with strengths in the motor block can be encouraged to trace the word.

Encourage your child to study a word, using the technique that seems most effective, as preparation for writing it successfully from memory. When your child feels ready to write the word, remove the card, and test whether the word can be written correctly from memory. As an alternative to writing words on index cards, use an erasable slate, which can be purchased in most toy stores.

If you understand your child's strengths and weaknesses within the processing blocks, and the difficulties experienced with decoding or encoding, you will be able to help by using the methods described in this chapter. Use them one-on-one with your child, or teach them to the tutor, if you employ one. But don't keep the emphasis solely on school skills. Whenever possible, relate your child's interests to the reading matter you select—whether it's a favorite magazine, a set of stories, or a newspaper feature. Make the exercises into games that everyone in the family can play.

Reading Fluency: Speed

Successful readers do not just recognize words; they do so quickly, automatically, and nearly effortlessly. This ability is referred to as *automaticity*. Readers who have become automatic do not need to pay a great deal of attention to word appearance. Some children develop accurate word recognition skills, but their decoding process is not automatic, and instead requires great effort. As a result, these children read materials at a slow pace; they are not *fluent* readers. Reading fluency refers to the reading speed or rate of reading, as well as to the ability to read materials with expression and comprehension.

Children who experience difficulty when they first learn to read often have slow reading rates; when they read aloud, they do so in a monotone and they have difficulty understanding what they are reading. They often need to reread in order to comprehend. Because they expend so much effort in decoding, they may have a hard time getting beyond word-by-word reading. As time goes on, their lack of reading fluency stops them from keeping up with assignments and they fall behind their classmates. If their fluency does not improve, their problems with learning to read impede their progress in reading to learn, and what begins as a problem in the processing blocks may affect performance in the thinking blocks and may also cause problems with self-esteem. Many nonfluent readers get referrals for help when they reach fourth grade and the reading demands accelerate.

Children whose reading rate is below grade expectation may take a much longer time than their peers to complete assignments; they may even avoid doing reading assignments altogether because they know they will not have enough time to finish. At least initially, they may need to be given either extra time to complete reading assignments or shorter assignments. However, there are a number of ways to help increase reading fluency.

Assessing Reading Rate

Growth in reading rate appears to be about 14 words per minute, in each year from grades 2 to 12. The figure at the bottom of the page can help you estimate whether your child reads at an adequate rate.[6] Ask your child to read a passage from a class text for one minute. Count the number of words read within that time. Compare this count to the typical rate of a student at that grade equivalent, as listed at the bottom of the page.

Typical Rates for Reading with Understanding		
Grade Equivalent	Standard Words per Minute*	Standard Sentences per Minute*
2.5	121	7.2
3.5	135	8.1
4.5	149	8.9
5.5	163	9.8
6.5	177	10.6
7.5	191	11.5
8.5	205	12.3
9.5	219	13.1
10.5	233	14.0
11.5	247	14.8
12.5	261	15.7

*A standard word is 6 letter spaces including punctuation and spacing, and a standard sentence is 16.7 standard words.

STRATEGY   You can help increase your child's reading fluency by teaching how and when to use different rates of reading. Over time, most people develop and use a fairly consistent rate of reading—a pace at which they can understand complete thoughts in successive sentences of relatively easy material. When the material is more difficult, however, or when they are performing different tasks, readers often alter their rate.

As a skilled reader, you know how to adjust the gears of your reading to suit your purpose. If you are trying to memorize material for an exam, your pace is slow and reflective; you stop and review as you progress. If you are reading a novel for pleasure, your pace is steady and fluent. If you are searching for information in a catalog, your pace is rapid.

Dr. Ron Carver, an expert in reading fluency, uses the analogy of shifting the gears in a car. The lower gears, first and second, are the slowest but most powerful gears. Readers use first gear when they are trying to memorize materials, and second gear when they are trying to learn material. Third gear represents a person's normal reading rate. The fourth gear, for skimming, and the fifth gear, for scanning, are the fastest but least powerful gears. Readers use them when they are trying to locate a specific piece of information or need only the general sense of a passage without reading every word.

Some children use one reading rate for all tasks. They may attempt to read information in an encyclopedia at the same pace that they read a story, because they have not learned how to adjust their reading rates. To help develop this skill, encourage your child to change gears, depending on the purpose for reading. Show the difference between skimming through a chapter to get a sense of the information it contains, and studying that chapter for a weekly test. Encourage using varying rates, depending on the purpose for reading.

Activities for Increasing Reading Rate

There are many ways to help increase your child's reading rate. The methods described below are easy to use. To make the experience enjoyable, keep the sessions short (10 to 15 minutes), select books that your child finds interesting to read, treat mispronunciations as part of learning, and smile a lot. Some children who are reluctant to practice reading can be motivated by knowing that a treat, such as a piece of pizza or 15 minutes of rollerblading, will follow the session.

Memorizing a Book   One of the most important things you can do to help your child become a more fluent reader is to encourage reading and rereading. By reading the same material over and over, a beginning reader learns to associate the sounds of words with their appearance and to recognize them instantly.

Select a favorite simple book and read the book aloud to your child several times. Then read it together several times. Gradually, let your child pronounce words that seem familiar. As skill improvement occurs, take turns reading sentences and then alternate pages. Continue practicing until your child is able to read the story aloud without any help.

Predictable Books   If your child is just beginning to learn to read, the most helpful choices are predictable books, such as *The House that Jack Built* or many of the books by Dr. Seuss. Their repetitive patterns make it easy for children to guess what comes next. Limited background knowledge is not a problem because the authors introduce simple ideas and then build on them, incorporating familiar words and ideas into the text. As you read these stories again and again, encourage your child to join in and supply any anticipated words.

The Presenting Technique   The Presenting Technique[7] is a prereading method that is particularly useful for children with weaknesses in the auditory processing or language thinking blocks. To begin, select a simple story and sit across from your child. Read aloud, three times, a short paragraph or two from a story, then summarize the paragraph(s), using vocabulary that you know your child will understand. Reread the same segment and ask your child to retell as much of its content as possible. Read a short phrase or sentence and ask your child to repeat back the material. Next, read short phrases or sentences in unison from the rehearsed passage. When your child can recognize some words without assistance, pause and encourage pronouncing them. Once your child gains skill with this technique, move on to the Neurological Impress Method,[7] or choral reading, which is an allied part of the Presenting Technique.

Neurological Impress Method (Choral Reading)   The Neurological Impress Method is a fancy name for choral reading. With this method, you and your child read a book together, aloud, for 10 to 15 minutes daily. To begin, select or have your child select a high-interest book—one that your child will find very enticing and enthralling. Sit side by side and point to the words with your index finger as you read them aloud. Read at a slightly accelerated pace and ask your child to try and keep up with you. The rules are: don't worry about mistakes, and keep the eyes on the words. After you have finished reading for the day, ask your child to guess what will happen next in the story you are reading.

Repeated Readings   The repeated readings technique is designed for children who read slowly despite having adequate word recognition.[8] In this procedure, the child reads the same passage over and over.

To begin, select a book that is slightly above your child's reading level, and find a passage 50 to 100 words long. Have your child read the selection aloud; record the reading time and the number of words pronounced incorrectly. Set a realistic goal for speed and number of errors, using the averages in the figure on page 192.

Next, have your child look over the selection, reread it, and practice the words that caused difficulty in the initial reading. When ready, have your child reread the same passage. Time the reading again, and record the number of errors. Continue to practice reading the selection. Chart the progress after each trial until the predetermined goal is reached or your child is able to read the passage fluently, with few mistakes.

Taped Books   Another way to help your child practice reading is to use taped books. Have your child listen to the reading while following along with an unabridged copy of the book. Most public libraries loan a wide selection of recorded books.

Unabridged audio books are also available for rent from Books on Tape or Recorded Books. Selections include best-sellers, classics, history, biographies, and science fiction. Books may be rented for one month and then returned by mail. Prices vary according to the length of the books. If your child has been diagnosed as having a vision disability or dyslexia, consider ordering taped books from Recording for the Blind. Sources for obtaining books on tape are listed in Appendix A.

Great Leaps in Reading

A commercially available program called Great Leaps in Reading is designed to improve fluency and rate of reading. This program balances phonics instruction, sight phrase reading, and story reading, to offer children practice in the three most important skills related to fluent, automatic reading. In addition, the program's graphing procedures and interesting stories have proved motivating to children. The Great Leaps program is easy to learn and can be implemented by a parent or a tutor in less than 10 minutes daily (see Appendix A).

Selecting Books for Practice

At Home   Keep in mind two important guidelines when you are selecting reading materials: (a) choose high-interest materials whenever possible, and (b) make sure that your child is able to read the book and does not feel frustrated by the difficulty level. Before you visit the library or go to a bookstore, consider your child's interests and look for reading materials that are a good match.

Choose magazines or books containing material that will entice your child to keep reading. Even slow or hesitant readers will push themselves to read when the subject material is sufficiently interesting. For instance, Aaron was fascinated by all kinds of sports. When he received his first copy of *Sports Illustrated,* he was determined to read every article, even though the level of language was slightly above his present skill level. Kristen, on the other hand, loved horses. With her mother's help, she manages to read every classic book about horses that she can find.

Be sensitive to a frustration factor, however. If your child hesitates while reading or mispronounces too many words, look for easier books or make the book a choral reading project. As a rule of thumb, count out a passage of about 100 words, and have your child read it aloud. If more than five words are missed, the reading selection is too difficult.

At School   When children are given books to read that are too difficult, learning is actually prevented. This is always the case when a teacher uses the same textbook for all children in the class.

Make sure that the assigned classroom books are not too difficult for your child to read. If you notice many mistakes when your child reads textbooks from school, share your concerns with the teacher. Ask whether materials at an appropriate level are available so that your child can practice reading independently.

The Importance of Regular Reading Time

The most effective way for your child to improve in reading is to spend time reading. If fluent decoding skills have not developed, set aside time each day for reading aloud to you. Even a few minutes daily can have a positive impact on overall performance.

Show that reading is important to you. Try to schedule regular family reading time, read aloud to your children, and model reading yourself. Reading aloud to children is particularly important for improving their reading, listening, and comprehension skills; putting them in touch with their own emotions in a nonthreatening way; enlarging their vocabulary and firing their imagination; and creating opportunities for enjoyable time with their parents. Share your own enjoyment of what you read

YOUR CHILD'S READING LEVEL

A major component of appropriate reading instruction is an accurate determination of your child's present reading level. Experts generally describe three levels of performance that should be considered when selecting reading materials:

Independent level: The child can read the material with ease and expression. Accuracy is close to 100 percent.

Instructional level: The child can read the material with some assistance from a better reader. Accuracy is close to 95 percent.

Frustration level: The child is unable to read the material. Accuracy is below 90 percent, and reading is filled with hesitations and mistakes.

When nine words in ten are being read with accuracy, is your child doing well? Not really. Consider what happens to you when you are reading something unfamiliar—how to set up a new piece of electronic equipment, or the instructions for filing a complicated tax form (unless you're an accountant). You may be reading nine out of ten words accurately, but if you don't understand the important words, you become frustrated. The same things happens when your child is reading something beyond his or her skill level.

Ideally, when your child is reading alone and silently, the material should be at the *independent level.* When your child is receiving help from you or from a teacher, the material should be at the *instructional level.* Your child should never have to cope with the *frustration level* unless the material is highly motivating, or your child has selected it, and is determined to read it (with your help). The best reading instruction is only slightly above your child's present performance level.

by talking about the books and magazines you have read and how you have reacted to them. Emphasize that many movies, songs, dances, plays, and cartoons are derived from written sources. Make visits to libraries and bookstores part of your family's regular schedule. Provide space for your child's books either in or near the area set aside for doing homework; or alongside your own books.

When learning and books are part of everyday life, children thrive. And when a child has mastered the basic skills and can read fluently and spell consistently, more energy can be devoted to the next level of learning—the reading and writing tasks that involve the thinking blocks.

Chapter

9

Reading Comprehension and Writing

Teaching the Skills Your Child Needs for Reading to Learn and Writing for Self-Expression

From your parents you learn love and laughter and how to put one foot before the other. But when books are opened, you discover you have wings.

Helen Hayes

When children have learned to read with reasonable fluency, they are ready to move on to *reading to learn*. When they have learned to spell, they are ready to move on from simply forming words to using them to express their ideas. Reading and spelling draw on skills in the processing blocks. Reading to learn and writing to express ideas draw on skills in the thinking blocks as well as mastery of skills in the processing blocks.

Weaknesses in the skills of any of the thinking blocks—language, images, or strategies—may affect children's reading and writing performance. If your daughter's profile revealed several weaknesses in the skills that comprise the thinking blocks, she is likely to struggle with activities that involve comprehending and using language. She may memorize correct spellings easily but have trouble using those same words in writing assignments. She may sound like an expert reader when reading aloud but be unable to tell you what happened in the story that she just read. She may have trouble figuring out what to write about; or, she may have plenty of ideas but no notion of how to organize them.

If you're not sure where the problems with reading and writing originate, pay attention to your child's *oral* language abilities. If your son struggles with reading but speaks easily and coherently, is able to listen well, and understands and can explain to others what's being read or said, then his problem probably lies within the processing blocks. (See Chapter Eight.) If he reads well but can't comprehend what he has read or can't express himself verbally, his problem is likely to be in the thinking blocks.

Many of the methods used to build a child's skills in understanding what is read and expressing ideas in writing are directed toward developing the skills of the thinking blocks of both language and images. These methods also emphasize the use of skills from the thinking block of strategies, such as self-monitoring and evaluating one's own performance when reading and writing. The techniques presented in this chapter are designed to assist children in thinking about what they are doing as they attempt to understand text and to organize and express their ideas in writing. Although the information here will be of particular help to children who have distinct problems in the thinking blocks, the techniques are useful for many other children.

HELPING YOUR CHILD BECOME A GOOD READER AND WRITER

Throughout this chapter, we will be talking about the skills needed to become a thoughtful and attentive reader, and an effective and analytical writer. Keep in mind that these are fundamental life skills, not just school or academic skills. In other words, acquiring these skills is not an end in itself; good reading and writing skills are important throughout life.

Instruction in the classroom is very important, but, in the development of these skills, you play a major role. Make sure that your child sees that you read often, critically, and attentively, and that you strive to write letters, messages, and instructions clearly. Your example will encourage best efforts in all of these areas.

Building Language Skills through Modeling

Oral language forms the basis for our understanding of what we read and for how we express our ideas in writing. This means that, through conversational give and take, we can help our children build skills in understanding and expressing themselves. In our day-to-day activities, we are can show them the kind of thinking that we do while reading and solving problems, and we can help them build their skills in the thinking block of language. This is called *modeling,* a fancy term for old-fashioned parental "Show and Tell."

When you are reading a newspaper headline, or trying to figure out the instructions for a new appliance, or writing a letter to protest being overcharged on a bill, share your thoughts in terms your child can understand. You will be modeling the behaviors that good readers and writers use. Modeling is simple: you talk while your child watches and listens to you. By imitating you, your child will become more strategic in approaching language and will learn to employ these and similar strategies independently. You can also help increase understanding by describing your child's actions while they are being performed.

Most parents use, quite naturally, two other simple techniques for boosting language knowledge and comprehension: *expansion* and *elaboration.* In expansion, you extend a child's remark, making it more complete and correct. If your child says "I shutted it," you remark: "Oh, you shut the door?" In elaboration, you take the child's response, expand it to a more correct form, and provide some additional information. In the example above, you might say, "I am glad you shut the door. It was getting rather cold in here." Use of these and similar techniques will help increase your child's language development and knowledge of the world.

The Role of Background Knowledge

One critical factor influences oral expression, reading comprehension, and written expression: *background knowledge.* We understand most easily and write most fluently when the subjects at hand are relevant to our background and experiences. When we do not understand what we have heard or read, or we do not have much to write about when asked, it is usually because we have limited background knowledge about a particular topic.

We've all heard the protest—or even said ourselves—when yet another new technology appears: "It's just beyond me." In one way, the statement is an accurate description of the speaker's feelings. Technology changes rapidly, and it is hard to keep up. In another way, however, the statement is misleading. The new technology is not "beyond" the speaker's intellectual grasp, but there is a need to invest time in studying the subject more, in order to catch up. This process reflects what children face in learning. Life situations require expansion of the present store of knowledge and skills. To increase understanding and the ability to function well in the world, there is a constant need to evaluate the present level of knowledge and to study and learn so that it is expanded as needed or desired. Knowledge expansion is more work for a child than an adult, because children know less about the world. Seeing that you are a constant learner will give a natural boost to your child's efforts.

STRATEGY One of the easiest ways to increase understanding of a topic is by talking to others who know more about it. The next section describes strategies you can use to help your child build background knowledge.

Building On and Expanding Background Knowledge

Children who have difficulty in understanding ideas when reading and in generating ideas when writing need more experiences involving feeling, hearing, and seeing. When these children are given a framework or structure for arranging what they know and don't know *before* they are asked to read or write, they are better able to establish concepts, and their performance improves. Practically speaking, this means that your child will benefit from having a general idea of what a story is about, and a sense of its plot, before reading the story. As we will explore, children benefit from having a sense of what they know and don't know before they begin to read or write.

Simply asking your child to read or write more will not improve these skills; instead, structure and feedback are needed. All children benefit from activities that help them develop, expand, and organize their ideas prior to reading and writing. In fact, some experts believe that over half of all instructional time should be spent on preparing children for their reading and writing assignments. Lengthy preparation is even more critical for young learners who have weaknesses in the thinking blocks.

Fortunately, many strategies exist to help children increase their ability to organize their ideas in a logical sequence. As a parent, you can have your child do these prereading and prewriting activities for any type of assignment—or even when reading for enjoyment. Remember, when you are not working with your child on specific homework assignments, try to select materials that are highly motivating. High-interest materials will engage your child's attention, which is a necessary prerequisite for reading for learning.

Prequestions, Previewing, and Predicting   Research has demonstrated that asking questions *before* reading is a far more effective tool for improving comprehension than asking questions *after* reading. Prereading questions, or *"prequestions,"* alert readers to what the writer wants them to know. The questions encourage active thinking while reading. As the prequestions become a routine step, your child will become a critical reader who can apply the skills of the thinking blocks to the processes of reading and writing.

Children's ability to understand what they read is improved by talking with them about a book or article before they start reading it. When your child starts a new book, talk about the title, look at some of the pictures, identify the main characters, and make predictions in regard to the plot. Ask your child questions such as:

- What do you think the title means?
- What do you think this book will be about?
- Whom do you think the book is about?
- What do you think [this character] is like?
- What do you think [this character] looks like?
- What do you think may happen to [this person]?
- What are some things that [this person] may do?
- Can you guess how the story will end?

Ask similar questions when your child is assigned to read a section of a science or social studies textbook. The prequestions will help develop a general understanding of the content and will teach how to make predictions about the material to be read. Direct attention to the important points of a chapter. Review any questions at the beginning or end. Establish a pattern of *previewing* any assigned reading. Help your child form the habit of prereading and prequestioning by modeling it yourself with the books, newspapers, and magazines you read.

Finding material that is of interest to your child makes the reading-for-learning process easier. If your child is a sports fan, for instance, it's a natural step to scan the headlines of the sports section of the newspaper, or the cover of a sports magazine, and ask the questions aloud. If you both love movies, look at movie reviews in the same fashion. Through this process, you engage your child in thinking about the reading. What will happen in the story that is about to be read? What mental images of the characters can be created? By the time the questioning is finished, your child should have a general idea of what the book or article is about.

STRATEGY   Research has demonstrated that children benefit from forming and answering more in-depth or "guiding" questions, such as: Why do you think the main character acted the way he did? What do you think would have happened if he had followed his original plan? Before you discuss a reading unit with your child, analyze the material yourself, to determine the significant points. Try writing down specific questions that your child should answer while reading—questions that direct attention to specific details and facts. (You may want to break longer assignments or stories into smaller blocks of reading. Making the sections more manageable is particularly necessary if your child has trouble with comprehension because of attentional problems or becomes overwhelmed when too much material is presented at one time.)

It is also important to help your child learn how to make *predictions*. As you are reading a book with your child, or when your child has completed the nightly reading, reexamine together what has happened so far in the story. Then ask for predictions about what will happen next. If your child cannot make a prediction, make up a few of your own and have your child select the one that seems most likely. You may want to write down the prediction and have your child use it as a bookmark. As the reading progresses, the story line can be compared with the prediction.

Ask your child postreading questions, to evaluate comprehension and the ability to recall what has been read. If the questions cannot be answered, help your child locate the answers in the text, and then review the information.

THE VALUE OF PREDICTIONS

The ability to make predictions is important because it means your child is an involved reader—one who is curious, who thinks about what is being read, and who considers what is going on and whether it makes sense. These are the skills of a good reader, and they are key to increasing reading comprehension.

Self-Monitoring Your Reading

STRATEGY   Research has demonstrated that good readers share several characteristics. They think about what they already know as they read. They make and revise predictions as they go through a story. Most importantly, they monitor their understanding. In other words, they run comprehension checks on themselves periodically while reading.

We have all had the experience of reading several pages, only to find that our brain has not been participating. Suddenly, we stop and ask: "What did I just read?" Then we go back several pages and reread, this time paying closer attention. Children need to learn how to check their understanding during reading, reread if they don't understand, and ask for help when necessary.

If children do not learn this self-check strategy, a moment's lapse of attention, a challenging concept, or too much information coming at them at one time may make them feel like failures. These worries, when added to attentional and comprehension problems, cause children to begin to give up; they feel sure that they will never really understand. This is especially true for children who have comprehension problems as they enter the mid-elementary years, when classroom texts begin to contain more advanced concepts.

Monitoring Strategies for Comprehension

Comprehension is not an isolated skill. A child needs to learn several strategies to use when reading, to ensure understanding and recall of the important ideas. Here are some simple ways to help your child improve the ability to comprehend what he or she reads.

Paraphrasing   The ability to *paraphrase,* or translate into one's own words what someone else has said or written, is critical for success in both reading and writing. To understand what you read, you must be able to transform into your own interpretation the words another person has chosen. To express yourself in writing, you must be able to analyze, evaluate, and synthesize your own ideas and the ideas of others.

After your child has finished a story or passage, ask for a restatement of what has happened in the story, in your child's own words. If this is too difficult, explain the concept in simple terms, and then ask for a paraphrasing of what you have just said. Explain that this is the kind of thinking that you do when reading or writing; then ask for another try, with a story recently read.

STRATEGY   If your child is in upper-elementary school or middle school, "RAP," a simple paraphrasing strategy developed by researchers at the University of Kansas,[1] may be beneficial. RAP is an acronym representing these steps:

Read the paragraph.

Ask: What were the main ideas and details in this paragraph?

Put the main ideas into your own words.

By applying this strategy to each paragraph in a passage, your child will be more actively involved in reading and will better understand the material.

Reciprocal Teaching   To understand what we read, we need to revise and reevaluate the text constantly. Reciprocal Teaching is a technique that uses active involvement with another person to help children improve in reading comprehension.[2] As the name suggests, each person in the pair has to teach the other what has been learned from reading. This activity aids in the development of critical skills in the thinking blocks by teaching the skills of questioning, summarizing, clarifying, and predicting.

The technique has these steps:

1. Sit with your child and read a paragraph or passage together.
2. Generate questions together about what you have read.
3. Summarize the content in a sentence or two.
4. Discuss with your child any difficult sections; clarify any concepts or vocabulary that your child may not understand.
5. Encourage a prediction of what will happen in the next passage. This will help create a link between background knowledge and the new information being learned.

As you practice reciprocal teaching, aim to increase your child's involvement gradually. Encourage developing questions, summarizing content, and making predictions about the next section. Self-questioning and comprehension monitoring promote active involvement with the reading process.

If your child is in kindergarten or first grade, or has trouble with reading, make reading a regular listening activity. Read the text aloud and then discuss it with your child.

Directed Reading–Thinking Activity (DRTA)   Like other self-monitoring reading strategies, the purpose of the DRTA is to help your child develop critical reading skills.[3] Using this strategy, your child predicts or sets purposes for reading, reads to process ideas, and then tests those ideas for their validity. Follow these steps:

1. Have your child read the title of a story, then ask how the title might relate to the story. Once a prediction has been made and discussed, have your child read part of the story.

2. When the assigned amount has been read, close the book for a comprehension check. Ask three questions:
   a. "Were you correct about the meaning of the title? Which part shows that you were right?"
   b. "What do you think about what you have read?"
   c. "What do you think will happen next?"

3. Ask your child to stop two more times partway through the story. Ask similar questions about the most recent predictions.

Building Visual Thinking Skills

Though it may not seem obvious, the ability to think with images is critical for effective reading and writing. Readers need visual thinking skills to understand story action and visualize characters' relationships; writers need those same skills to describe experiences prior to writing. Furthermore, visual thinking skills are important strategic tools that allow readers and writers to organize their thinking and to clarify what they do and don't know.

Mapping and Graphic Organizers

A simple procedure that draws on the block of thinking with images is called *mapping*. Maps or webs are graphic organizers that help children develop and organize their thoughts during and after reading, or before writing. Mapping is similar to the outlining procedure many of us were taught for organizing our thoughts and ideas before writing or when taking notes. The framework for mapping, however, is more flexible and adaptable; there is no need to have two subordinate ideas under a heading.

Picture a spider web, with all the intertwining threads connected. Like a web, graphic organizers show connections. Through visual display, they depict the important ideas and illustrate their relationships. These illustrated relationships help children link pieces of information. Consequently, their understanding and their ability to recall and use information improve.

Mapping or webbing begins with brainstorming—free-associating to produce idea after idea rapidly. Suppose your daughter has an assignment to write a report about the planet Saturn. Before she begins, sit down with her and say: "Tell me everything that you already know about Saturn." All ideas are acceptable, even those that don't seem to be related. For example, your daughter might mention that Saturn is a type of car. Write that idea down. Later, you can discuss why that name might have been given to a car.

When your daughter cannot think of any more ideas, return to each idea and ask questions that will help expand her knowledge. (You may have to do a little research yourself.) For instance, your daughter may have noted that the planet Saturn has rings. Using expansion and elaboration, you might ask: How many rings does Saturn have? What are the rings made of?

Once you have a list of ideas, the two of you can use crayons or markers to color-code the ideas that can be grouped or categorized together, or connected on a map. As your child becomes more familiar and confident with the use of cognitive mapping and graphic organizers, help her learn to categorize the ideas as they are generated. At this point, color-coding will become unnecessary. After practicing mapping on several assignments, Jamie was able to produce the map shown in the figure on page 209 before she started to write a description of her new pet cat.

K-W-L Procedure

Used with or without mapping, a very simple procedure called K-W-L helps children see how new information affects what they already know. K-W-L increases knowledge and allows more active participation in the reading and writing process.[4] To begin, write the following three column headings across the top of a piece of paper:

K—What I *know* **W**—What I *want* to learn **L**—What I *learned*

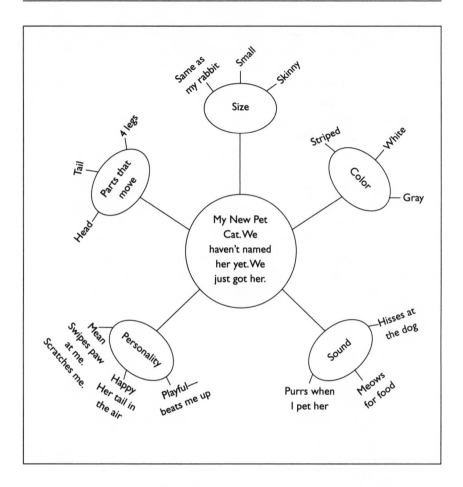

To complete the worksheet, choose a topic and then ask your child to:

1. Brainstorm, and list in the first column any information already known about the topic.
2. Develop questions about what might be learned about the topic, and record them in the second column.
3. Record in the third column what has been learned from reading and library research.

After the worksheet has been completed, help your child write a paragraph that summarizes what has been learned about the topic. At first, you may want to be the "secretary" and do the note taking for your child. Later, encourage your child to take more responsibility for the writing.

An adaptation of the K-W-L strategy adds both mapping and summarization, by organizing and categorizing the information listed under L.[5] (This procedure works even better when a writing activity is added, because it allows children to summarize the new information they have learned, and to organize it more efficiently in their own words.) To transform the K-W-L strategy into a map, make the topic the centerpiece. As an example, let's go back to the writing assignment about the planet Saturn. Your daughter would write "Saturn" in the center of the map. She would then add lines to show the relationships between the main topic and the facts that she learned—details about the planet's rings and their characterization, for instance.

Children then use the map to summarize. When writing is added, the center of the map becomes the title of the essay or report, and each category listed becomes the topic for a new paragraph. Supporting details are then added to expand or explain the topic further. After practice with this procedure, some children are able to omit the mapping step and write their summaries directly from the K-W-L worksheet.

Language Experience Approach (LEA)

The Language Experience Approach (LEA) is a procedure designed to engage children in reading and writing at any age. Because it draws on children's natural language as a basis for reading and writing instruction, some children can actually learn how to read and write using this very simple procedure. For all children, however, the LEA can help increase comprehension and build skills in the thinking block.

The basic procedure of the LEA is as follows:

1. Have your child share an experience.
2. Write (by hand or using a word processor) a record of the ideas as your child dictates a story about the experience. Say each word as you write it down.
3. Ask your child to read the story back to you. Help with any words that cause trouble.
4. Save the story and have your child practice reading it on subsequent nights.

Throughout this process, use modeling techniques and questioning to increase your child's involvement and background knowledge. Draw on your child's emotions and senses. Ask questions such as: What did you like about the experience? What did you see? hear? smell? taste? touch? Many children enjoy illustrating their stories when they are finished.

Adaptations of the Language Experience Approach   You can combine the LEA with several other strategies, to improve your child's reading and writing skills. For example, LEA plus mapping would have these steps:

1. Ask your child to describe an experience.
2. Draw a circle in the middle of a page, and write a word that is central to the experience.
3. Have your child suggest different words or ideas that can be arranged as categories around the topic.
4. After the map has been developed, have your child dictate a story about the experience into a tape recorder.
5. Listen to the taped text together, and evaluate the story for clarity and organization.
6. Help with writing a final version of the dictated story.

Vocabulary improvement can be coordinated with using the LEA. After your child has developed the story, help with brainstorming words that are more precise and descriptive. Discuss differences in word meaning. Additional activities for vocabulary development are described in the next section.

Vocabulary Development

A child who has a rich and varied vocabulary is likely to succeed in school. In fact, the breadth and depth of a child's vocabulary are often described as the best predictors of school performance, from kindergarten through college. Knowing the meanings of a wide variety of words will help your child to understand what is read and to express ideas more clearly in writing.

Children are wired to learn and use language; they pick up its underlying rules intuitively, as part of everyday life. As an example, this conversation took place between four-year-old Ryan and his father one night as Ryan was finishing his bath. His father told him it was time to get out of the tub. Ryan replied, "Daddy, first you must unsoap me." "Unsoap" is not an actual word, but Ryan understood the use of the prefix *un-* to change a word's meaning.

As a parent, you can use a variety of strategies to help your child build on this natural tendency to enrich and increase vocabulary. Make a point of exposing your child to new words, using them in a variety of different contexts, and introducing active involvement in learning word meanings. One of the easiest and most natural ways to boost your child's vocabulary is by consciously using more complex vocabulary, in natural contexts, in your interactions. Never talk down to your child—but don't search the dictionary for new vocabulary, either. Instead use the appropriate language for each conversation's context. For example, when out on a tennis court, Ms. Ambers pointed and said to her five-year-old son: "Michael, would you please get the tennis ball? It just rolled under the gazebo." Michael skipped over and retrieved the ball. A few minutes later, he remarked: "Mommy, I am leaving my toys under the gazebo. Will you watch them for me?" *Gazebo* had not been a word in his vocabulary, but his appropriate use of it showed that he not only understood its meaning but was willing to incorporate it into his everyday speech.

The most effective way to increase your child's vocabulary is to integrate new words into the pool of words that is already known. Parents tend to do this naturally. When a child asks the meaning of a word, a parent will try to pair the new word with one that is familiar. Another simple way to help expand vocabulary is to define words that are new or unfamiliar through explanation and elaboration. Use an unfamiliar word in a sentence, and then follow it with a sentence that defines the word. For example, when answering her son's question about a friend, Ms. Nye replied: "That information is confidential. I really can't share it with anyone."

TEACHING GRAMMAR NATURALLY

If your child makes a grammatical error when speaking, do not label it as an error. Repeat the sentence back, using the correct form. If your five-year-old daughter might say, "I taked the books back." You would reply: "I am glad you took the books back." Through modeling and listening, your child's ability to use correct forms will increase. Children are very creative in their use of language, and their knowledge of language rules seems to increase daily through exposure and practice.

STRATEGY   Study one new word each day. Select the word from your child's reading material, or use a word-a-day calendar that introduces new vocabulary. (Some word-a-day calendars are general; others follow themes, such as particular sports.) Each morning, discuss that day's word, post it on the refrigerator or the family bulletin board, and make a point of providing opportunities for using it when your child is present. Turn the process into a game, or give your child points for every correct use of the word in speaking or writing during that day. The points can later be exchanged for a treat or small prize.

When reading with your child or helping with homework, review any vocabulary that might be new. After the reading is finished, discuss again the meanings of the new or unfamiliar words.

Using Visual Imagery to Build Vocabulary

Encourage use of the thinking block of images by helping your child learn to visualize words, settings, or scenes. Consider the expression: "A picture is worth a thousand words." When your show and discuss a picture, you help to expand your child's understanding. You can also help with forming mental scenes. For example, suppose your daughter has been asked to write a story about traveling to the moon. You might say: "Close your eyes and imagine you are in a spaceship on your way to the moon. Tell me everything you see." Write down her observations so that she can integrate them into the assignment. Ask questions that will help her expand and elaborate new elements.

At times, you will have to help your child recall more difficult terminology, such as new words to be learned for a science or history class. Researcher Dr. Margo Mastropieri[6] has developed a highly successful method for tying new words to visual images, as a way of helping children recall word meanings and learn new vocabulary. Mastropieri's method involves three steps: (a) recoding, (b) relating, and (c) retrieving.

To use this method, begin by defining and discussing the meaning of a new word with your child. Choose a *keyword*—a word that evokes specific visual imagery, or one that rhymes with the new word. Then have your child make a mental picture of the definition, involving the *keyword* in some way. Have your child study the mental picture until the definition is easily recalled. For example, Mr. Ames was trying to help his daughter Christina learn the meaning of the word *apex*. Christina created an image of an ape standing on a spot marked with the letter *X*, on top of a mountain. When she was asked to produce the definition later, the image—and the meaning of the word—came easily to mind.

Using Prefixes, Suffixes, and Root Words

As school progresses, you can help increase the size and depth of your child's vocabulary by teaching the meanings of the most common *prefixes* (syllables attached to the front of the root word) and *suffixes* (syllables attached to the end of the root word). Begin by explaining to your child that many words consist of prefixes and/or suffixes, and roots. Then give examples of common prefixes and suffixes, such as those in Appendix C, and teach the meanings:

STRATEGY You can use graphic organizers to help increase your child's understanding of the relationships among prefixes, suffixes, and root words. Write the root word in a circle at the middle of the map, and then add various prefixes, in circles, connected to the root word on the left side, and suffixes, in circles, connected to the root word on the right side. For example, draw a centered circle and write the word *cover* inside it. Connect, on the left side, circles containing prefixes such as *dis-*, *un-*, and *re-*, and on the right side, suffixes such as *-ing* and *-ed*. Or, as an alternative, write a prefix or suffix in the center of the map and attach a variety of root words.

In another approach, you can make a horizontal list of common prefixes, suffixes, or roots. For example, across the top of a page you might write

UN-   *DIS-*   *FRIEND*   *-TION*   *-LY*

Under the headings, have your child list several words that use that syllable or root, such as *unhappy, disagree, friendless, action, sadly.* Encourage your child to "mix and match" roots and affixes, forming words such as *unfriendly, disagreeing.* The visual nature of writing provides an excellent opportunity for helping children to expand their vocabulary.

Boosting the Use of Synonyms/Antonyms

While working on vocabulary, one central goal should be to reduce overreliance on common words and substitute more precise terms. Encourage your child to think of a variety of optional words *before* starting to write. For example, you might ask for a list of synonyms for *said,* such as *shouted, observed, questioned, suggested, whispered.*

You can also use graphic organizers to teach word meaning. In the center of a drawing shaped like a spider or a star, write a word your child tends to overuse. Then help to brainstorm synonyms that can be written on each of the arms. For example, for the word *ran,* you might write *galloped, cantered, skipped, loped, fled, scampered.*

Repeat the procedure, substituting antonyms for the synonyms. If the center word is *happy,* you might write *unhappy, sad, miserable, glum,* and *depressed* on the spider legs. As this skill improves, draw a ten-pointed star or an octopus, and have your child research synonyms or antonyms in a thesaurus.

For a greater challenge, have your child list the words by degree of meaning, and place them on a graphic organizer that is shaped like a pyramid. For example, *glum, unhappy, sad, miserable,* and *depressed,* in that order, describe increasing degrees of severity. After your child has ordered the list, ask how the meanings make the words seem right, in that order.

Cloze Procedure

The cloze procedure is a technique to help your child's overall comprehension and build vocabulary. The word *cloze* is derived from the psychological concept of closure—the ability of the brain to supply information that is missing. Most of us do this quite naturally. If we hear only a part of a word during a conversation, or if we see only part of a picture or object, we are able to complete the word or image. For instance, when we see a cat's tail rounding a corner, we can supply the mental image of the cat; when we hear someone say, " The doctor says I suffered a drop in blood pres . . . ," we can fill in the concept of "blood pressure."

The cloze procedure helps increase children's awareness of word meaning and encourages learning to use the context to arrive at the right word while reading or writing. The procedure is particularly effective in teaching children self-monitoring for comprehension. They learn to stop, evaluate (for sense) what they are reading, and then correct any mistakes. Let's take as an example the sentence "The cowboy rode away into the sunset on his _____." Using the context to help you predict word meaning, you would fill in the blank easily with the word *horse.* However, when Bruce, a third-grade student, read the sentence, he mistook the word *horse* for *house,* and did not stop reading to ask himself whether this made sense. Bruce would benefit from doing some cloze exercises.

You can use the cloze procedure to work on vocabulary development or to increase your child's ability to predict and use context clues. Begin with passages that are at an easy reading level for your child, and then delete certain words—for instance, every tenth word, or specific types of words, such as nouns or verbs. After the deletions have been made, have your child first read the passage all the way through once, and then reread the passage and suggest, or write in, possible responses. As a final step, discuss your child's choices. If a particular response does not make sense, help to determine why this is so, and decide on a better answer.

If your child is in preschool or kindergarten, an oral cloze procedure may work better. Read a story to your child and point at the words while you are reading. When you get to a word that is easy to predict, pause and then ask your child to guess the word. This type of oral procedure is particularly useful for children with weaknesses in the thinking block of language.

Many younger children like cloze exercises because they can be made into games, but they needn't be drudgery for older children, either. You can make up cloze games to play with your child, using newspaper headlines, movie titles, or song lyrics. As one variation, try doing cloze exercises where you pick a wrong ending, to demonstrate how jarring— and sometimes hilarious—this can be.

Synonym Cloze   You may also use the cloze procedure to help your child change words after the first draft of a story or an assignment is complete. Read through the draft and help to identify words that are redundant, overused, or imprecise. With an eraser or correction fluid, delete the word from the line, leaving a blank space, and then write the original word below the blank for reference. For example, when Omar, a fifth-grade student, went over a story he had written, he noticed that he had used the word *nice* six times. When he and his dad were working on the final draft, they noted each use. Initially, Omar had begun his story with the sentence: *It was a nice day.* Using the cloze procedure, his dad changed the sentence to:

It was a _____ day.
                    nice

Then his dad asked Omar to brainstorm a more descriptive adjective. They decided on: *It was a glorious day.*

Sentence Expansion

Some children have trouble understanding the meaning of long sentences. They also tend to use very simple sentences when they are writing. The reason could be one of several conditions: weaknesses in the thinking block of language, limited background knowledge, or fear of misspelling when writing long sentences. Sentence-combining strategies can help to improve your child's understanding of more complex sentence patterns and encourage the use of longer sentences.

To begin, write two or three simple sentences on a piece of paper, or take sentences directly from your child's written work. Ask your child to combine the sentences to form one longer and more elaborate sentence. Encourage the production of several different acceptable sentences. Teach how to join short sentences by using a variety of conjunctions, such as *because*, *but*, and *or*.

Another easy way to help your child expand written sentences is to insert blanks where the sentence can be elaborated. Have your child brainstorm descriptive words, phrases, and clauses that could be added to make the writing more interesting and varied, then discuss which choices would make the writing most precise and readable. For instance, if your daughter wrote, "The man left town that day," you could ask her to think about descriptions of the man, the town, and the day. Martina worked with her mother on this sentence and ended up with "The short, sad man slunk out of the unfriendly town that stormy day."

Writing with Purpose

Expanding vocabulary and learning to use various sentence patterns are prerequisites to writing with purpose. Over time, your child will be asked to do two main types of reading and writing in school: *narrative* and *expository*. Narrative text is largely fiction and consists of stories that emphasize events or experiences. Expository text is nonfiction and consists of factual information and explanations.

The abilities to comprehend and write expository text increase in importance as your child progresses through school. In high school, writing is the major basis for evaluation in classes. Therefore, to succeed in school, your child must learn how to understand and write both well-structured essays and well-organized stories. The section that follows directly explains how to use a process-oriented approach for helping your child with writing. The next two sections provide overviews of techniques for using and understanding narrative and expository text structure. Using these strategies at home will help your child increase both reading comprehension and writing skill.

Writing Process Approach

In the past two decades, the approach to instruction in written language has changed in most schools. Formerly, teachers emphasized the basic, more mechanical details of writing: handwriting, spelling, and punctuation. Today, teachers emphasize the use of writing to express and communicate ideas. Because reading and writing skills are generally taught together, even very young students do a considerable amount of writing. Don't be overly alarmed if your child brings home papers that seem to be filled with uncorrected spelling errors or poor punctuation. What you are seeing are first drafts of compositions. The corrections will be made at a later time.

Thanks to the work of authors like Donald Graves writing is now viewed as an activity that incorporates thinking, planning, composing, revising, editing, and sharing—what teachers call the "writing process approach." As you are helping your child develop and write papers, essays, and reports for school, you also will want to follow this process, first acting as your child's coach and editor, and then teaching your child to do the process alone.

Stage One: Prewriting   Before beginning a writing assignment, your child must have ideas to write about. The easiest way to generate ideas is to spend time with your child and encourage brainstorming and recording ideas. Organization of the ideas will come later. Review the section on building background knowledge (pages 201–204). After your child has decided what to write about, help with listing and organizing the ideas that will be included; there may also be a list of words that your child wants to use. Help with grouping ideas on a graphic organizer, or organize them in a sequence on a piece of paper.

Stage Two: Drafting or Composing   During this stage, your child should begin writing or composing a first draft. The stress should be on content rather than on the processing skills of spelling or the motor skills of handwriting. Give help if your child asks how to spell a word, but encourage focusing on capturing ideas. Remind your child that you will help correct the spelling at a later date and that you are more concerned about recording ideas.

STRATEGY On the first draft, encourage writing on every other line so that it will be easier to make revisions and edits. If your child is working at a word processor, make sure you both know how to use the editing functions.

Stage Three: Revising During this stage, your child seeks feedback from others about the content of the paper. Again, keep attention directed toward the meaning of the piece, not its form. Begin the discussion with your child by telling what you really like about the piece, such as: "You've done a really nice job of describing this character. You gave me a clear picture of exactly how he looks." After sharing what you like about the paper, note any areas where the content could be altered or the organization improved. If necessary, return to the prewriting stage and help your child brainstorm some more ideas.

A more formal approach, which works best with older children and more complicated projects, is to prepare a list of questions and comments about the draft. Examples of topics you may discuss include: How well does the draft adhere to the assignment? Is the information well organized? Is the vocabulary descriptive and appropriate? Have all the relevant topics been included? For some children, you may have to make your questions more specific, indicating that they must reevaluate what they've done. You may want to look at the assignment closely in order to prepare appropriately specific questions.

Next, have your child read the draft to you aloud. Discuss the questions and comments. View this as a conference where your child, as an author, and you, as a friendly and helpful editor, share your ideas. In your role as editor, identify the sections that seem problematic and then explain why. Discuss strategies for improving and clarifying the writing. Have your child make revisions and then review and discuss them. Ideally, your child will be working on a word processor, so that changing and moving sections of text are accomplished easily.

Stage Four: Editing In this stage, you direct attention to the conventions of writing. Help your child correct errors in grammar, spelling, punctuation, or capitalization, keeping in mind the necessary level of guidance. Some children will need line-by-line guidance; others will need only a checklist of general reminders. Be careful not to expect your child to correct errors that are beyond his or her current skill or knowledge level. You may, however, use these as "teachable" moments—for instance, to show an inexperienced young writer how to use commas or quotation marks to denote dialogue.

To help your child improve in detecting and correcting errors, review the paper and identify all errors. If there are only a few errors, try writing their number at the top of the paper, and see whether your child can locate them. If there are many errors, place a checkmark (√) alongside each line that contains an error. If a line has more than one error, note the number alongside the line, in parentheses. After your child attempts to correct the errors, review the assignment and help correct any remaining errors.

STRATEGY Teaching your child the COPS mnemonic (memory guide) will help with learning to identify the following types of errors:[7]

C CAPITALIZATION—check for capitalization of first words in sentences and proper nouns.

O OVERALL appearance of work—check for neatness, legibility, margins, indentation of paragraphs, and complete sentences.

P PUNCTUATION—check for commas and appropriate end punctuation.

S SPELLING—check whether all words are spelled correctly.

This strategy helps children learn to check their writing independently before they submit their work—to become their own editors.

STRATEGY Help your child improve in editing skills by teaching how to use a spell-checker. Use of a spell-checker is also the single most important way your child can improve in spelling.

A spell-checker may be in a word processing program or it may be a small hand-held instrument. Underline some (or all) of the misspelled words from one of your child's writing samples. Type the incorrect spellings into the spell-checker. If the program presents several choices, help with selecting the correct spelling. Some spell-checkers pronounce the choices aloud.

A word of caution is in order: You have to be a fairly accurate speller in order to use a commercial spell-checker. In other words, your child has to be able to come up with fairly close approximations of the correct spelling. For children with consistent spelling difficulties, a better choice may be a personal list that contains the words listed alphabetically that he or she misspells frequently.

Stage Five: Publishing The final stage of the writing process approach is called publishing—sharing the writing with others. This may be as simple as your child's letting someone else read the finished work, or as elaborate as putting together a bound book, newsletter, or magazine.

This writing process approach can be used with all types of writing, fiction and nonfiction. Additional strategies for working with a variety of texts are presented in the next section.

Teaching Narrative: Story Grammars

The easiest way to increase your child's understanding of narrative text and improvement in narrative writing is to teach the use of story grammars. *Story grammar* simply refers to the underlying structure of a story—the characters, setting, and action.

Simple Story Grammars It's not uncommon for children with weaknesses in the thinking blocks to read an entire book but not be able to tell where the story took place, or describe any of the characters, or tell what happened. Research has shown that direct teaching of story grammar can help children of all ages improve both their reading comprehension and their writing skills.

You can introduce your child to the concept of story grammar as early as kindergarten or first grade. Teach that every story has three parts: a beginning, a middle, and an end. Review a common fairy tale or fable, such as *The Tortoise and the Hare,* and ask your child: What happened at the beginning? In the middle? How did the story end? You can draw three circles and connect them with arrows to illustrate this sequence. Or you may give your child a series of prompts or questions for guiding organization, such as: Who? Did What? And then what happened? Or ask your child to tell you:

- Who is the story about?
- What is that person trying to do?
- What happens to that person at the end?

Advanced Story Grammars As your child enters second or third grade, you can introduce more detailed story grammars, which can include the following general elements:

- The setting: Where and when does the story take place?
- The main characters: Who is the story about?

- The problem: What happens to the main character?
- The solution: What does the main character do to solve the problem?
- The ending: How is the story resolved?

When you are helping children to increase their understanding of a story that they have read or to prepare for writing a story, try to include elements of story grammar as guiding points for your discussion.

The Story Grammar Marker The Story Grammar Marker™ is a comprehensive program designed to help children who have trouble comprehending what they read or hear, as well as organizing their thoughts for speaking or writing. In other words, children who need extra support in developing the skills of the thinking blocks. The program focuses on teaching the child the underlying organizational structure of stories and provides practice activities for identifying significant ideas, sequencing story details, and reflecting upon a character's actions. Although this program was designed primarily for classroom use, it is an excellent resource if you are home schooling your child or helping your child with oral or written language development over the summer break. By reviewing this program, you will become an expert in teaching children the important aspects of story grammar.[8]

Story Maps

Mapping and graphic organizers can also help your child develop a story. Similar to the example seen on page 209, story maps can be created by following these simple steps:

1. Have your child brainstorm ideas.
2. Help to organize the ideas on the map. These ideas can be subcategorized under: characters, setting, problem, and ending.
3. Help to incorporate the information on the map into a story.

As their skills increase, children should be encouraged to take more responsibility for developing and organizing a story map. They can then use it as a guide when reading.

STRATEGY You can use maps to help your child with a certain aspect of story grammar. For her English class, Drew was reading a novel that involved many characters, and she had trouble remembering the relationships among them. To help her organize the characters mentally, Drew and her mother made a character map. They wrote each character's name in a circle and then drew lines between characters and wrote their relationship, such as "sisters," on the connecting line. Whenever she needed clarification while she was reading, Drew consulted the map.

Questioning

After reading or before writing a story, your child may benefit from answering specific questions pertaining to the characters, setting, problem, and ending. Here are some guidelines:

1. Ask questions about the *characters:*

   Who is the main character?

   Who are the other characters?

   What do you know about these characters?

   Encourage your child to discuss the social/emotional as well as the physical traits of the characters.

   Ask:

   What does this person look like on the outside?

   How does he feel in the inside?

2. Next, have your child consider the *setting,* including the time and place:

   When does the story occur?

   What is the time of year?

   Where does the story occur?

3. Ask questions about the *problem:*

   What is the main problem?

   Are there other, minor problems?

   How does the main character plan to solve the main problem?

   How do the other characters respond?

4. Ask questions about the *ending:*

   How does the story end?

   How do the characters feel at the end?

Character Development

In addition to strategies to assist with organization, your child may benefit from instruction in character development. When your child is attempting to understand a character in a novel or to create a character for a story, ask questions that will help define and describe this person more precisely. For example, you might ask:

> What does the person look like?
>
> What does the person do?
>
> How does the person feel about what is happening?
>
> What emotions does the person display?

Story Grammar Frameworks

STATE the Story   Because some children can remember story grammar strategies more easily if an acronym illustrates the steps, we suggest "STATE the Story," which uses a first-letter mnemonic to help children remember story elements:

> **S = Setting** (Who? What? Where? When?)
>
> **T = Trouble** (What is the trouble or problem?)
>
> **A = Action** (What happens?)
>
> **T = Turning point** (What is done to resolve the problem?)
>
> **E = End** (How does the story end?)

While reviewing a story (or when planning to write a story), your child can use this acronym to make sure each element is accounted for.

STORE the Story   The technique of reviewing story elements is helpful for providing writing structure. "STORE the Story"[9] incorporates elements of the writing process. STORE is an acronym for:

> **S = Setting** (Who? What? Where? When?)
>
> **T = Trouble** (What is the trouble or problem?)
>
> **O = Order of events** (What happens?)
>
> **R = Resolution** (What is done to solve the problem?)
>
> **E = End** (How does the story end?)

To teach your child this strategy:

1. *Introduce the acronym STORE.* Discuss the meaning of the verb "to store" (save, hold, keep for a while, put away) and the purpose of "STORE the Story," which is to help understand and remember—to store—any story you read by recognizing and recalling each part. Next, remind your child that just as every story has a beginning, middle, and end, it also has a *Setting, Trouble, Order of events, Resolution,* and *Ending.*

2. *Show your child how to use STORE.* Make up a story yourself, and use it to set up a STORE cue sheet. Write the headings of the five story parts on a page. Leave extra room under the order of events so that you and your child can number the events as they will occur. Explain this purpose as you demonstrate the technique. Begin at the prewriting stage of the writing process. Select a topic and then brainstorm ideas. Fill in the STORE cue sheet, crossing out some ideas and adding others until you are satisfied. Next, read over the cue sheet to make sure that all parts of the story make sense and fit in with the other parts. Proceed through the writing stage of the writing process approach, and then through the stages of revising, editing, and rewriting. Explain how the use of STORE ensures continuity of the story line.

3. *Provide guided practice with the store format.* Following the steps above, help your child create a story using the STORE format.

4. *Provide independent practice with store.* Have your child create his or her own story.

For extra support or as a variation, fill in a STORE The Story frame, using a familiar story. Or, provide picture cards to aid in generating story ideas. If your child is having trouble getting started, provide the Setting and Trouble parts of the process, and perhaps some events, and then tell your child to add more events and finish the story; or, provide the Setting or the Trouble and have your child generate all of the other parts of the story.

SPOT the Story   For a younger child, you may want to use "SPOT the Story."[10] For this strategy, your child may picture a dog named Spot. The letters in this acronym represent:

S = Setting

P = Problem

O = Order of action

T = Tail end

As your child discusses a story or prepares to write one, ask for a summary of the events in the story. Until your child memorizes the strategy, write the steps on an index card for reference.

Shared Writing

An enjoyable way to help increase your child's writing skill is to write stories together. Explain that you will be writing this story together and that your goal is to make it sound like the story has been written by one person. After you discuss and choose a topic:

1. Write the initial sentence of the story.
2. Ask your child to read the sentence and then to add another sentence.
3. Take turns contributing sentences and discussing the additions, until you agree that the story is complete. At intervals, encourage your child to stop and read the entire story before adding a sentence.
4. When the story is complete, read the story together.

You can modify this activity by alternating sentences, single words, or paragraphs. Most children like this method of storytelling, which is especially effective with reluctant writers. As a variation, try recording the story on tape or revising it on a word processor.

Expository Writing

In addition to comprehending and creating stories, children must be able to convey factual information and opinions through their ability to write clear and effective sentences, paragraphs, essays, and reports. Many children are spontaneous and natural storytellers, but research has shown that many others benefit from formal instruction in expository writing, including methods of organization, and practice in writing a variety of paragraphs.

A child who has weaknesses in the skills of the thinking blocks is likely to have trouble developing and organizing ideas. Fortunately, many strategies can help to improve skills in collecting and organizing the factual information needed to write paragraphs, essays, and reports.

Paragraph and Essay Structures

Children must develop several different types of expository styles to succeed in higher grades. The most common types of expository paragraphs are described; each is followed by a sample opening sentence.

- *Sequential writing* describes a process in a step-by-step fashion. "In order to make a peanut butter and jelly sandwich, you must follow several steps."
- *Descriptive writing* presents the physical appearance or characteristics of something. "Imagine what you will see when you step into my messy room."
- *Enumerative writing* provides reasons for beliefs. "There are many reasons for saying 'No' to drugs."
- *Chronological exposition* recounts an event across time. "The first day of their journey, they crossed the mountain range."
- *Compare–Contrast writing* explains how two things are alike and how they differ. "There are many differences and similarities between the states of California and Arizona."
- *Problem–Solution writing* offers directions for solving a problem. "If your car breaks down and it's late at night, you should do several things."
- *Opinion* expresses a personal attitude in regard to an issue. "Some people believe that teachers should not assign homework over the weekend."
- *Cause–Effect exposition* explains the results or impact of an event. "The closing of the factory created an economic disaster in the small town."
- *Persuasive* writing attempts to convince the reader that a particular stance or option is correct. "Before buying a new car, you must consider the merits of a Ford Taurus."

Begin by teaching your child how to write one type of paragraph. When that format is mastered, proceed to the next.

Organizing Ideas in Expository Writing

When children start writing exposition, they need to learn how to organize their ideas within paragraphs and then within essays. The following strategies will help to develop this skill.

Power Writing   Power Writing is a structured program designed to teach children how to categorize and subordinate ideas,[11] moving from the level of single words all the way through to writing essays. By adapting the formal course of instruction, you can easily use this concept at home. Essentially, the term "powers of writing" refers to the following levels of organization:

> *1st Power:* Main idea statements.
>
> *2nd Power:* Major details or subtopics.
>
> *3rd Power:* Minor details about the subtopics.

To teach the concept, start with simple words. Give your child a category, such as farm animals, toys, or ice cream flavors, and ask the names of two members of that category (e.g., cows and chickens; dolls and building blocks; or chocolate and strawberry).

When your child is comfortable with the idea of a major category—1st power—and subcategories—2nd power—introduce practice in writing simple paragraphs. For the purposes of this program, a simple paragraph consists of one main idea or 1st-power sentence, followed by two 2nd-power sentences. Start by giving your child the opening 1st-power sentence: "There are two things I like to do when I go on vacation." Or, "I really like two types of ice cream." Andrea's mother gave her the following 1st-power sentence: "I love to do two things at the beach." Andrea then wrote two 2nd-power sentences: "I love to make sand castles. I like to jump into the waves."

After writing a simple paragraph is accomplished, teach how to write longer passages. To help your child create an essay:

1. Begin by writing a general main-topic sentence at the top of the paper. When starting out to generate topic sentences, have your child keep the first sentence short. Make sure that it contains only *one* statement. For example, Jack wrote: "Skiing is my favorite sport."

2. Have your child write three sentences about the original statement. Each of these sentences should provide more specific information about the main topic. Encourage the use of simple declarative

statements. Write the first of these three sentences directly after the topic sentence. To allow enough space for 3rd-power sentences, write the next 2nd-power sentence about one-third of the way down the page, and the third 2nd-power sentence two-thirds of the way down the page. Jack's three 2nd-power sentences were: "I like the feeling of going down a hill fast. " "I enjoy cold weather." "I like going into the lodge at the end of the day."

3. Have your child write two to three 3rd-power sentences to follow each of the three sentences in step 2. The sentences in step 3 must be specific and concrete. Encourage your child to go into detail and use examples. Underneath the sentence "I like going into the lodge at the end of the day," Jack wrote: "It feels great to take off your ski boots and relax. Then I get a cup of hot cocoa. I put my feet up and sit by the fire."

4. Have your child rewrite the first sentence in a new way to complete the essay. Jack wrote: "These are the reasons I enjoy a day on the slopes."

5. At this point, help your child review the content to ensure that the subject has not changed, and that the central idea or theme is obvious from the first paragraph.

This type of structure will help your child learn to write a coherent essay. Both in and out of the classroom, your child will be able to construct messages that communicate with clarity. As this skill improves, your child will become more flexible in approaching writing assignments. Later, you may want to review the material on sentence expansion (see page 217).

STRATEGY   If more structure is needed when learning to write paragraphs, try giving your child *paragraph frames* to complete. To create a frame for any kind of expository writing, outline several key words or phrases that may be used in a paragraph, and, around each one, allow space for writing. When constructing these frames for your child, provide surrounding words that will help to identify what should be written in the spaces. Some children benefit from combining the ideas of a paragraph frame with some kind of graphic organizer. For instance, to help your child learn to write a sequential paragraph, you might fold a piece of paper into four squares and ask your child to write one step in each square. Or, for cause-and-effect writing, suggest that your child first draw an event, then add connecting events with arrows, and finally proceed to describe what happens.

MY FAVORITE SPORT [JACK'S ESSAY]

Skiing is my favorite sport. I like the feeling of going down a hill fast. I don't like lift lines, but I look forward to steering around trees and other skiers on the way down.

I enjoy cold weather. I like to feel the wind on my face when I'm dressed warmly. I also like wearing cool ski goggles to keep the sun out of my eyes.

I like going into the lodge at the end of the day. It feels great to take off your ski boots and relax. Then I get a cup of hot cocoa. I put my feet up and sit by the fire.

These are the reasons I enjoy a day on the slopes.

Cohesion

Cohesion, which refers to the patterns and linking words that writers use to connect the sentences and paragraphs within their compositions, is an important element of writing. You can use a variety of strategies to help your child increase skills in sequencing, organizing, and connecting thoughts. These strategies aid in understanding the underlying organization of what your child reads, as well as how to tie together what your child writes.

The specific words used to show organization or the organizational pattern within a passage are called *cohesive ties.* Examples of cohesive ties include:

- Words signaling sequence, such as *first, next,* or *finally.*
- Words signaling time order, such as *before, after,* or *when.*
- Words signaling comparison–contrast, such as *however, but, as well as,* or *yet.*
- Words signaling cause–effect, such as *because, therefore,* or *consequently.*

Your child can learn to use these cohesive ties in writing by keeping a list of them as part of a graphic organizer; in your role as friendly editor, you can point them out as part of the writing process approach. You can also point them out in the books your child reads.

Writing Reports: Note Cards and Organizational Charts

As your child's school career progresses, research-oriented reports will be required. To learn how to structure a report, most children benefit from the direct teaching of age- and skill-appropriate organizational strategies, such as K-W-L, mapping, the writing process approach, and Power Writing.

Direct explanations or reminders of some mechanical skills and strategies are also in order. Review skimming and paraphrasing with your child, as well as note-taking techniques. One mother called us in regard to her fourth-grade son, Steven, who was supposed to write information on index cards for a report he was preparing on Africa. When his mother asked to see a note card, she noticed that he was copying information verbatim from the encyclopedia. When she told Steven that this was not the way to do note cards, he responded: "Yes, it is. My teacher told me to just take the information right out of the encyclopedia." Steven had not spent enough class time learning about the process of taking notes on index cards. Skimming is not easy for children who read slowly; review the idea that different reading speeds are like gears (see Chapter Eight). Have your child practice skimming with easy material; teach how to go through a chapter and read just the headings and all underlined words. Eventually, as the complexity of assignments increases, your child may have to rely on others and/or on technology—that is, on reading the material with others, or listening to it on an audiotape.

If your child is going to use index cards to gather information for a report, review how to paraphrase and how to create an organizational system. Help to identify key words and subtopics for the report; a graphic organizer may be helpful. See that one key word is written in the top right-hand corner of each index card. As information is gathered it should then be noted on the card that has the closest descriptive heading (key word). When needed, sub-subtopics can be added under the subtopics.

Teach your child how to color-code the headings in the right-hand corner to indicate their level of subordination. For each major topic, use a different color such as blue or red; for subtopics, use a different shade of the color such as light blue or pink. Color-coding will facilitate sorting the collected information at a later date. A graphic organizer can help with viewing and reviewing the various heads and subheadings.

STRATEGY   A similar strategy can be used with stick-on notes.[12] Children can write several topics on a piece of paper or a poster board, and then record and place their notes under the appropriate headings. An especially handy feature of this strategy is that the stick-ons can easily be moved from category to category as your child attempts to create an organizational structure for a report.

Communication with a Purpose

The strategies of this chapter are designed to help your child develop the skills of the thinking blocks and use them more effectively. Remember, when working on reading and writing, you're helping your child to develop skills that are needed throughout life. Therefore:

- Remind your child that the purpose of reading and writing is communication.
- Offer opportunities to increase your child's background knowledge, and model this activity yourself—continuously.
- Use questioning techniques to help your child participate actively in the reading and writing process.
- Teach your child how to paraphrase and monitor his or her own reading and writing.
- Think of ways to enhance motivation; use games and other materials that build on your child's interests. Make sure that reading materials are at an appropriate instructional level.
- Read yourself, read to your child, encourage reading, and give plenty of nonacademic opportunities to write.

You will find that, by using these techniques, your child will become a more effective and efficient reader and writer.

▼
Chapter

10

Addition, Subtraction, Multiplication, and Division

Helping Your Child to Understand and Master the Basic Concepts and Operations of Mathematics

If your assessment showed weaknesses in many of the skills related to the processing blocks, your child is likely to have difficulty memorizing math facts and recalling all of the steps needed to complete various calculations.

David, for instance, had strengths in the thinking blocks but difficulty learning to read, spell, and calculate. By the time he was in fifth grade, he understood how to complete long division problems, but got lost when faced with the multiple steps required to complete these problems. If he paused while solving a problem, he forgot what he was supposed to do next. And once his train of thought had been interrupted, he could not reconstruct his thinking but instead had to start solving the problem over again from the beginning. If this occurred several times, David became so frustrated that he would rip up his math paper. David's story will be familiar to many readers whose children have processing block weaknesses.

Like learning to recognize and spell words, performing computations involves the skills of perceiving, memorizing, and visualizing, and fine motor control. Let's look at the steps involved in completing the following calculation:

$$
\begin{array}{r}
45 \\
+\ 29 \\
\hline
\end{array}
$$

1. Add 9 + 5 and remember the answer: 14.

2. Record the 4 in the ones column.

3. Carry the tens place digit (1) and write it above the 4.

4. Add the three digits in the tens column.

5. Write the answer 7 in the tens column.

When you consider these multiple steps, it is easy to understand why children who experience trouble with memory and visualization can experience difficulties in computation.

If your child has computational difficulties, your first step should be to acquaint yourself with the school's math curriculum. An understanding of the curriculum will help you recognize the approach your child's teacher takes, the expectations for your child, and the purpose of the homework assignments.

The Mathematics Curriculum

When many of us attended elementary school, 90 percent of our math instructional time was spent on learning and performing pencil-and-paper computations. A typical homework assignment would be: "Complete 50 addition problems." We were sometimes given story problems to solve, but all of the story problems in a unit required the use of the same math operation—the addition chapter had ten story problems involving addition, the subtraction chapter had ten story problems requiring subtraction, and so on. Most of our time was spent memorizing facts, completing math worksheets, and learning that there was only one right answer and one way to reach it.

Then things began to change. The "new math," with its emphasis on "base 2" and "base 8" came into vogue—and then departed, leaving in its wake bewildered parents who could no longer help children with their math homework. Even more changes have occurred in the past decade. Most teachers now use a problem-solving approach to math instruction. Instead of repetitive calculations, they emphasize estimating, determining the reasonableness of answers, and studying patterns and relationships. Children learn math concepts by using manipulatives—concrete objects, such as tiles, beads, balls, or sticks, that they can touch and move to aid them in solving math problems—to demonstrate mathematical relationships.

In other words, today's teachers focus less on the secretarial skills of the processing blocks and more on the comprehension and application skills of the thinking blocks. Most teaching involves setting up opportunities for children to discover mathematical principles. Depending on your child's learning profile, this change in focus may increase or decrease the chances of success with math.

For instance, using manipulatives can be very helpful to children as they encounter and begin to use math concepts. The theory is that by learning to perform problems with concrete objects, your child will gradually come to understand how numbers (abstractions) relate to objects. Sometimes, however, children do not fully grasp the connection between manipulatives and math facts. Thus, when Amy, a second-grader, was asked to solve some simple addition and subtraction problems, she crossed her arms, sighed, and then implored in a patronizing tone, "How do you expect me to solve these problems without my manipulatives?" Amy did not understand that if she didn't have her tiles, she could simply use her fingers.

Most (but not all) schools feature a balanced curriculum; the emphasis is on understanding mathematical concepts, but paper-and-pencil computations are also taught. However, if the approach used in your child's school is directed primarily toward problem solving with manipulatives, you may have to teach or review paper-and-pencil computations with your child. If, on the other hand, the school's approach involves mostly computational drilling, you may have to spend more time making sure that your child understands the underlying principles behind the calculations as well as their application to problem solving.

Math Prerequisites

Unlike instruction in reading and writing, instruction in computation must follow a specific sequence. A child has to master certain skills before moving on to try understanding others. For example, to understand multiplication, a child must (a) grasp the idea that numbers represent objects; (b) know how to count and how to add numbers together; and (c) understand that multiplication is just a faster way for doing repeated additions. If any of these foundational skills is missing, the child will not understand the fundamental process of multiplication.

Many children receive failing grades in mathematics because they have not achieved an understanding of basic concepts or mastered the underlying prerequisite skills. A child first fails in math when the instruction received is inappropriate or too limited to develop the skill or incorporate the concept being taught. Unfortunately, in some classrooms, instruction proceeds entirely from the math textbook, regardless of whether students have in fact mastered the concept being taught. For example, a child who gets only 30 percent of the problems on a chapter review correct may nonetheless be assigned problems from the next chapter, along with classmates. Without help in mastering the missing skills, this child will continue to fall further behind.

Ideally, mastery should be assured before your child is asked to move on to new information or to read the next chapter. However, this is not always the case. In an effort to keep all students in a classroom on the same page of a textbook, the teacher may set a pace that is too fast for some and too slow for others. If your child appears to be struggling, it is important for you to intervene and discuss your concerns with the teacher. Your child may need special accommodations to get caught up—and plenty of practice at home.

Beginning Mathematical Concepts

Children naturally develop many math skills in their preschool years; depending on the child, these skills range from counting by rote to grasping the idea that each number corresponds to a certain amount. By the age of 4 years, many children can count from 1 to 10, can count several objects accurately, and are starting to write numbers. Children usually acquire these skills at home or at day care; in any case, they have them before formally starting school.

Readiness Skills

To be ready to learn math—and to keep up with classmates—your child needs to develop a foundation for basic concepts even before entering kindergarten.

Fortunately, preschoolers are happy to learn about numbers when someone will play number games with them. Being "ready" for kindergarten means being able to do the following tasks with a group of objects:

- Match and sort the objects by size, shape, and color.
- Compare sets of objects by quantity and size.

- Arrange a series of objects by size.
- Match a group of objects to a spoken number.

Shortly after entering kindergarten, your child will be asked to match a group of objects to written numbers, and soon after that, to count objects and pictures and record the numbers without help.

One-to-One Correspondence

Accurate counting is based on the idea of one-to-one correspondence: each number corresponds to a certain amount, and two sets of objects with the same number can be matched (two cookies can be matched to two glasses of milk). Children soon begin to realize that as each object is added to a set, the number increases by one. Most children grasp this concept between the ages of 4 and 5 years.

You can help with understanding one-to-one correspondence by having your child match every object of one group with an object in another group. Start with common matching objects, such as socks or marbles. As your child is matching the objects, ask whether one group has the same number as the other group, or fewer, or more. Use the terms "the same as," "more than," and "less than." As this skill progresses, have your child match different objects in the same category such as a fork and a spoon.

STRATEGY   Give your child plenty of opportunities to count objects that are used daily, such as tableware, books, and shoes. As counting skills improve, have your child count tokens, poker chips, or beads. Show how to move each counted item slightly away from the group, to avoid counting the same item twice.

For additional practice, show your child how to use an abacus. Touching and moving the beads will reinforce the concept of one-to-one correspondence and help to develop an initial understanding of place value. Playing certain games will also reinforce number recognition and counting skills. When using dice or playing with dominoes, encourage accurate counting. Make comments like: "Check to see if you have a domino with three dots just like this one."

Do not introduce written numbers or math facts until your child is developmentally ready to understand symbols or graphic representations. Dr. Cecil Mercer, an expert in learning problems and mathematics, emphasizes an important fact: When it comes to math, *understanding precedes memorization.* Your child cannot begin to master computation before understanding the meaning of the numbers. In other words, even if your child has a great memory, don't spend time using math fact flashcards if he or she does not understand what the problems mean.

Some parents jump the gun and try to introduce computation before their children are ready. The parents of 6-year-old Jon, for example, were thrilled that he had memorized many math facts. They didn't realize that he had no idea what the numbers represented. If he forgot the answer to a problem, he could not arrive at the solution in an alternative way, nor could he check to see whether his answers were reasonable. The goal is for children to be able to use abilities in the thinking blocks in computation. To ensure that your child understands the meaning of computations, you'll need to follow a specific instructional sequence.

Sequence of Instruction

As a general rule for teaching math concepts, the sequence of instruction should go from *concrete* (objects) to *semiconcrete* (drawings or representations) to *abstract* (numbers).[1] With this progression, children develop mental representations of the meaning of numbers and expand their ability to think with images.

Children with weaknesses in either the processing or the thinking blocks need a lot of experience at the concrete and semiconcrete levels before they can use numbers meaningfully. When working with manipulatives and pictures, be sure to show your child how these representations relate to actual numbers.

Concrete

In the earliest stage of mathematical understanding, children must see and manipulate objects—the "manipulatives" we mentioned earlier—to solve problems. To teach her to count from 1 to 10, you would ask your daughter to move and count 10 objects. To teach addition, you would have her put together 2 or more objects or groups of objects and then count the total number. To subtract, she would remove a specified number of objects from the group. The basic purpose of manipulatives is to help your child form mental images of these processes.

In practicing subtraction with her son, Spencer's mother placed 10 gummy bears on the table. She then invented a series of word problems. "One day, Spencer had 10 gummy bears for a treat. He ate 2 of the bears.

How many did he have left?" At this point, Spencer ate 2 bears and counted the remaining bears. His mother then gave him another problem: "Spencer now had 8 gummy bears, but he was not very hungry and only ate 1. How many did he have left?" Drawing on his experience in manipulating—counting and eating—the gummy bears, Spencer quickly learned the concept of subtraction. He also learned what it meant when there were zero gummy bears left.

Semiconcrete

In the semiconcrete stage, children learn that pictures or tallies can be drawn to represent objects. Help your child develop mathematical understanding at this level by using pictures, dots, lines, or sticks to represent physical objects. Show how to set up a tally system wherein a popsicle stick or a toothpick represents each member of a set of objects. This will encourage a focus on the *number* properties of sets rather than on their color, size, or flavor. The purpose of teaching mathematical concepts at the semiconcrete level is to help in making associations between visual pictures and symbolic processes. Thus, a child who counts fingers when solving simple addition and subtraction problems can learn to draw lines and use them instead, for adding or subtracting.

STRATEGIES   Mr. Lawson explained to his son, Robby, how the problem 12 − 8 could be represented with lines. After writing the problem vertically, he drew one long vertical line to represent the tens place, and then 2 horizontal lines to represent the ones. Because 8 cannot be subtracted from 2, the tens line had to be exchanged for 10 horizontal lines and added to the 2 lines. Mr. Lawson told Robby to cross out 8 lines and to count the remaining lines for the answer. Similarly, to teach Robby how to perform a simple division problem, such as 15 divided by 3, Mr. Lawson drew 15 lines. He asked his son to draw circles around groups of 3 lines, and then to count the number of circles for the answer. By using drawings and tallies, Robby was able to understand how to solve basic math problems.

STRATEGIES   Ms. Ames used a slightly different procedure for teaching the concept of simple division to her daughter, Anda. She showed Anda the problem: 15 divided by 3. She had Anda point to the number 3 and then count up, by 3s, until she reached 15. Each time she counted three numbers, Anda made a mark. Anda then counted the number of marks to get her answer. Using these types of simple strategies can help prepare your child for the use of symbols in the abstract level. Before working exclusively with numbers, make sure your child is able to represent a problem with pictures.

Abstract

At the abstract level of reasoning, children learn to solve problems by using numbers. They understand that numbers represent objects, and they can work with them—6 always represents the same number of objects, whether the objects are eggs or cookies or horses or trees. At this point, memorization of math facts becomes important for calculation.

Some children are asked to use numbers to solve problems when they really do not understand their meaning. Their first experience with numbers is at the abstract level, rather than at the more useful concrete level. For instance, in first grade, Marla's teacher showed the class the number 4 and said: "This is the number 4." Although she had learned to count by rote from 1 to 20, Marla did not understand that the number 4 represented 4 objects. To her, numbers were no different than letters of the alphabet. Sometimes, when she was writing, she created words composed of letters and numbers. Before engaging in problems with numbers at the abstract level, Marla needs to go back to the concrete and semiconcrete stages to learn that numbers represent a set of objects. Once she has mastered this concept, she will be ready to solve problems using numbers.

Instruction in Basic Math Facts

When children begin school, they are expected to learn the four basic operations of mathematics: addition, subtraction, multiplication, and division. An important way to help at home is to ensure that your child has a strong conceptual understanding of each operation.

Addition and Subtraction

Addition and subtraction are related processes. Addition means combining objects into a group; subtraction means removing objects from a group. When you introduce the concept of addition and subtraction to your child, start at the concrete or semiconcrete level, and use objects or pictures rather than numbers. As a conceptual basis for addition, demonstrate how two groups of objects can be combined to form a new group.

For instance, show one group consisting of 2 pencils and another group consisting of 3 pencils. Put all the pencils together and ask your child to count the total number in the group. Repeat the process several times with pennies, paper clips, poker chips, toy race cars, or any other objects. When your child thoroughly understands this concept, show how to draw lines to represent an addition problem. Finally, teach how to write numbers to represent the two groups and find the answer to the problem.

Use similar activities to form the conceptual basis for subtraction. With manipulatives or pictures, show your child how one subset of a group may be removed, leaving behind a second subset. For example, show your child 5 marbles. Pull 2 away from the group and ask your child to count the marbles that are left. Teach how to draw pictures to represent the problem. Once your child understands the concepts, show how to write the problem using numbers, and then teach additional strategies that will shorten the time a calculation requires.

STRATEGY   Some children learn faster if simple facts are paired with pictures. When Pat was practicing her addition facts, her mother used common objects to help her remember all of her doubles facts. She showed her that 2 + 2 was a car with four wheels, 3 + 3 was two clovers, 4 + 4 was an octopus with four legs on each side, 5 + 5 was both hands; 6 + 6 was an egg carton, 7 + 7 was two weeks, 8 + 8 was two boxes of crayons, and 9 + 9 was like two baseball teams.[2]

Counting Up and Counting Down

When Zachary was first learning to add, he would begin counting from 1, regardless of what numbers were presented. For example, when asked to add 4 + 2, he would quickly put up four fingers and then two fingers, and then would count all ten fingers. Although this approach to counting is a normal stage of math development, Zachary needed to understand that he could start by just saying the name of the larger number and then count on from there. In other words, to add 6 + 3, Zachary can say: "Six" and then count on three more: "Seven, eight, nine." Knowing that this is the basis of useful strategies for adding and subtraction, Zachary's parents gave him lots of practice, first starting out with full rolls of candies and then adding on individual pieces.

Children who have trouble recalling basic math facts can use "count up" and "count down" strategies to lessen their difficulties.[2] As Zachary learned, to count up you say the name of the larger number and then count up to the value of the smaller number. When your child is learning this strategy, allow using the fingers while counting up to the value of the number. Show a math fact like 5 + 2, and have your child say: "Five," and then, lifting two fingers one at a time, ". . . Six, seven."

Similarly, basic subtraction facts can be recognized quickly by using a counting down strategy. Children who have trouble counting backward will need to practice this first. Sean was one such child. He often became confused when counting backward; after one or two numbers, he would skip a number or start counting forward. Before teaching a counting down strategy to help Sean learn to subtract, Sean's mother helped him with activities that involved counting backward. For example, they set up a rocket ship and pretended they were doing the countdown for the launch: "10, 9, 8, 7 . . . ." Another day, his mother set up 10 Legos® and asked her son to point to each one as he counted backward. She also had him work with a number line, which allowed him to actually see the numbers as he counted backward. Once he had mastered counting backward, he was able to use a counting down strategy for subtraction.

Multiplication and Division

Multiplication and division are related mathematical processes that involve groups equal in number. To multiply, we put together equal-sized groups and then determine how many in all. To divide, we break a number apart into equal-sized groups and then tell the total number of groups.

Use simple stories to teach your child the basic concepts behind these operations. For example, her mother showed Carol how she could solve basic multiplication and division problems with manipulatives. She began by asking Carol to solve problems like these:

- You have 3 packs of gum, and each pack has 5 sticks. How many sticks of gum do you have in all?

- Jill had 12 pencils that she wanted to share with her friends, Sally and Jane. She divided her pencils into three equal groups. How many pencils did she give to each of her friends?

After Carol solved the problems with pencils and sticks of gum, her mother showed her how she could perform these operations with pictures or using a number sentence. When Carol was sure she understood the processes, she was able to start to memorize the facts.

As with addition and subtraction, understanding *must* precede memorization. Dana, a third-grade student, was trying to memorize multiplication facts, but she did not understand what they meant. When asked to make a picture of the problem 4 × 3, she drew four dots and then three dots. Although she knew that the correct answer to the problem was 12, Dana did not understand that the problem 4 × 3 means four groups of three, or three groups of four. Make sure that, before starting to memorize the multiplication tables, your child understands that multiplication means repeated additions of an equal group.

Memorizing Math Facts

Memorizing math facts is still viewed as essential in most school programs. However, because of the time involved in arriving at solutions, memorizing simple addition and subtraction facts is not as important as committing multiplication facts to memory. Children who have not learned multiplication facts by heart often struggle with math-related activities throughout school, at least partly because, without knowing multiplication facts, they find it is hard to solve problems involving division.

By third grade, most schools begin to teach children math facts; the idea is to give children enough practice so that they can recall them automatically. By fourth grade, many children are able to retrieve these facts from memory. As with the skill of reading rapidly, *automaticity* is the term used for the speed at which a child can recall math facts. A child is said to have automaticity when answers can be produced rapidly, with little effort. When asked the answer to 7 × 6, can your child produce the correct answer in less than two seconds? Or does your child pause and perform mental additions before responding? Ideally, children should be able to retrieve the solutions to facts quickly, effortlessly, and without error.

If your child has trouble memorizing, there are several methods for minimizing the amount of memorization he or she will need to do to learn math facts. When you are sure that your child understands the process of multiplication, teach the following strategies but not all at one time.

- 0 × any number is zero.
- 1 × any number is the number.
- 2 × any number is double the number.
- 5 × any number involves counting by 5's, as when telling time from a standard clock. An even number times 5 is written as half that number with a 0 added. For example, 4 × 5 = 20; 6 × 5 = 30.
- 9 × any number is magic and can be solved with a simple trick: Take 1 away from the multiplier and then add a number to form

9. For example, to calculate 9×7, you would say: $7 - 1 = 6$, and $6 + 3 = 9$, so the answer is 63. Or to multiply 9×8, you would say: $8 - 1 = 7$, and $7 + 2 = 9$, so the answer is 72.

Betty Sheffield in the Ohio Valley Orton Dyslexia Society newsletter described this memory trick for the even 6s. $2 \times 6 = 12$ – half of the 2 followed by the 2 itself; $4 \times 6 = 24$ – half of the 4 followed by the 4 itself; $6 \times 6 = 36$ – half of the 6 followed by the 6 itself; $8 \times 6 = 48$ – half of the 8 followed by the 8 itself

When your child has mastered the facts above, only 12 basic multiplication facts are left to memorize. Use the following chart, and cross out the facts as each is mastered:

3×3	4×4		7×7	8×8
3×4		6×7	7×8	
3×6	4×7			
3×7	4×8			
3×8				

For memorization of the additional facts, teach how to recognize patterns that will reduce the demands on memory. For example, if your child knows 8×8, but is stuck on 8×9, present it as $8 \times 8 + 8$, and allow counting up with fingers. Help your child learn how to think of easy or already known math facts to help recall other facts—for instance, the answer to 3×4 is also the answer to 4×3.

Using Language Cues If your child has strengths in the thinking block of language, these remaining 15 facts may be learned most easily with the use of music or rhyme. Make up a silly song or a rhyme for each fact. Draw a picture together to illustrate the rhyme. Here's an example that Lonnie and her mother composed: "3×3 was feeling fine, until it turned into number 9. When 3×4 came out the door, it turned into 12 and sat on the floor. . . . 3×6 said: What have I seen and then turned quickly into 18. Then 3×7 said: Look what's been done and turned into number 21." Your child may find it easier to use songs or rhymes with only one fact at a time, such as "7×8 got in a fix and then turned into 56." Inexpensive commercial rhyme cards are also available.[3] An example from these cards is: "8×7 were nifty chicks until they became 56."

Times Table Triangle Another simple, inexpensive tool to help your child memorize multiplication facts is called the Times Table Triangle™. This plastic coated, colored triangle was developed by a teacher, Brenda Batten, who was home schooling her son. When she tried to teach him the times tables, he became discouraged and said there were just too many facts to learn. To ease his frustration, she invented the triangle. All of the times facts are on one side with a small hole above each fact. The answers are written on the other side. To identify the answer to a fact, the child places a pencil through the hole and then flips the triangle to find the correct solution on the other side. Brenda found that her son smiled when using this aid and gradually learned his multiplication facts.[4]

Multisensory Cues Children with weaknesses in the processing blocks often benefit from a multisensory approach to learning math facts. As is the case when learning reading and spelling, your child may need to use a combination of the visual, auditory, and motor skills of the processing blocks to help with memorizing. Depending on your child's learning style, different approaches will be more effective. For instance, Rebecca found it easiest to learn math facts if she made a point of saying the facts aloud while looking at them. Taylor, on the other hand, needed to look at the fact, say it, trace it, and then write it.

For many children, saying the facts aloud and then trying to write them from memory will enhance learning. As with teaching spelling, make sure your child tries to write the answer from memory rather than simply copying. Use this simple procedure:

1. Have your child look at a fact with the answer.
2. Remove the fact.
3. Ask your child to write the fact and the answer.
4. Hold up the fact and have your child check it.

Touch Points Cues If your child makes frequent errors in computation but understands the basic operations, try placing dot patterns on numbers—for example, four dots on the number 4—to help improve accuracy in addition and subtraction. As that accuracy grows, your child can just tap a pencil on each number as she counts, to solve simple addition and subtraction facts.

One multisensory approach for teaching four basic computational skills is called Touch Math™.[5] Using a touch points approach, you may teach your child to touch the dots on each of the numbers when counting. The process includes several steps. For example, to add a series of numbers, your child would touch the dots on the numbers and count forward. To subtract, your child would say the name of the larger number and then touch the dots while counting backward. The sequence for touching the dots in the Touch Math program is shown in the figure on page 246.

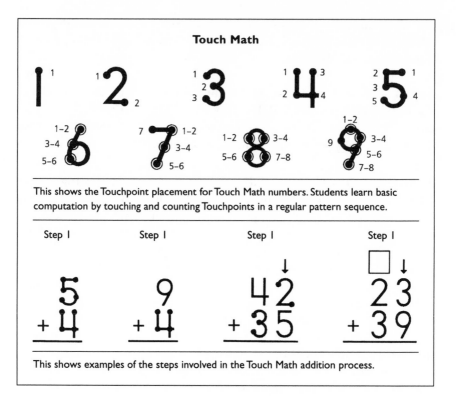

This shows the Touchpoint placement for Touch Math numbers. Students learn basic computation by touching and counting Touchpoints in a regular pattern sequence.

This shows examples of the steps involved in the Touch Math addition process.

Many first- and second-grade teachers use this type of method, in conjunction with existing math programs, to help students improve their accuracy in addition and subtraction and to aid with memorization of basic facts. Children are encouraged to eliminate touching the points as they become more proficient.

Flashcards Another way to help your child master math facts is to practice with flashcards. First, identify the facts that your child does not know. Then practice three unfamiliar facts at a time. Present the card and ask your child to respond. If the response takes longer than two seconds, say the answer and move on to the next card. After your child has mastered these three facts, place them in a pile for review the following day. An alternative is to place three possible answers on the table and have your child point to the correct one. Once this can be done successfully, present the cards one at a time. If your child has weaknesses in memory, keep in mind that you will need to reduce the number of facts expected to be learned at any one time, and that you will have to repeat and practice the facts more often.

Remember, the difference between children with weaknesses in memory and normal learners is not the process by which they learn, but the number of trials necessary for mastery. Patience, persistence, and frequent praise are essential in helping motivate your child to keep at it, even though mastery seems like a slow and laborious process. Many computer software programs are available to help your child practice and master basic math facts. Some provide game formats that are quite engaging for some children. You may find that your child is more willing to practice with a computer than with you; after all, a computer-teacher has unlimited patience. If your child needs a lot of practice, it's a good idea to plan on incentives to keep interest high. (See Chapters 5 and 6 for ideas.)

Math facts are tools to help your child learn to reason and solve problems. However, if your child has severe weaknesses in the processing blocks, memorization of math facts can seem impossible. When some children return to school after summer vacation, they have genuinely forgotten all the facts that they learned. Others persist in using a counting strategy to solve problems involving multiplication facts, though this is an imperfect and time-consuming solution.

Despite the application of persistence and creativity, some children never manage to learn math facts automatically. For instance, in third and fourth grade, Roxanne spent hours and hours with her parents, trying to learn the multiplication tables. Her parents tried flashcards and computer games—and even a tutor—but she continued to struggle. Finally, recognizing her hard work in the face of great difficulties, her parents and teachers decided that Roxanne would be allowed to use a calculator for all her math assignments. They ultimately had to recognize that focusing on Roxanne's memorizing the math facts was stopping her from making progress in the math program and would continue to hold her back unnecessarily.

Calculations and Visual and Motor Problems

In addition to problems with memorization, some children with weaknesses in the visual and motor processing blocks have trouble learning to form numbers or to align them properly for calculations. When Carlos solved math problems, his columns would often wind down the page like a snake. The solution to this problem was simple: Carlos needed to use

THE RIGHT PAPER FOR THE JOB

Graph paper is really the paper of math. The boxes formed by the grids help keep the numbers lined up correctly. The grids on graph paper comes in many different sizes. Try to select paper with grids that yield boxes that are about the same size as your child's numbers. Encourage using this type of paper in the classroom as well.

graph paper for his math assignments, rather than the lined paper he used for his writing.

Children with weaknesses in the visual processing block may also have difficulty remembering the direction that certain numbers face and/or the correct order for writing the digits. A child may know the right answers to problems, but write the digits in the wrong order. For instance, when asked to solve 7 + 6, a child may say the answer is 13 but then write 31. Mistakes of this sort usually arise from confusion about left-to-right progression. A teacher might recognize the difference between incorrect answers and transposed answers when marking papers, and might then introduce corrective exercises.

Tracing numbers and saying visual clues aloud can help children with this kind of confusion. When writing a 6, these children might say: "Go down and then make a circle around." Or, parents can use color as a prompt for which way the pencil should go; a green dot would show where to start the number, and a red dot would show where to stop. As these children write numbers in the teens, they can remind themselves that these numbers are different from others: the number heard first is written last. The number 14, although pronounced "four-teen," is written with a 1 and then a 4, rather than the reverse. In addition, cueing the child to think about place value will reduce the confusion and aid in learning to write the answers in the correct order.

STRATEGY   Children with weaknesses in the visual processing block also may have difficulty paying attention to computational signs. They do not look at the signs prior to performing an operation; consequently, they often add instead of subtract. If your child has this problem, you might try using color-coding to denote the sign: Green for addition signs and red for subtraction signs. Or, have the child circle the problem's sign as the first step in performing a calculation.

Place Value Concepts

After children understand the basic math operations, they need to learn the concept of place value; that is, they must understand that the value of a digit changes, depending on where it is in a number. For example, the number 589 means that there are 5 hundreds, 8 tens, and 9 ones; 895 means that there are 8 hundreds, 9 tens, and 5 ones. At a basic level, your child should be able to explain to you that the number 12 represents one 10 and two 1's.

When Linda was in fourth grade, her teacher dictated numbers for the class to write. Three of the numbers she read were: 5,489, 892, and 7,023. When she heard the numbers, Linda wrote on her paper:

5000,400,89

800,92

7000,23

Her paper came back with the problems marked as incorrect. In analyzing Linda's responses, her father could readily see that though she had listened carefully to the numbers, she was confused about place value concepts. Linda did not understand that, in a four-digit number, the fourth column on the left represents 1000's; the third column, 100's; the second column, 10's; and the first column, 1's. Unfortunately, because the teacher had so many papers to grade, she failed to notice the reason Linda's answers were incorrect.

If your child does not understand place value concepts, you need to return to the concrete stage of instruction. Use manipulatives—blocks, Legos™, or popsicle sticks—to teach the concept of place value. Show your child how 10 units or 10 separate Legos™ can be exchanged for 1 unit of 10, or 10 joined Legos™. For example, to solve 15 − 8, place one 10-unit group and 5 blocks before your child. Below that unit, place 8 blocks. Show that because 5 blocks are a smaller unit than 8, the 10-unit group must be separated into 10 blocks and added to the 5 blocks. Only then are you able to subtract 8 blocks. Or, try using an abacus to help your child visualize the amounts. Once your child understands this process, you can show how to do the computation with pencil and paper.

Successful regrouping, commonly called borrowing and carrying, is based on firmly established concepts of place value. When first learning to subtract, a common error children make is to just proceed the easiest way, regardless of the sign. When Misty was asked to solve:

$$\begin{array}{r} 63 \\ -\ 25 \\ \hline \end{array}$$

she wrote the answer as 42. She noted that 5 cannot be taken away from 3, and decided it would be easier to just go in the other direction.

If your child makes this same mistake, review adding and subtracting with manipulatives. Show how to exchange 10 cubes for one 10-cube unit, and break one 10-cube unit into 10 separate cubes. Children who gain a firm understanding of these concepts will comprehend that they cannot switch directions to make the problem easier.

Children with weaknesses in memory also make errors in regrouping or borrowing. Even when they understand place value concepts, they often forget to cross out and reduce a number when they borrow, or to record the digit when they carry.

When Mike was adding 29 + 86, he added 9 + 6 to get 15, and wrote down the 5. But as he moved over to the numbers in the next column, he forgot to carry the 10 and wrote the final answer as 105. After looking at his homework, Mike's father could see where he was making errors. He showed his son that when the answer was 15, he should split the number by writing the 1 in the tens column and recording the 5 in the ones column. In this way he would not forget to carry.

Estimation

Once children can perform elementary operations with numbers, they need to know how to estimate answers. This skill is actually an important part of the thinking block of strategies, because it involves monitoring the reasonableness of solutions. Most day-to-day math applications involve estimation of some kind. As you shop at the grocery store, you may check whether you have enough money for your purchases; when you look at your checkbook or monthly bank statements, you calculate whether the balance makes sense.

To compute successfully, your child needs to become good at estimating and then at checking answers to problems. If, in practicing the multiplication tables, your son wrote that 8 × 4 was 86 and that 4 × 7 was

98, he will be ahead of the game if he has learned to consider whether those answers make sense. When he realizes that these solutions are impossible, he will go back and rework the problems.

To be able to estimate, your son needs to know how to "round" a number—to recognize that 42 is closer to 40 than to 50, and that he can do the calculation with 40 to get a rough idea of the answer. Children are often taught that if the last digit in a number is 5 or higher, they should round up; otherwise, they round down. To help your son with the concept of rounding, show him a number line and ask him to locate where a number would fall on the line. For example, after presenting a line from 60 to 70, ask him to find where the number 67 would fall. Because it falls nearer to the 70 than to 60, 67 would be rounded up to 70.

STRATEGY To get your son in the habit of estimating answers when solving math problems, have him estimate the answer and tell it to you, or write it by the side of a problem, before he computes the answer. After he has learned to estimate, teach him to ask: "Does this answer make sense?" after he solves a problem. Using estimation will help him learn to use the thinking block of strategies to monitor his performance.

Assessing and Correcting Errors

Most of the mistakes children make on math problems are not random; rather, they are repetitive and of one or another type: not paying attention to the sign, changing the operation in the middle of the problem, or forgetting to regroup (borrow or carry). Usually, children are confused about some part of the process. Or, they may not securely understand some basic concept, which trips them up time and again.

One of the most effective ways to help your children master mathematics is to analyze or review any mistakes made on school papers or homework assignments. Try to determine why your child missed certain problems. If a child makes a mistake but does not get feedback about the error, he or she will continue to make the same type of errors until the problem is identified and intervention occurs.

Error Analysis

To gain an understanding of your child's computational difficulties, perform an error analysis. Look at your child's errors, and attempt to determine whether they have a specific pattern. The last step is to devise a way to resolve your child's problem. Study the problems presented below. Can you identify what the child did in each problem that resulted in an error? Check your analysis against the answer key.

Once you have become a computational detective, you are well on the way to helping your child resolve confusions. If your child has many errors, refer to Chapter Five for advice on communicating with his or her teacher.

Problems for Error Analysis

1. 58 × 6 64	2. 46 +69 25	3. ⁵59 +14 91	4. ⁴56 × 8 98	5. 84 −36 52
6. 73 −46 37	7. 37 +82 110	8. ¹42 × 4 178	9. 69 +48 1017	10. 401 +263 604

Answer key to the problems:

1. The child did not pay attention to the sign and added instead of multiplying.

2. The child added all of the digits in the problem together.

3. The child put down the tens unit and carried the ones unit, instead of vice versa.

4. The child multiplied and then added within the same problem.

5. The child did not borrow and subtracted the 4 from the 6.

6. The child borrowed from the tens unit but did not change the number.

7. The child added the digits from left to right and then carried the number to the next column on the right.

8. The child carried and added in a number unnecessarily.

9. The child did not regroup.

10. The child is confused about the properties of zero.

Talking a Problem Through

When you cannot determine why your child made an error, talk through the solution step by step together. Encourage your child to state how the problem was understood, and then to say aloud everything done to solve the problem. If you listen carefully to the explanation, and ask questions as needed, you will discover the source of the error.

For instance, her mother noticed that when Shelley did addition or subtraction problems where a zero was present, she always came up with the wrong answer. Thus, she answered that $7 + 0 = 0$. When asked to explain her thinking, Shelly reported: "Zero means that there is nothing there, so you can't have anything when there is a zero." Using manipulatives, Shelly's mother then showed her that, when adding or subtracting 0, the number of objects in the set remains the same.

Using "Show and Tell" to Help Your Child Learn Math

When your child is struggling with new concepts and skills, you can help by using modeling and demonstrations—an instructional version of "Show and Tell." Have your child listen to you talk yourself through a problem and solve it. Then talk your child through performance of the task. Finally, have your child talk through and perform the task. Through this method, your child will learn how to approach the solution of problems.

Debra was having trouble understanding how to do division problems. By verbalizing each step, her mother showed her how to solve:

$$3\overline{)250}$$

1. Ask whether 3 goes into 2. Since the answer is "No," ask whether 3 goes into 25. Since the answer is "Yes," count how many times 3 goes into 25.

2. Record 8 on the top of the line, above the 5.

3. Multiply 8×3 and record 24 below 25.

4. Subtract.

5. Check to make sure that 3 cannot go into the remainder (1).

6. Bring down the 0.

7. Ask whether 3 goes into 10. Since the answer is "Yes," count how many times 3 goes into 10.

8. Record 3 on the top of the line.

9. Multiply 3×3 and record 9 below 10.

10. Subtract.

11. Check to make sure that 3 cannot go into the remainder.

12. 3 can't go into 1, so the answer is 83, with a remainder of 1.

After they had talked through several different examples, Debra's mother summarized the steps of division on an index card.

1. Ask how many.

2. Write the number.

3. Multiply and write.

4. Subtract.

5. Check.

6. Bring down.

Debra then used this card to talk herself through the steps of the division problems that she was attempting to solve.

To increase understanding, children need to see, hear, perform, and talk about what they are learning. In some families, parents solidify concepts by asking an older child to test newly mastered skills by trying to explain them to a younger sibling.

Reinforcement

Once children know how to perform a task and can come up with the correct solutions, providing positive reinforcements will increase their motivation to practice and to improve in accuracy and speed. Motivate younger children by awarding a small candy, a raisin, or a peanut for every correct answer when they are learning math facts; older children might be motivated by seeing their progress represented by stars pasted on a chart or color bands in a graph. Reinforcement is particularly important when children have to struggle hard to learn facts and operations. For these children, motivational rewards should be given often. (See Chapter Five for more on this.)

Advanced Computation: Fractions, Percentages, and Decimals

Some children continue to have difficulties with calculations even after they master the basic math facts and operations. They have trouble with division, multiplying numbers, and operations that involve fractions, percentages, and decimals. Unless they learn how to perform these operations, they will continue to struggle throughout their school years.

As when teaching the basics, when you help your child with more advanced computations, begin with concrete objects, progress to semiconcrete representations, and then introduce numbers.

STRATEGY When teaching your child about the concepts of fractions try beginning the lesson with an edible object. Jason was perplexed by fractions until his mother brought in a pepperoni pizza to help him understand. First, she showed him how the pizza could be cut in half, then into quarters, and then into eighths. She then showed him how to draw a circle to represent a pizza, and to add lines to represent the slices. When Jason understood these concepts, she explained the fraction ½ this way: The bottom number tells how many portions the pizza has been cut into, and the top number tells how many of those portions Jason was given. She showed Jason how being given ¼ of a pizza is less than being given ½.

STRATEGY When trying to help your child understand the decimal system, the easiest way to begin is with American money. Explain that one U.S. dollar bill represents the whole unit and is written as 1.00. With the exception of silver dollars and Susan B. Anthony dollars, all *coins* represent less than 1.00 and so are written as fractions or decimals. A quarter is written as .25 and has the same meaning as ¼. A half-dollar is written as .50 and has the same meaning as ½. A dime is written as .10 and has the same meaning as ¹⁄₁₀. If you follow this sequence of instruction when explaining new information, your child will gain increased understanding of decimals and fractions.

Many children have difficulty acquiring the concept that fractions, percentages, and decimals can be used interchangeably when stating a quantity; in other words, ¼, 25%, and .25 all mean the same thing: one quarter of a whole. Jessica, a fifth-grade student, understood the meaning of ¼ but she did not understand the use of a decimal point. She needed to review the concept of place value and remember that numbers to the right of the decimal referred to: tenths, hundredths, thousandths, and so on. After several demonstrations, she began to see that .50 and ½ have the same meaning.

Calculators

Today, most schools encourage students to use calculators and computers for complex computations. In fact, many of the standardized tests that are administered at the secondary level encourage or even require the use of calculators. When Ben, a fourth-grade child, was asked to explain how he had solved a certain problem, he wrote: "I youst a calqulayter." His teacher wrote back: "Good use of a calculator, Ben."

The popularity and increased acceptance of teaching the use of calculators arose from two factors: the increasing emphasis on problem solving rather than paper-and-pencil calculation, and the fact that calculators reduce the drudgery of math. As teachers began to make math more of a "real world" subject, they had to recognize that, in the real world, most people would rather spend five minutes searching the house for a calculator than adding up a column of numbers " by hand." Most people are capable of doing the paper-and-pencil computation, but they find it a tedious chore.

Every child should learn how to use a calculator, but this skill is critical for children with severe memory weaknesses. These children may need to learn to use a calculator as an alternative to pencil-and-paper computation so that their progress in math is not derailed.

Before using a calculator, your child needs to be able to come up with accurate estimates, and to judge whether the calculator's answers are

---

SUBTLE CHEATING?

Some teachers resist using calculators in the classroom because they feel students "do not have to work to get the answers." They may even believe that using calculators is a subtle form of cheating. However, most teachers will bend on this point, particularly for students whose learning problems are severe enough to require Individual Educational Plans (IEPs) or Section 504 accommodations that specifically call for their use.

reasonable. Ideally, your child will understand how to perform a backup check, using pencil and paper, if a calculator answer seems suspect.

STRATEGY   Your child should learn how to use a calculator to check answers to problems via a reverse operation. For example, when dividing $8\overline{)56}$, your child can check the answer by multiplying the divisor (8) by the dividend (7). Or, when calculating $49 - 26$, adding the answer of 23 to 26 will verify the result.

Many different types of calculators exist, varying in size, shape, and number of functions. You may find that your child benefits most from a talking calculator: the numbers and answers to problems are heard as well as seen. Although a few children will need to use a calculator throughout their school years, most can become proficient in basic math skills and will require calculators only to perform more complex operations.

One fact is clear: Children's later achievement will be compromised if they fail to acquire sufficient skill in performing basic operations, with or without a calculator. In other words, limited fluency with the recall of basic facts will hinder the development of higher-level math skills. Increasing children's problem-solving skills is of the utmost importance, but they must also master basic math skills. Failure to master basic skills usually leads to paralyzing math anxiety, which can cause otherwise good students to fail.

Once children understand and become good at computational skills, they will be able to direct their attention to the skills of the thinking blocks required for math problem solving.

Math Problem Solving

Boosting Your Child's Skills at Using the Basics of Mathematics to Solve Problems

If you checked that your child has weaknesses in the thinking blocks, especially thinking with images, the odds are that your child will struggle with math problem solving—the most important aspect of math. Like reading comprehension and writing, success in solving math problems relies on the skills of the thinking blocks. The purpose of this chapter is to explain why children have difficulties in math problem solving and to offer interventions that will allow for their correction.

The Building Blocks and Math Problem Solving

Weaknesses in the thinking blocks of language, images, or strategies account for most of children's struggles to solve problems in math. Language weaknesses make it difficult for them to understand verbal and written instructions and the information in a textbook. Weaknesses with images make it hard for them to picture problems, to think in spatial terms, or to interpret charts and graphs. Weaknesses in strategic thinking limit their resourcefulness when faced with new problems to solve or when monitoring their performance.

As children progress through school, the math concepts they are taught increase in difficulty. Thus, if your child has strengths in the processing blocks but weaknesses in the thinking blocks, the difficulties with mathematics may take you by surprise. Math facts may have been learned in the early years of school, but later attempts to apply them to story problems and real-life situations may be only causing confusion.

Brenda is a fifth-grader who has trouble understanding language and thinking with images. When she reads math story problems, she does not know where to begin. When the teacher showed her a picture of four trees recently and asked her how many one-half of them would be, Brenda replied: "You mean if you cut them this way?" Then she made the motions of drawing a horizontal line through the middle of the four trees. Brenda needs help in both interpreting language and learning to use strategies.

Some children have trouble solving math problems because of factors unrelated to their reasoning skills. If they have strengths in the thinking blocks but weaknesses in the processing blocks, they may understand mathematical concepts but still do poorly because they have trouble reading the directions in the math textbook or writing out answers to problems. If your child has these kinds of difficulties, consult Chapters 7 and 8 for help.

Today's Math Curriculum

As we noted in Chapter 10, the focus of the math curriculum in the past decade has shifted away from paper-and-pencil computations and toward activities involving logical thinking and problem solving. As a result, the skills and abilities of the thinking blocks have become even more critical for math performance.

The job of the math teacher today is to stimulate students to come to their own understanding of math through observations and experiences. A good teacher provides opportunities to identify, solve, and evaluate problems. (Though this approach works for many students, some children cannot construct their "own" important mathematical concepts without very specific instruction, which is where the building block assessment and interventions come in.)

In the past, many people without good math problem-solving skills could "get by." Even today, a few people—including some parents and teachers—may not view mathematics as an essential life skill, believing that only a few people will really need to be proficient in math. This perspective is incorrect.

In today's world, every child needs to become competent in math. Recent findings from the Third International Mathematics and Science Study (TIMSS) showed that U.S. eighth-graders scored below average in math, in comparison with students in 40 other nations. As technology becomes an ever larger part of our world, most jobs will require some form of math problem-solving ability.

In a Report to the Nation on the Future of Mathematics Education, the National Research Council (NRC) stressed the urgent national need to revitalize math education. From major studies, the NRC identified weaknesses in our present system and then made recommendations for rebuilding and restructuring mathematics education in the United States. The report stated: "It is mistakenly thought, even by otherwise well-informed adults, that the mathematics they learned in school is adequate for their children."[1] The message is clear: The skills that we learned as children are not sufficient to take our children into the twenty-first century, and changes in the math curriculum have begun to address this challenge.

Practically speaking, this means that although children must learn to add, subtract, multiply, and divide, they will spend less time on worksheets and more time learning to use calculators to solve problems. Using a calculator will allow them to concentrate on how a problem should be solved (using the skills of the thinking blocks), rather than on the actual solution (using the secretarial skills of the processing blocks). Another major change is that there is greater emphasis on using mathematics to solve everyday problems. Increased attention is being directed to the problem solving skills of the thinking blocks, and less attention is being devoted to mastery of basic skills. Substantial research supports approaches that build on a foundation of work with strategies and concepts.[2] The types of approaches will lead to greater comprehension, more effective learning, and the development of math skills useful throughout life. Because of these changes, the goal today is to help children build a strong foundation in mathematical concepts and relationships, many of which can be taught in the home in real-world contexts.

Teaching Basic Real-World Math Concepts

Some children have trouble learning the basic math concepts used in everyday life, such as telling time, using money, or measuring. Fortunately, these essential life skills can be taught by parents and reinforced in the home. A few strategies for working with these skills are described in the next three sections.

Telling Time

Some children, particularly those with weaknesses in the thinking block of images, have trouble learning to tell time on a standard clock. They may be able to read the time on a digital clock or watch, but they do not transfer this skill to a standard clock.

To learn to tell time on a clock face, your child must be able to count by ones and fives to 60, to identify the numbers from 1 to 12, and to differentiate the hour hand from the minute hand. Teaching how to tell time can be accomplished most easily using a paper-and-pencil clock or a model clock with movable hands.

1. To begin the paper-and-pencil instruction, draw a large clock face. Write the numbers from 1 to 12 in black, in their proper places. Around the outer edge of the clock face, use red to write the numbers for minutes. Move by 5's from 00 (placed above the 12) to 55 (placed above the 11). On narrow strips of paper, draw the long minute hand and the shorter hour hand. Anchor them with a toothpick at the center of the clock.

2. Explain the different speeds of the clock hands. Then practice reading and writing various times, using the principle of counting by 5's. Continue to use black and red to differentiate the hours and minutes, move the clock hands randomly, and record each new time on paper. Separate the hour and the minutes with a colon so that the written time resembles a digital clock—for example, 2:20, 3:30, 5:45.

3. Have your child practice setting the hands on the paper clock to match various times on a digital clock.

As you help your child learn to tell time, start with the simple and progress to the more complex. First teach how to tell time to the hour; next, to the half hour; and then, to the quarter hour. After your child has mastered five-minute intervals, teach how to count by ones to read the minute hand—for example, 2:15, 2:16, 2:17.

In addition, teach the different ways that people express times before and after particular hours. For example, explain that 8:30 can be referred to as "eight-thirty," "half-past eight," or "thirty minutes past the hour." Review specific vocabulary phrases that are often associated with telling time, such as "almost eleven," "ten-past nine," "a quarter after ten," "a little after eight," "noon," and "midnight."

Understanding and Dealing with Money

Another important life skill is understanding money concepts. Children need to be able to count money and make change correctly. They also must be able to estimate approximately how much various items cost, and about how much change they should expect to get when they pay for something.

Many children with weaknesses in the thinking blocks don't know how to make change efficiently. For example, when 17-year-old Conrad got his first job as a cashier at a fast-food restaurant, he was expected to know how to make change. When a customer's change was 14 cents, he began counting out pennies. The customer asked whether the restaurant was out of dimes. Conrad replied, "No, but doing it this way will be faster." He clearly had not mastered the skills needed for operating a cash register and making change.

Conrad needs someone to help him understand why the change given to customers is usually the combination that requires the fewest coins. He needs practice with assembling coins for different money amounts, and combining coins with dollar bills, to determine the most appropriate ways to provide change. The best way to do this is to follow basic instruction with substantial practice.

Counting money can also be a problem for children who have weaknesses in the processing blocks. The reason for these children's difficulty is different, however. Even though they have a clear understanding of the concepts, they may have difficulties performing mental computations, visualizing problems, or remembering the sequence of steps involved. For instance, by age 11 years, Eric still could not count change accurately. He could add together 6 dimes, but got lost when he tried to add together coins of different value. Although he could identify the various coins and understood their monetary value, he had trouble changing from one value to another. He is going to need more instruction and practice.

When teaching money concepts, use real money. Encourage your child to touch and move the money as part of the lesson. As with other areas of math, start with the simple and move toward the more complex. Begin with pennies, then nickels, dimes, and quarters. Make sure that your child understands the value of each coin and how combinations of different coins can result in the same value—that is, both ten pennies and two nickels equal one dime.

STRATEGY   Teach your child the value of coins and bills by playing money games. Quote money amounts and have your child "pay" them with various combinations of currency. Or, set out an amount one way, such as 50 cents with two quarters, and ask your child to come up with another way to make 50 cents. Or, using pennies, nickels, dimes, and quarters see how many ways your child can make 42 cents.

When you teach how to count and make change, start with small sums (under $1.00). First teach how to add pennies, then nickels, dimes, and quarters. Practice counting by 5's and 10's, so that when several nickels or dimes, are received together, they can be counted rapidly.

Use the principle of counting-on when you teach your child how to add together a set of coins. Have your child say the value of the largest coin—for example, 25 cents—and then add on the remaining coins, from largest in value to smallest in value. Encourage counting aloud; for instance, in adding a quarter, two dimes, one nickel, and four pennies, your child might say: "25 cents plus 20 makes 45, plus 5 makes 50, and plus 4 makes 54 cents."

Provide your child with lots of opportunities to make and count change. For example, after grocery shopping, ask your child to check the change you received. Or, after buying an ice cream cone, have your child confirm that the correct amount of change was received. Play games such as Monopoly,™ and discuss money in relation to objects that are desired or must be purchased.

Eventually, your child will need to learn the skills involved in money management, such as comparison shopping, setting up a bank account, balancing a checkbook, determining interest on a loan, writing checks, and using a credit card. To prepare your child for these life skills, talk about your actions and decisions when you are performing these money tasks.

Measurement

Children need and will benefit from many concrete and realistic experiences in measuring objects, liquids, and solids, including reading the fractional parts of an inch ruler. If your child is age 10 years or younger, you may want to start out with a simplified ruler that shows only quarter, half, and whole inches. Begin with measurement of objects that are an exact number of inches. Gradually teach how to measure to the half inch and quarter inch. Show your child how to write measurements in fractions.

An easy way to teach estimation of size is to compare objects with the dimensions of familiar objects. For example, a regulation baseball bat is about one yard in length; a standard notebook is approximately one foot from top to bottom.

Some schools provide instruction in use of the metric system; other schools do not. Depending on where you live and travel, your child may need some understanding of the basic units of the metric system. Because this system is based on 10, the units are easy to express and understand. Difficulty arises when the metric system and the systems based on feet, gallons and miles must be mutually translated.

Measurement of liquids and solids is very easy to teach at home: have your child assist you in the kitchen. For instance, ask your son to help you measure a liquid to add to a recipe or to determine the number of eggs needed when a recipe is doubled. Take advantage of children's cookbooks that provide simplified recipes for treats and everyday family fare. Most children enjoy learning the measurements when they get to eat the results of their work!

Even in these days of digital read-out thermometers, your child should learn how to read regular thermometers—for cooking, for reading the outside temperature, or for finding out whether someone has a fever. Again, depending on the school and where you travel, metric measurement of heat and cold may be an issue. Consider making a game out of reading the national and international weather maps. On paper, plan a vacation trip with stops in countries that use the metric system, and record your "travel" distances in miles and kilometers.

Math Vocabulary

Children who have a weakness in the thinking block of language and have difficulty learning vocabulary are likely to have trouble mastering the meanings of specific math terms. Difficulties with math vocabulary can persist into secondary school. In addition to the ideas presented here, you may want to review the suggestions for learning general vocabulary, presented in Chapter 9.

Some important terms for addition are: *plus, sum, total, more than,* and *greater than.* Important terms for subtraction include: *take away, minus, less than,* and *subtracted from.* If you aren't sure which terms your child should know, consult the math textbook or look at the glossary and make a list of the terminology. Or, if the class doesn't use a textbook, ask the teacher to provide you with a list. Identify, teach, and then review the specific math vocabulary that your child will be expected to know. By the time they reach the sixth grade, children should understand the meaning of most of the common mathematical terms.

STRATEGY   Help your child learn the meaning of important math terms by developing a personal dictionary file that contains math vocabulary. On a 3 x 5 index card, have your child write a word and its definition, and then, to illustrate the meaning, draw a picture or label the elements of a problem. Have your child arrange the cards alphabetically in a recipe file or shoe box, and review the words periodically.

STRATEGY The word *mnemonics* simply refers to memory aids used to help recall information. When first introduced to fractions, Russell, a fifth-grade student, was having trouble remembering the meaning of the words *numerator* and *denominator*. When his teacher gave the class directions to multiply the numerator of a first fraction by the denominator of a second fraction, Russell often got confused. He knew one word meant the number at the top of the fraction and the other meant the number on the bottom, but he was not sure which was which. Then his mother taught him an easy way to remember: the word *denominator* begins with the letter *d*, the first letter in the word *down*. With the help of this little memory tip, Russell was able to keep the two terms straight.

Steven was having trouble remembering the meaning of the word *percentage*. His father reminded him that *cent* means 100: there are 100 years in a century and 100 cents in a dollar, and a centennial marks a 100-year celebration. His father explained to him that *percent* means "out of 100." Steven was then able to remember that 25 percent means 25 out of 100.

Word or Story Problems

Among the most important components of math instruction are word or story problems. A student must analyze the information presented, decide on a procedure for solving the problem, and then determine the answer.

Most of us do not have fond memories of these problems and would find it difficult to solve, in a timely way, the story problems presented in an introductory algebra textbook. Try it yourself: take 3 minutes and try to answer the following problems:

1. There are 15 jelly beans in a jar. Five are yellow, 6 are black, and 4 are red. If you take out one jelly bean, what is the probability it will be either yellow or black?

2. When Carleton led the troops, they marched 24 miles in 6 hours. Then he left, and the troops reduced their speed by 1 mile per hour. How long did it take them to march the last 18 miles?

3. Five times a certain number is 35 greater than 2 times the negative of the number. What is the number?

4. A baseball team started the season by hitting 1.875 times their previous season's average. If that season's average was .368, what was the beginning average this season?

Answers:

1. 11/15
2. 6 hours
3. 5
4. .690

If you were successful, you remember more than the average adult about how to solve word problems. If you were unsuccessful, you probably read the problem several times and thought: "I really don't remember how to do those." Or, you may have just felt annoyed at your first reading and skipped over the problems. Let's face it: solving story problems is not a process that many of us approach eagerly. However, solving story problems does provide practice for real life, which is why they are part of the school curriculum.

Solving story problems places great demands on the thinking blocks and requires the use of several distinct skills in a particular sequence. To solve story problems with ease, your child must be able to: understand the problem, identify relevant and irrelevant information, select the correct operation, perform the necessary calculations, and evaluate the correctness of the solution.

Let's look at these steps in some detail.

Understanding the Problem

First and foremost, children need to understand the language and the meaning of a problem well enough to be able to restate the problem in their own words and draw pictures to aid in solving it.

In years past, if children were struggling with the statement or the vocabulary of story problems, teachers sometimes taught them to attend to cue or key words to help them choose an operation—for instance, the phrase "How many in all?" always means to add. This type of strategy may have worked well enough when math was taught chapter by chapter—an addition chapter whose story problems all involved addition was followed by a subtraction chapter that had only subtraction problems. It often wasn't necessary for students to read the problems; all they had to do was find the numbers and then add or subtract. Math instructional series are not set up that way anymore. In most programs today, the emphasis is on flexibility and comprehension; children need to be able to think a problem through.

Dr. John Cawley,[3] an authority in the area of mathematics, advises that children should not be taught a "key word" or cue strategy to solve problems, because doing so encourages the children to bypass the reasoning requirements associated with good problem solving. Furthermore, in real-life problems, the language cues are not always helpful in selecting the proper operation. Consider the following problem: "Emily had 4 pencils that she wanted to give her two friends, Amy and Jessica. If she split them evenly between the two, how many pencils do they have in all?" Solving this problem requires division, not addition. To solve problems successfully, children must be able to understand what the language of the problem is really asking.

Identifying Relevant versus Irrelevant Information

In this second important step for understanding story problems—identifying the relevant and irrelevant information—language abilities are an underlying factor.

Consider the following problem: "Jane walks 5 blocks to school. Terri walks 3 blocks to school. Sally walks 4 blocks to school. How many blocks do Jane and Sally walk altogether?" To solve this problem, your child must understand that the important information is the total number of blocks walked by Jane and Sally, and that the number of blocks that Terri walked is irrelevant.

Selecting the Correct Operation

After children have identified the important information in a story problem, they must select the appropriate mathematical operation. For some children, this is a major stumbling block, as serious a problem as poor reading or computational skills. A common question from a child who has just read a story problem is: "What am I supposed to do—add, subtract, or times it?" This question indicates a lack of comprehension of the nature of the problem. As they work through story problems, children need to learn how to identify and then initiate the correct operation.

Performing the Necessary Calculations

The next step in solving story problems involves actually performing the necessary math operations. Simple story problems involve one calculation;

more advanced problems might require several sequential computations. The greater the number of steps and computations, the greater the demands placed on both the processing and thinking blocks.

Evaluating the Answer

Evaluating the reasonableness of an answer is the final step of problem solving. More than simply checking the answer is involved. Instead, children must reread the problem, rephrase the question in their own words, and then decide whether the solution makes logical sense.

Strategies for Solving Story Problems

When helping children improve their skill in solving word or story problems, a basic rule is to start out with simple problems and gradually progress to more challenging ones. The difficulty of story problems is influenced by several factors: the complexity of the language, the presence of unnecessary or extraneous information, the number of required operations, and the familiarity of the vocabulary.

Simplify and Then Expand Language

If your child is having trouble understanding the language of word problems, begin by reducing the demands on language comprehension. Start with short phrases and sentences that represent simple computations:

- One apple plus three more. . . .
- Six pencils, take away two. . . .

Gradually increase the amount of context as your child's skill improves. Next, provide complete sentences with increased detail:

- Betty had two apples and ate one. How many are left?
- Jimmy started the game with ten marbles. He lost three to Peter. How many marbles does he have left?

When your child is able to solve one-step problems, move on to two-step problems such as:

- Serena had 20 tennis balls in a basket. She accidentally hit 2 of these balls over the fence. She then opened 2 cans of new balls, each containing 3 new balls, and added them to the basket. How many tennis balls does she now have in the basket?

As another activity, present simple number equations and ask your child to invent word problems. You might say: "Make up a problem that has this for the answer: $4 - 1 = 3$." Your child might then say: "Sally gave her dog, Kelly, 4 dog biscuits. Kelly ate 1. How many are left?" Encourage your child to make problems varied and eventually more complex.

If your child has trouble creating story problems, begin with several examples. As you are developing a problem, ask your child to select the correct word: "Tony had 4 postcards. He (bought, mailed, found) 1. He now has 3 postcards." The examples will acquaint your child with the format and language of the problems and the vocabulary commonly used. Try to create story problems that reflect real life. Another technique is to write each step of a story problem on a different piece of paper. Ask your child to read the steps, and then to put the sentences into the correct order.

Your child may have trouble discovering and then eliminating the irrelevant information from word problems. This is a common problem for children with weaknesses in the thinking block of language. To help with learning to attend to the language of story problems, present problems that contain unnecessary information.

STRATEGY   To begin, develop problems that have only one type of extraneous information. Do not ask your child to solve the problems. Instead, have your child highlight the needed information and cross out what's unnecessary. Next, move on to problems with two different kinds of extraneous distractors: irrelevant numbers, and irrelevant added information about a person, place, or thing mentioned in the problem. For example:

- Marcos, Steven, and Dominique were all on the swimming team. Marcos swam the freestyle event in 5 minutes and the butterfly event in 8 minutes; Steven swam the freestyle event in 7 minutes and the breast stroke event in 14 minutes; and Dominique swam the freestyle event in 4 minutes and the butterfly event in 7 minutes. How much faster was Dominique at the butterfly than Marcos?

The information about Steven and about the freestyle races can be eliminated before solving the problem. Adequate practice with this sifting procedure will help develop an understanding of the sequence of story problems and a method for attending to important information while ignoring irrelevant facts.

Using Manipulatives to Understand Language

When children continue to have difficulty understanding language unless the instruction is supplemented with visual materials, the use of manipulatives (concrete objects) and pictures can clarify the meaning of the word problems.

Studies conducted at the University of Florida by Drs. Cecil Mercer and Susan Peterson suggest that teaching that moves sequentially from the concrete stage to the abstract stage helps children not only to learn and but also to retain and apply mathematical concepts. The concrete stage involves the manipulation of objects. The semiconcrete or representational stage involves using drawings or pictures to represent a process. The abstract stage requires the use of numbers. (For a full review of the different levels of reasoning, see Chapter 10.)

Now let's take another look at the problem presented earlier, involving Serena and the basket of tennis balls. Here is how the three stages of instruction could be used to show children how to solve the problem:

1. *Concrete (use of actual objects):* Put 20 tennis balls in a basket. Take out 2. Add 2 sets of 3. Count the balls by physically removing them one at a time from the basket.
2. *Semiconcrete (use of visual representations):* Draw the 20 balls. Cross out 2. Then draw and add in two sets of 3.
3. *Abstract (use of numbers):* Write the equation: $20 - 2 + 3 + 3 = 24$.

Depending on their developmental level and understanding of symbolic operations, different children will apply varying strategies to solve story problems. Consider the ways that three fifth-graders solved the following problem: "Mr. Jones wanted to show some friends his slides from his vacation. He was expecting 50 people, and he wanted to make sure that everyone had a chair. If he set up 5 chairs in each row, how many rows of chairs would he have?"

Joe, who was operating at the abstract level, divided 5 into 50 and got 10 rows as his answer. Jake, who was operating at the semiconcrete level, recorded his first row of 5 chairs with a 1, and then proceeded to count by 5's, making a tally each time, until he reached 50. He then counted the total number of rows to get 10. Sandra, who was operating at the concrete/semiconcrete level, drew 5 chairs in 10 rows and then counted the total number of chairs. Although all three children came up with the right answer, the differences in their problem-solving abilities are obvious. Sandra and Jake need specific instruction to help them move from the concrete and semiconcrete levels to the abstract level of problem solving.

Some children can successfully make the transition from concrete materials to abstract numbers without training with semiconcrete representations, such as drawing sticks to represent numbers. Your child's learning characteristics will dictate the steps used. If your child does not understand the meaning of problems or how to use computations to solve problems, more practice with manipulative materials is essential.

Creating Problems with Manipulatives To develop adequate mathematical foundations, your child needs to spend a lot of time performing activities in the concrete, manipulative realm. In most schools, children learn how objects or manipulatives can be used to solve story problems; a few teachers may skip this step.

Initially, give your child short problems orally, to be solved using manipulatives. Even children as young as 6 years can grasp the concepts of the four major math operations as long as concrete objects are used. Younger children often love to work out the answers to story problems when the manipulatives are edible—peanuts, raisins, small candies, or gummy bears. Ask your child to add together two sets of peanuts, then take away—and eat!—a certain number of peanuts from the set. Or ask how many peanuts would be in each of the four shares if your child was given three times as many peanuts and divided them among three friends.

Practice with both oral and written problems. Play a game in which your child separates objects into sets while you make up a story problem to solve, based on the arrangement of the objects. Then encourage inventing story problems for you to solve.

Drawing Pictures to Solve Problems After succeeding in using manipulatives to solve problems, your child is likely to benefit from engaging in activities at the semiconcrete or representational level of instruction. To help increase your child's understanding of problems read a simple story problem together and then ask your child to draw a picture that will help visualize the problem.[4]

For example, you may say: "Last week, Betty bought 5 new *Goosebumps* books. She now has read 2 of the books. How many more does she have to read?" Your child would draw a picture of the 5 books and then cross out the 2 books that Betty has read. Alongside the picture illustrating the problem, have your child identify the relevant numbers and write a number sentence: $5 - 2 = 3$. Ideally, this will help with learning how to use the thinking block of images. The goal is to be able to form a mental image of the problem that acts as a guide for thinking through the necessary steps.

If your child is younger or has trouble drawing pictures, prepare several illustrations yourself and then ask your child to choose the picture that best illustrates a problem. Gradually, as your child becomes more proficient, help with developing original drawings.

After your child can successfully make and use pictures to solve problems, substitute simple representations for the pictures. For instance, the next time Susan was given the story problem about Betty and the *Goosebumps* books, she drew 5 sticks to represent the books, crossed out 2 sticks, and then counted the remaining 3.

Problem-Solving Strategies

As the problems presented become more complex, children are likely to need additional structure. Many children benefit from having index cards on which the proper series of steps is written. Using such cards reduces the demands on memory and helps children organize their thoughts before solving.

One simple strategy is to write the steps for a math operation on a card and have your child cross out the number or place a check beside it when the step has been performed.[4] Have your child:

1. Read the problem.
2. Draw a picture of the problem.
3. Estimate the answer.
4. Write the problem.
5. Solve the problem.
6. Check the answer.

Researchers J. Fleischner, M. Nuzum, and E. Marzola[5] found that children with learning disabilities could be helped to solve story problems if they were given index cards that listed the steps to be followed. A slightly modified version of this strategy contains the following five steps:

1. **Read:**   What is the question?
2. **Reread:** What is the necessary information?

   (Do I need all the information that's supplied?)
3. **Think:**   Putting together = add.

   Finding the difference or taking apart = subtract.

   Is there more than one step in the problem?
4. **Solve:**   Write the calculation.
5. **Check:**   Recalculate.

   Label the answer.

Sally used this strategy, putting a check by each step as she solved the following: "Mia walks 8 blocks to school, Ruth walks 6 blocks to school, and Peter walks 13 blocks to school. How many more blocks does Peter walk than Mia?"

First, Sally reviewed the question: How many more blocks does Peter walk than Mia? Then she reread the problem and identified the important information: Mia walks 8 blocks and Peter walks 13. She underlined these two numbers. She realized that she did not need to know how many blocks Ruth walked. She next thought about whether she needed to add or subtract. Because she was asked how much farther Peter walked than Mia, or the difference, she knew she needed to subtract. She then wrote the calculation and the answer: $13 - 8 = 5$. She added together $8 + 5$ to check her answer. When she was sure her answer was correct, she wrote the solution: 5 blocks.

STRATEGY   Another simple procedure developed by Drs. Cecil Mercer and Susan Peterson is called the DRAW strategy:[6]

Discover the sign.

Read the problem.

Answer or draw and check.

Write the answer.

Using this strategy, children are encouraged to perform the operation mentally if possible, and to use a drawing strategy if they don't know the answer or can't perform the calculation in their heads.

Terry, a third-grade student, was asked to solve the following problem: "In Farmer John's barnyard, there were 3 cows, 2 pigs, and 4 chickens.

Amy, his young daughter, wanted to know how many legs the animals had. Help Amy determine the number of legs."

Terry thought about what operations would be required as she read the problem. She decided that she would have to add. She tried to get a mental image of the animals and to count the legs. To check herself, she then drew a simple sketch and counted the number of legs on the barnyard animals.

If your child is in upper elementary school or middle school, you may want to teach a more detailed strategy—for example, an eight-step strategy for verbal math problem solving developed by Drs. Marjorie Montague and Candace Bos.[7] The steps of this strategy are as follows:

1. **Read the problem aloud.** Discuss with your child any unknown words.

2. **Paraphrase the problem aloud.** Have your child reread the problem, identify the question being asked, and summarize the information that will be important for solving the problem.

3. **Visualize.** Have your child draw a picture of the problem or visualize the situation and tell what it is about.

4. **State the problem.** Have your child underline the most important information in the problem and then complete the sentences: "What I know is . . ." and "What I want to find out is. . . . "

5. **Hypothesize.** Have your child complete the sentence: "If . . . , then. . . . " For example, "*If* 7 people each want to buy 20 tickets, *then* I need to multiply to determine the number of tickets." For multistep problems, have your child think through the series of steps and write the operation signs in the order they will be used.

6. **Estimate.** Ask for a written estimate of the answer.

7. **Calculate.** Ask your child to calculate the answer and label it (e.g., 140 tickets).

8. **Self-check.** Have your child review the problem, check the computation, and review whether the answer makes sense.

Adjust or modify the steps of the strategy to suit your child's age and learning characteristics. It may be helpful to put the steps on an index card for easy reference.

Most strategies for solving story problems encourage children to paraphrase, draw, plan, and then evaluate their performance—to practice using the skills of the thinking blocks. Make sure that your child gets plenty of practice in applying whichever strategy is used.

STRATEGY Don't put the emphasis solely on school math work or formal problems. Use board and family games and computer technology to help your child get enjoyable practice in these skills.

Many of the strategies presented in this chapter involve reasoning and decision making. Learning to make correct decisions involves application of skills in the thinking blocks. Parents can help children observe and discover mathematical relationships by providing learning opportunities with some structure.

Jean Piaget, the renowned French developmental psychologist, stated: "It is a great mistake to suppose that a child acquires the notion of number and other mathematical concepts just from teaching. On the contrary, to a remarkable degree he develops them himself independently and spontaneously. . . . When adults try to impose mathematical concepts on a child prematurely, his learning is merely verbal; true understanding of them comes only with his mental growth."[8]

The ability to solve problems is an essential skill in life as well as in school. As Piaget noted, we should not hurry our children. Instead, we should help them come to view themselves as competent problem solvers. In this way, they will improve their abilities to reason and will develop a true understanding of mathematical concepts. Placing an emphasis on everyday problem solving in your home will help your child develop the life skills that are needed to face the demands and challenges of the classroom and the community.

Final Words
for the Journey

As the result of his school struggles, Christopher began to question whether a higher power could help him. Facing adversity, feeling helpless and hopeless in school, Christopher wrote the following plea in his daily diary:

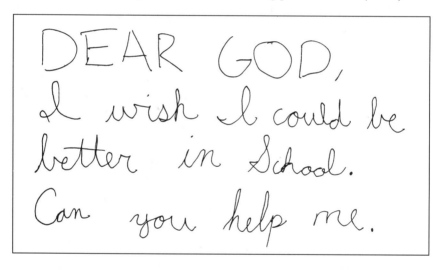

DEAR GOD,
I wish I could be
better in School.
Can you help me.

Being a parent is seldom easy. This is especially true when your child feels badly, underachieves, or misbehaves at school. Those struggles and failures become yours. As the world becomes ever more complicated and the necessity for a sound education becomes more apparent with every passing day, school problems loom large and threatening.

The Bad News and the Good News

Learning is such a large part of a child's life that school failure can affect self-esteem irrevocably, leaving devastating and even lifelong scars.

Unchecked, the downward spiral of school failure can lead to desperation, hopelessness, anxiety, and depression—for both children and parents. That's the bad news. The good news, as we have demonstrated, is that learning difficulties do *not* inevitably lead to failure in school and in life. By identifying learning weaknesses and selectively employing interventions that draw on specific learning strengths, parents can help their children break the cycle of underachievement.

However, it's important for both you and your child to understand that complete solutions and quick cures to learning problems do not exist, and finding effective strategies for dealing with even a minor learning difficulty does not guarantee a trouble-free educational future. The very nature of learning ensures that your child's educational needs will change as he or she progresses through school. What works in the early grades may not suffice later. Middle school may require more reliance on learning compensations and study strategies than on specific interventions. The type of compensations employed will differ with each individual. Some children will require books on tape. Others will need to be classroom notetakers. Still others will need specific instruction in time management, organization, and setting priorities. All children, however, need to become polite, effective advocates for themselves. They must learn how to discuss their strengths and weaknesses clearly and objectively, and how to request adjustments from others when a task is too difficult or impossible for them to perform.

Battling Discouragement

Even when your child is able to be a self-advocate and to make the most of specific interventions, strategies, and compensations, some rough spots are inevitable, and it's natural to become discouraged from time to time. When this happens, remember that your child's attitude toward school and its problems is affected by your perceptions and beliefs. If parents believe their children can succeed, the children will believe it, too. As one child told us, "My mom always tells me that I can be anything I want to be—but I might have to find a different path for getting there." You need to strike a balance between optimism and realism, and impart the attitude that although finding the right path may not be easy, it is possible.

To fight discouragement, remind yourself that, ultimately, what your child *can* do is more important than any deficiencies. That is why it's as important to focus on your child's special talents and abilities as it is to recognize and help with problems in behavior, emotions, or academics.

The same child who has great difficulty with reading or math may be an outstanding athlete, artist, or musician—and deserves credit and recognition for these talents. Positive out-of-school experiences and recognition can go far toward counteracting the effects of negative school experiences. All children want to do well and desire acceptance, approval, and recognition from others. Knowing that there are activities at which they can excel will allow them to take adversity in stride and remain willing to keep trying. Most of the children we know who have overcome or compensated for weaknesses in the building blocks of learning have parents who recognized and nurtured their special talent and interests.

Striking a balance is essential. Cheer each accomplishment and victory, both in school and out, but remember that learning problems inevitably bring inconsistencies in performance. When your child succeeds, don't assume that the problems have been solved once and for all. And when your child stumbles, guard against the temptation to attribute the lack of success to lack of effort.

Be alert for this attitude in your child's teachers as well. Confronted with your child's perplexingly uneven performance, teachers may fall back on the explanation of laziness: "He could do if he just tried," or "If she applied herself to reading as much as she does to drawing, . . ." Don't get caught in this trap. Lack of effort is a secondary symptom caused by discouragement with unacceptable performance or difficulty with a task. It is *not* the primary reason that a child does poorly in school. No child chooses to fail. Remind yourself of this often, and, if necessary, remind your child's teacher as well.

The Importance of Persistence and Love

Ultimately, the successes of children with marked school problems stem from a mixture of hard work and persistence. All children require empathy, understanding, and support as they are learning how to solve problems and how to learn. Remind your child frequently that persistence will be rewarded. Keep in mind that school problems do not necessarily become life problems. School difficulties and failure can be devastating, but each of us knows highly successful adults who performed poorly in school.

As you and your child travel the road of education, both of you will learn much. When your child hits a bump or pothole, remember:

- Common sense is a great ally. If all else fails, confront the problem from a commonsense stance and stop worrying about what others—even so-called experts—may think.

- As a parent, you know your child best. Rely on that knowledge as you attempt to help solve your child's problems. If you feel that something is wrong, chances are that your perception is accurate.

- Life is complicated. Biology is *not* destiny. Though it may set and define the boundaries of the playing field of each individual's life, unique character and life experiences can affect outcomes powerfully.

- A child with learning problems is, first and foremost, a child. In addition to help with learning problems, that child needs all the things that every child needs—love, acceptance, respect, and empathy.

Your influence on your child cannot be overestimated. Research has begun to validate what parents know in their hearts: Children's ability to cope with adversity is best predicted by the strength of their emotional ties to their parents and the quality of the parent–child relationship.

Be assured that your patience, persistence, and commitment to your child will be rewarded. Your ability to provide support as an advocate and friend will help your child become happy, confident, and well-adjusted—while struggling to learn now, and while maturing into adulthood—despite any school problems. Over many years, working with thousands of parents and children, we have seen consistent evidence that parental support, constant encouragement, and steadfast love are the main ingredients for helping a child overcome underachieving.

Good luck on your journey.

▼

Appendix A

Resources

Books

Archer, A., & Gleason, M. (1989). *Skills for School Success.* North Billerica, MA: Curriculum Associates, Inc.

Barkley, R. A. (1995). *Taking Charge of ADHD—The Complete Authoritative Guide for Parents.* New York: Guilford Press.

Bornstein, S. J. (1988). *Memory Techniques for Vocabulary Mastery.* Canoga Park, CA: Memory Improvement Programs.

Bos, C. S., & Vaughn, S. (1998). *Teaching Students with Learning and Behavior Problems* (4th ed.). Boston: Allyn & Bacon.

Brooks, R. (1991). *A Self-Esteem Teacher.* Circle Pines, MN: American Guidance Service.

Conners, C. K. (1990). *Food Additives and Hyperactive Children.* New York: Plenum Press.

Custer, S., McKean, K., Meyers, C., Murphy, D., Olesen, S., & Smoak, S. (1990). *SMARTS: Study Skills Resource Guide.* Longmont, CO: Sopris West, Inc.

Dendy, C. A. C. (1995). *Teenagers with ADD—A Parents' Guide.* Bethesda, MD: Woodbine House.

Forte, I., & Schurr, S. (1993). *The Definitive Middle School Guide.* Nashville, TN: Incentive Publications.

Fowler, M. C. (1990). *Maybe You Know My Kid: A Parent's Guide to Identifying, Understanding and Helping Your Child with Attention Deficit Disorder.* New York: Carol Publishing Group.

Fry, E. B., Kress, J. E., & Fountoukidis, D. L. (1993). *The Reading Teacher's Book of Lists* (3rd ed.). Englewood Cliffs, NJ: Prentice-Hall.

Garber, S., Garber, N., & Spizman, R. (1987). *Good Behavior—Over 1,200 Sensible Solutions to Your Child's Problems from Birth to Age 12.* New York: St. Martin's Press.

Goldstein, S. (1995). *Understanding and Managing Children's Classroom Behavior.* New York: Wiley.

Goldstein, S. (1997). *Managing Attention Disorders and Learning Disabilities in Late Adolescence and Adulthood.* New York: Wiley.

Goldstein, S., & Goldstein, M. (1992). *Why Won't My Child Pay Attention?* New York: Wiley.

Goldstein, S., & Goldstein, M. (1998). *Managing Attention Deficit Hyperactivity Disorder: A Guide for Practitioners* (2nd ed.). New York: Wiley.

Hallowell, E. (1996). *When You Worry About the Child You Love: Emotional and Learning Problems in Children.* New York: Simon & Schuster.

Ingersoll, B. (1998). *Your Hyperactive Child* (2nd ed.). Doubleday.

Ingersoll, B., & Goldstein, S. (1993). *Attention Deficit Disorder and Learning Disabilities: Realities, Myths and Controversial Treatments.* Garden City, NY: Doubleday.

Ingersoll, B., & Goldstein, S. (1995). *Lonely, Sad and Angry: A Parent's Guide to Depression in Children and Adolescents.* Garden City, NY: Doubleday.

Jenson, W. R., Rhode, G., & Reavis, H. K. (1995). *The Tough Kid Tool Box.* Longmont, CO: Sopris West, Inc.

Jones, C. B. (1991). *Sourcebook for Children with Attention Deficit Disorder: A Management Guide for Early Childhood Professionals and Parents.* Tucson, AZ: Communication Skill Builders.

Jones, C. B. (1994). *Attention Deficit Disorder: Strategies for School-Age Children.* Tucson, AZ: Communication Skill Builders.

Katz, M. (1997). *On Playing a Poor Hand Well—Insights from the Lives of Those Who Have Overcome Childhood Risks and Adversities.* Chicago: Norton.

Lerner, J. W., Lowenthal, B., & Lerner, S. R. (1995). *Attention Deficit Disorders: Assessment and Teaching.* Pacific Grove, CA: Brooks/Cole.

Levine, M. (1993). *All Kinds of Minds.* Cambridge, MA: Educators Publishing Service.

Levine, M. (1994). *Keeping A Head in School: Student's Guide about Learning Abilities and Learning Disorders.* Cambridge, MA: Educators Publishing Service.

Mather, N., & Roberts, R. (1996). *Informal Assessment and Instruction in Written Language: A Practitioner's Guide for Students with Learning Disabilities.* New York: Wiley; 1-800-225-5945. (ISBN 0471162086)

Parents Educational Resource Center (1993). *Bridges to Reading.* Belmont, CA: Charles and Helen Schwab Foundation. (A comprehensive kit of step-by-step strategies to address reading problems; 1–800-471–9545.)

Parker, H. (1988). *The ADD Hyperactivity Handbook for Parents, Teachers and Kids.* Plantation, FL: Impact Publications.

Parker, H. C., Davis, L., & Sirotowitz, S. (1996). *Study Strategies Made Easy: A Practical Plan for School Success.* Plantation, FL: Special Press.

Rhode, G., Jenson, W. R., & Reavis, H. K. (1995). *The Tough Kid Book.* Longmont, CO: Sopris West, Inc.

Rief, S. (1993). *How to Reach and Teach ADD/ADHD Children.* West Nyack, NY: Center for Applied Research in Education.

Rief, S. (1993). *Simply Phonics—Quick and Easy.* Birmingham, AL: EBSCO Curriculum Materials; 1-800-633-8623.

Rief, S., & Heimburge, J. (1996). *How to Reach and Teach All Students in the Inclusive Classroom.* West Nyack, NY: Center for Applied Research in Education.

Rodriguez, D., & Rodriguez, J. (1994). *Times Tables the Easy Way—A Picture Method of Learning the Multiplication Tables.* Sandy, UT: Key Publishers, Inc.

Schumm, J. S., & Radencich, M. (1992). *School Power—Strategies for Succeeding in School.* Minneapolis, MN: Free Spirit Publishing.

Shure, M. B. (1994). *Raising a Thinking Child.* New York: Henry Holt.

Silver, L. B. (1992). *The Misunderstood Child—Guide to Parents of Children with Learning Disabilities.* Blue Ridge Summit, PA: TAB Books.

Smith, C., & Strick, L. (1997). *Learning Disabilities A to Z: A Parent's Complete Guide to Learning Disabilities from Preschool to Adulthood.* New York: The Free Press.

Spizman, R., & Garber, M. (1995). *Helping Kids Get Organized.* Carthage, IL: Good Apple Press.

Stern, J., & Ben-Ami, U. (1996). *Many Ways to Learn—Young People's Guide to Learning Disabilities.* New York: Magination Press.

Stowe, C. (1995). *Spelling Smart! A Ready-To-Use Activities Program for Students with Spelling Difficulties.* West Nyack, NY: Center for Applied Research in Education.

Turnbull, A. P., & Turnbull, H. R. (1997). *Families, Professionals and Exceptionality: A Special Partnership* (3rd ed.). Upper Saddle River, NJ: Prentice-Hall.

Vail, P. I. (1990). *About Dyslexia: Unraveling the Myth.* Chicago: Modern Learning Press.

Walker, H. M., & Walker, J. E. (1991). *Coping with Non-Compliance in the Classroom.* Austin, TX: PRO-ED.

Waring, C. C. (1995). *Developing Independent Readers: Strategy-Oriented Reading Activities for Learners with Special Needs.* West Nyack, NY: Center for Applied Research in Education.

Videos

Barkley, R. (1992). *ADHD—What Can We Do?* New York: Guilford Press.

Barkley, R. (1992). *ADHD—What Do We Know?* New York: Guilford Press.

Brooks, R. (1997). *Look What You've Done—Learning Disabilities and Self-Esteem: Stories of Hope and Resilience.* Alexandria, VA: PBS Video.

Goldstein, S. (1994). *Why Isn't My Child Happy?* Salt Lake City, UT: Neurology, Learning and Behavior Center.

Goldstein, S., & Goldstein, M. (1989). *Why Won't My Child Pay Attention?* Salt Lake City, UT: Neurology, Learning and Behavior Center.

Goldstein, S., & Goldstein, M. (1990). *Educating Inattentive Children.* Salt Lake City, UT: Neurology, Learning and Behavior Center.

Goldstein, S., & Goldstein, M. (1991). *It's Just Attention Disorder* (video and user's guide). Salt Lake City, UT: Neurology, Learning and Behavior Center.

Lavoie, R. (1989). *How Difficult Can This Be? The F.A.T. City Workshop.* Alexandria, VA: PBS Video; 800-424-7963.

Lavoie, R. (1997). *Learning Disabilities and Discipline: When the Chips are Down.* Alexandria, VA: PBS Video.

Phelan, T. (1990). *Attention Deficit Hyperactivity Disorder* (two-part video and book). Glen Ellyn, IL: Child Management, Inc.

Rief, S. (1995). *ADHD: Inclusive Instruction and Collaborative Practices.* Portchester, NY: National Professional Resources, Inc.

Rief, S. (1997). *How to Help Your Child Succeed in School—Strategies and Guidance for Parents of Children with ADHD and/or Learning Disabilities.* San Diego: Educational Resource Specialists.

Robin, A., & Weiss, S. (1997). *Managing Oppositional Youth: Effective Practical Strategies for Managing the Behavior of Hard to Manage Kids and Teens.* Detroit: Specialty Press Videos.

Organizations

American Psychiatric Association
1400 K Street, NW
Washington, DC 20005
202-682-6000

American Psychological Association
750 First Street, NE
Washington, DC 20002-4242
202-336-5500

American Speech, Language and
    Hearing Association
10801 Rockville Pike
Rockville, MD 20852
800-638-8255

Center for Development and Learn-
    ing (CDL)
208 S. Tyler Street, Suite A
Covington, LA 70433
504-893-777

Children and Adults with Attention
    Deficit Disorder (CHADD)
499 NW 70th Avenue, #308
Plantation, FL 33317
954-587-3700

Council for Exceptional Children
    (CEC) and
Division for Learning Disabilities
    (DLD)
1920 Association Drive
Reston, VA 22091-1589
730-620-3660 or 800-328-0272

Council for Learning Disabilities
    (CLD)
PO Box 40303
Overland Park, KS 66204
913-492-8755

Educational Resources Information
    Center (ERIC)
ERIC Clearinghouse on Disabilities
    and Gifted Education
1920 Association Drive
Reston, VA 22091
800-328-0272

Franklin Learning Resources
122 Burrs Road
Mount Holly, NJ 08060
800-525-9673
(Markets a number of electronic
aides, including spell-checkers)

International Dyslexia Association
Chester Building, Suite 382
8600 LaSalle Road
Baltimore, MD 21204
800-ABCD123

Learning Disabilities Association
    (LDA)
4156 Library Road
Pittsburgh, PA 15234

412-341-1515

National Alliance for the Mentally Ill
800-950-NAMI (6264)

National Alliance for the Mentally
    Ill—Children and
    Adolescent Network
703-524-7600

National Attention Deficit Disorder
    Association (ADDA)
9930 Johnnycake Ridge, Suite 3E
Mentor, OH 44060
216-350-9595

National Center for Law and Learn-
    ing Disabilities (NCLLD)
PO Box 368
Cabin John, MD 20818
301-469-8308

National Center for Learning Disabil-
    ities (NCLD)
381 Park Avenue, Suite 1420
New York, NY 10016
212-545-7510

National Foundation for Depressive
    Illness
800-248-4344

National Information Center for
  Children and Youth with
  Disabilities (NICHCY)
PO Box 1492
Washington, DC 20013-1492
800-695-0285

National Right to Read Foundation
Box 490
The Plains, VA 20198
800-468-8911

Parents' Educational Resource Center
  (PERC)
1660 South Amphlett Boulevard,
  Suite 200
San Mateo, CA 94402-2508
415-655-2410

Recordings for the Blind and Dyslexic
20 Roszel Road
Princeton, NJ 08540
800-221-4792

Tourette's Syndrome Association
4240 Bell Boulevard
Bayside, NY 11361-2874
718-224-2999

Sample Remedial Reading Methods and Programs

Books on Tape
PO Box 7900
Newport Beach, CA 92658
800-626-3333

Bridges to Reading
PO Box 389
Belmont, CA 94002-9998
800-471-9545

Great Leaps Reading Program
Diarmuid, Inc.
PO Box 138
Micanopy, FL 32667
352-466-3878
e-mail: KUC49@aol.com

Phonic Remedial Reading Lessons
Academy Therapy
20 Commercial Boulevard
Novato, CA 94949-6191
800-422-7249

The Reading Lesson
Mountcastle Company
Two Annabel Lane, Suite 130
San Ramon, CA 94583
510-830-8655; 800-585-READ (7323)

Recorded Books
PO Box 409
Charlotte Hall, MD 20622
800-638-1304

Recording for the Blind
The Anne T. MacDonald Center
20 Roszel Road
Princeton, NJ 08540
609-452-0606

Spalding Education Foundation
2814 W. Bell Road
Suite 1405
Phoenix, AZ 85023
602-866-7801

*The Writing Road to Reading: The Spald-
  ing Method of Phonics for Teaching
  Speech, Writing, & Reading,* in
  Spalding, R. B., & Spalding, W. T.
  (1990).
William Morrow and Company
105 Madison Avenue
New York, NJ 10016

Publishers and Distributors

ADD Warehouse: 1-800-233-9273

Castilia Press: 503-343-4433

Child's Work/Child's Play: 1-800-962-1141

Communication Skill Builders: 1-800-866-4446

Guilford Press: 1-800-365-7006

Hawthorne: 1-800-542-1673

John Wiley & Sons: 1-800-225-5945

Research Press: 217-352-3273

Sopris West, Inc.: 303-651-2829

Successful Student: 1-800-677-8839

University of Minnesota Continuing Education: 612-625-3504

Western Psychological Services: 1-800-222-2670

Internet Resources

American School Directory, http://www.asd.com. Lists all K–12 schools in U.S.

CHADD, http://www.chadd.org. Information on ADD/ADHD, child and adult

Council for Exceptional Children, Division for Learning Disabilities, http://curry .edschool.virginia.edu/~sjs5d/dld (CEC = www.cec.sped.org). Geared toward educators, good links; see parent site

LD Online, http://www.ldonline.org. Covers all aspects of LD; clearinghouse

LD Resources (was Poor Richard's Publishing), http://www.ldresources.com (Note new address). Many subjects; learning disabilities software

Learning Disabilities Association of America, http://www.idanati.org. Information, resources, local, state chapters

National ADD Association, http://www.add.org. Medications, support groups, links

National Adult Literacy and Learning Disabilities Center (NALLDC), http://novel .nifl.gov/nalldtop.htm. Publications, hot topics, links re LD and adult literacy

National Center for Learning Disabilities (NCLD), http://www.ncld.org. Information on all aspects of LD; resources; links

International Dyslexia Association (was Orton Dyslexia Society), http://interdys.org. Information on dyslexia; research, legislation; state chapters

One A.D.D. Place, http://www.greatconnect.com/oneaddplace. Checklists, resources, products, conferences, more for ADD/ADHD

Parents Educational Resource Center (PERC), http://www.perc-schwabfdn.org. Resources by subject and type; services, publications; links

Parents of Gifted/Learning Disabled Children, http://www.geocities.com/athens. Information on gifted/LD children; parent, child, and educator support

Matrix Parent Network, http://marin.org/edu/matrix/index.html. Support for parents of children with disabilities

National Information Center for Children and Youth with Disabilities (NICHCY), http://www.nichcy.org. Information on all disabilities and related issues

Parents Helping Parents, http://www.php.com. Resources, links, technology

Recordings for the Blind and Dyslexic, http://www.rfbd.org. Information on materials on audiotapes and digital formats

D'Nealian Numbers and Letters

Number Descriptions

 Start at the top; slant down to the bottom.
[Top start; slant down.]

 Start a little below the top; curve up right to the top; curve down right to the middle; slant down left to the bottom; make a bar to the right.
[Start below the top; curve up, around; slant down left; and over right.]

 Start a little below the top; curve up right to the top; curve down right to the middle; curve down right again to the bottom; curve up left, and stop.
[Start below the top; curve up, around halfway; around again, up, and stop.]

 Start at the top; slant down to the middle; make a bar to the right. Start again at the top, to the right of the first start; slant down through the bar to the bottom.
[Top start; down halfway; over right. Another top start, to the right; slant down, and through.]

 Start at the top; make a bar to the left; slant down to the middle; curve down right to the bottom; curve up left, and stop.
[Top start; over left; slant down halfway; curve around, down, up, and stop.]

 Start at the top; slant down left to the middle; curve down left to the bottom; curve up right to the middle; curve left, and close.
[Top start; slant down, and curve around; up; and close.]

 Start at the top; make a bar to the right; slant down left to the bottom.
[Top start; over right; slant down left.]

 Start a little below the top; curve up left to the top and down left to the middle; curve down right to the bottom; curve up left; slant up right, through the middle, to the beginning, and touch.
[Start below the top; curve up, around, down; a snake tail; slant up right; through; and touch.]

 Start at the top; curve down left to the middle; curve up right to the beginning, and close; slant down to the bottom.
[Top start; curve down, around, close; slant down.]

 Start at the top; slant down to the bottom. Start again at the top, to the right of the first start; curve down left to the bottom; curve up right to the top, and close.
[Top start; slant down. Another top start, to the right; curve down, around, and close.]

286

Lowercase Manuscript Letter Descriptions

Start at the middle line; curve down left to the bottom line; curve up right to the beginning, and close; retrace down, and swing up.
[Middle start; around down, close up, down, and a monkey tail.]

Start at the top line; slant down to the bottom line; curve up right to the middle line; curve left, and close.
[Top start; slant down, around, up, and a tummy.]

Start a little below the middle line; curve up left to the middle line; curve down left to the bottom line; curve up right, and stop.
[Start below the middle; curve up, around, down, up, and stop.]

Start at the middle line; curve down left to the bottom line; curve up right to the beginning; touch, and keep going up to the top line; retrace down, and swing up.
[Middle start; around down, touch, up high, down, and a monkey tail.]

Start between the middle line and the bottom line; curve up right to the middle line; curve down left; touch, and keep going up to the bottom line; curve up right, and stop.
[Start between the middle and bottom; curve up, around, touch, down, up, and stop.]

Start a little below the top line; curve up left to the top line; slant down to the bottom line. Make a crossbar on the middle line.
[Start below the top; curve up, around, and slant down. Cross.]

Start at the middle line; curve down left to the bottom line; curve up right to the beginning, and close; retrace down to halfway below the bottom line, and hook left.
[Middle start; around down, close up, down under water, and a fishhook.]

Start at the top line; slant down to the bottom line; retrace up halfway; make a hill to the right, and swing up.
[Top start; slant down, up over the hill, and a monkey tail.]

Start at the middle line; slant down to the bottom line, and swing up. Make a dot above the letter.
[Middle start; slant down, and a monkey tail. Add a dot.]

Start at the middle line; slant down to halfway below the bottom line, and hook left. Make a dot above the letter.
[Middle start; slant down under water, and a fishhook. Add a dot.]

Start at the top line; slant down to the bottom line; retrace up halfway; curve right; make a small loop left, and close; slant down right to the bottom line, and swing up.
[Top start; slant down, up into a little tummy, and a monkey tail.]

Start at the top line; slant down to the bottom line, and swing up.
[Top start; slant down, and a monkey tail.]

Start at the middle line; slant down to the bottom line; retrace up, and make a hill to the right; retrace up; make another hill to the right, and swing up.
[Middle start; slant down, up over the hill, up over the hill again, and a monkey tail.]

Start at the middle line; slant down to the bottom line; retrace up; make a hill to the right, and swing up.
[Middle start; slant down, up over the hill, and a monkey tail.]

Start at the middle line; curve down left to the bottom line; curve up right to the beginning, and close.
[Middle start; around down, and close up.]

Start at the middle line; slant down to halfway below the bottom line; retrace up; curve down right to the bottom line; curve left, and close.
[Middle start; slant down under water, up, around, and a tummy.]

Start at the middle line; curve down left to the bottom line; curve up right to the beginning, and close; retrace down to halfway below the bottom line, and hook right.
[Middle start; around down, close up, down under water, and a backwards fishhook.]

Start at the middle line; slant down to the bottom line; retrace up; curve right, and stop.
[Middle start; slant down, up, and a roof.]

Start a little below the middle line; curve up left to the middle line and down left halfway; curve down right to the bottom line; curve up left, and stop.
[Start below the middle; curve up, around, down, and a snake tail.]

Start at the top line; slant down to the bottom line, and swing up. Make a crossbar on the middle line.
[Top start; slant down, and a monkey tail. Cross.]

Start at the middle line; slant down to the bottom line, and curve right; slant up to the middle line; retrace down, and swing up.
[Middle start; down, around, up, down, and a monkey tail.]

Start at the middle line; slant down right to the bottom line; slant up right to the middle line.
[Middle start; slant down right, and slant up right.]

Start at the middle line; slant down to the bottom line, and curve right; slant up to the middle line; retrace down, and curve right; slant up to the middle line.
[Middle start; slant down, around, up, and down, around, up again.]

Start at the middle line; slant down right to the bottom line, and swing up. Cross through the letter with a slant down left.
[Middle start; slant down right, and a monkey tail. Cross down left.]

Start at the middle line; slant down to the bottom line, and curve right; slant up to the middle line; retrace down to halfway below the bottom line, and hook left.
[Middle start; down, around, up, down under water, and a fishhook.]

Start at the middle line; make a bar to the right; slant down left to the bottom line; make a bar to the right.
[Middle start; over right, slant down left, and over right.]

Capital Manuscript Letter Descriptions

 Start at the top line; slant down left to the bottom line. Start again at the same point; slant down right to the bottom line. Make a crossbar in the middle line. [Top start; slant down left. Same start; slant down right. Middle bar across.]

B Start at the top line; slant down to the bottom line; retrace up; curve down right to the middle line; curve left, and close; curve down right to the bottom line; curve left, and close. [Top start; slant down, up, around halfway, close, around again, and close.]

C Start a little below the top line; curve up left to the top line; curve down left to the bottom line; curve up right, and stop. [Start below the top; curve up, around, down, up, and stop.]

D Start at the top line; slant down to the bottom line; retrace up; curve down right to the bottom line; curve left, and close. [Top start; slant down, up, around, and close.]

E Start at the top line; make a bar to the left; slant down to the bottom line; make a bar to the right. Make a bar to the right on the middle line. [Top start; over left, slant down, and over right. Middle bar across.]

F Start at the top line; make a bar to the left; slant down to the bottom line. Make a bar to the right on the middle line. [Top start; over left, and slant down. Middle bar across.]

G Start a little below the top line; curve up left to the top line; curve down left to the bottom line; curve up right to the middle line; make a bar to the left. [Start below the top, curve up, around, down, up, and over left.]

H Start at the top line; slant down to the bottom line. Start again at the top line, to the right of the first start; slant down to the bottom line. Make a crossbar on the middle line. [Top start; slant down. Another top start, to the right; slant down. Middle bar across.]

I Start at the top line; slant down to the bottom line. Make a small crossbar at the top line, and another at the bottom line. [Top start; slant down. Cross the top and the bottom line.]

J Start at the top line; slant down to the bottom line; curve up left, and stop. [Top start; slant down, and curve up left.]

K Start at the top line; slant down to the bottom line. Start again at the top line, to the right of the first start; slant down left to the middle line, and touch; slant down right to the bottom line, and swing up. [Top start; slant down. Another top start, to the right; slant down left, touch, slant down right, and a monkey tail.]

L Start at the top line; slant down to the bottom line; make a bar to the right. [Top start; slant down, and over right.]

M Start at the top line; slant down to the bottom line. Start again at the same point; slant down right to the middle line; slant up right to the top line; slant down to the bottom line. [Top start; slant down. Same start; slant down right halfway, slant up right, and slant down.]

N Start at the top line; slant down to the bottom line. Start again at the same point; slant down right to the bottom line; slant up to the top line. [Top start; slant down. Same start; slant down right, and slant up.]

O Start at the top line; curve down left to the bottom line; curve up right to the beginning, and close. [Top start; around down, and close up.]

P Start at the top line; slant down to the bottom line; retrace up; curve down right to the middle line; curve left, and close. [Top start; slant down, up, around halfway, and close.]

Q Start at the top line; curve down left to the bottom line; curve up right to the beginning, and close. Cross through the bottom line of the letter with a curve down right. [Top start; around down, and close up. Cross with a curve down right.]

R Start at the top line; slant down to the bottom line; retrace up; curve down right to the middle line; curve left, and close; slant down right to the bottom line, and swing up. [Top start; slant down, up, around halfway, close, slant down right, and a monkey tail.]

S Start a little below the top line; curve up left to the top line and down left to the middle line; curve down right to the bottom line; curve up left, and stop. [Start below the top; curve up, around, down, and a snake tail.]

T Start at the top line; slant down to the bottom line. Make a crossbar at the top line. [Top start; slant down. Cross the top.]

U Start at the top line; slant down to the bottom line; and curve right; slant up to the top line; retrace down, and swing up. [Top start; down, around, up, down, and a monkey tail.]

V Start at the top line; slant down right to the bottom line; slant up right to the top line. [Top start; slant down right, and slant up right.]

W Start at the top line; slant down right to the bottom line; slant up right to the top line; slant down right to the bottom line; slant up right to the top line. [Top start; slant down right, slant up right, slant down right, and slant up right again.]

X Start at the top line; slant down right to the bottom line; and swing up. Cross through the letter with a slant down left. [Top start; slant down right, and a monkey tail. Cross down left.]

Y Start at the top line; slant down right to the middle line. Start again at the top line, to the right of the first start; slant down left to the middle line; touch, and keep going down to the bottom line. [Top start; slant down right halfway. Another top start, to the right; slant down left, and touch on the way.]

Z Start at the top line; make a bar to the right; slant down left to the bottom line; make a bar to the right. [Top start; over right, slant down left, and over right.]

Lowercase Cursive Letter Descriptions

a — Go overhill; retrace halfway; curve down to the bottom line; curve up right to the middle line, and close; retrace down, and swing up.
[Overhill; back, around down, close up, down, and up.]

b — Go uphill to the top line; loop left down to the bottom line; curve up right to the middle line; curve left; and sidestroke right.
[Uphill high; loop down, around, up, and sidestroke.]

c — Go overhill; retrace halfway; curve down to the bottom line, and swing up.
[Overhill; back, around, down, and up.]

d — Go overhill; retrace halfway; curve down to the bottom line; curve up right to the middle line; touch, and keep going up to the top line; retrace down, and swing up.
[Overhill; back, around down, touch, up high, down, and up.]

e — Go uphill to the middle line; loop left down to the bottom line; and swing up.
[Uphill; loop down, through, and up.]

f — Go uphill to the top line; loop left down to halfway below the bottom line; loop right up to the bottom line; close; and swing up.
[Uphill high; loop down under water, loop up right, touch, and up.]

g — Go overhill; retrace halfway; curve down to the bottom line; curve up right to the middle line, and close; retrace down to halfway below the bottom line; and loop left up through the bottom line.
[Overhill; back, around down, close up, down under water, loop up left, and through.]

h — Go uphill to the top line; loop left down to the bottom line; retrace up halfway; make a hill to the right, and swing up.
[Uphill high, loop down, up over the hill, and up.]

i — Go uphill to the middle line; retrace down, and swing up. Make a dot above the letter.
[Uphill; down, and up. Add a dot.]

j — Go uphill to the middle line; retrace down to halfway below the bottom line; and loop left up through the bottom line. Make a dot above the letter.
[Uphill; down under water, loop up left, and through. Add a dot.]

k — Go uphill to the top line; loop left down to the bottom line; retrace up halfway; curve right; make a small loop left, and close; slant down right to the bottom line, and swing up.
[Uphill high; loop down, up into a little tummy, slant down right, and up.]

l — Go uphill to the top line; loop left down to the bottom line, and swing up.
[Uphill high; loop down, and up.]

m — Go overhill; slant down to the bottom line; retrace up, and make a hill to the right; retrace up; make another hill to the right, and swing up.
[Overhill; down, up over the hill, up over the hill again, and up.]

n — Go overhill; slant down to the bottom line; retrace up; make a hill to the right, and swing up.
[Overhill; down, up over the hill, and up.]

o — Go overhill; retrace halfway; curve down to the bottom line; curve up right to the middle line; close; and sidestroke right.
[Overhill; back, around down, close up, and sidestroke.]

p — Go uphill to the middle line; retrace down to halfway below the bottom line; retrace up; curve down right to the bottom line; curve left; close; and swing up.
[Uphill; down under water, up, around into a tummy, and up.]

q — Go overhill; retrace halfway; curve down to the bottom line; curve up right to the middle line, and close; retrace down to halfway below the bottom line; loop right up to the bottom line; close; and swing up.
[Overhill; back, around down, close up, down under water, loop up right, touch, and up.]

r — Go uphill to the middle line; sidestroke right; slant down to the bottom line, and swing up.
[Uphill; sidestroke, down, and up.]

s — Go uphill to the middle line; slant down to the bottom line; curve left, and close; retrace to the bottom line, and swing up.
[Uphill; down, around, close, and up.]

t — Go uphill to the top line; retrace down, and swing up. Make a crossbar on the middle line.
[Uphill high; down, and up. Cross.]

u — Go uphill to the middle line; retrace down, and curve right; slant up to the middle line; retrace down, and swing up.
[Uphill; down, around, up, down, and up.]

v — Go overhill; slant down to the bottom line, and curve right; slant up to the middle line; and sidestroke right.
[Overhill; down, around, up and sidestroke.]

w — Go uphill to the middle line; retrace down, and curve right; slant up to the middle line; retrace down, and curve right; slant up to the middle line; and sidestroke right.
[Uphill; down, around, up, down, around, up again, and sidestroke.]

x — Go overhill; slant down right to the bottom line, and swing up. Cross through the letter with a slant down left.
[Overhill; slant down right, and up. Cross down left.]

y — Go overhill; slant down to the bottom line, and curve right; slant up to the middle line; retrace down to halfway below the middle line; and loop left up through the bottom line.
[Overhill; down, around, up, down under water, loop up left, and through.]

z — Go overhill; curve down right to the bottom line; curve down right again to halfway below the bottom line; and loop left up through the bottom line.
[Overhill; around down, around again, and down under water, loop up left, and through.]

Capital Cursive Letter Descriptions

Start at the top line; curve down left to the bottom line; curve up right to the beginning, and close; retrace down, and swing up.
[Top start; around down, close up, down, and up.]

Start at the top line; slant down to the bottom line; retrace up; curve down right to the middle line; curve down right again to the bottom line; curve up left; touch; sidestroke right, and stop.
[Top start; down, up, around halfway, around again, touch, sidestroke, and stop.]

Start a little below the top line; curve up left to the top line; curve down left to the bottom line; and curve up right.
[Start below the top; curve up, around, down, and up.]

Start at the top line; slant down to the bottom line; curve left, and loop right; curve up right to the beginning; close; loop right, swing up, and stop.
[Top start; down, loop right, curve up, around, close, loop right, through, and stop.]

Start a little below the top line; curve up left to the top line; curve down left to the middle line; curve down left to the bottom line; and curve up right.
[Start below the the top; curve up, around to the middle, around again to the bottom line, and up.]

Start a little below the top line; slant down to the bottom line; and curve up left; sidestroke right. Make an overhill-underhill crossbar at the top line; and a straight crossbar on the middle line.
[Start below the top; down, around, up, and sidestroke. Wavy cross and a straight cross.]

Start at the bottom line; go uphill to the top line; loop left down to the middle line, and swing up; slant down to the bottom line; curve up left, across the uphill; sidestroke right, and stop.
[Bottom start; uphill high, loop through the middle, up, curve down, around, through the uphill, sidestroke, and stop.]

Start a little below the top line; curve up right to the top line; slant down to the bottom line. Start again at the top line, to the right of the first start; slant down to the bottom line; retrace up halfway; curve left, touch, loop right, swing up, and stop.
[Start below the top; make a cane. Top start, to the right; down, up, left, touch, loop right, through, and stop.]

Start a little below the middle line; sidestroke left; curve down right to the bottom line; go uphill to the top line; loop left down to the bottom line, and swing up.
[Start below the middle; sidestroke left, curve down, around, uphill high, loop down, and up.]

Start at the bottom line; curve up left to the top line; loop right down to halfway below the bottom line; loop up left, and through.
[Bottom start; curve up, around, touch on the way down under water, loop up left, and through.]

Start a little below the top line; curve up right to the top line; slant down to the bottom line. Start again at the top line, to the right of the first start; slant down left to the middle line, and touch; slant down right to the bottom line, and swing up.
[Start below the top; make a cane. Top start, to the right; slant down left, touch, slant down right, and up.]

Start a little below the top line; curve up right to the top line; loop left, and keep going down to the bottom line; curve left; loop right, and up.
[Start below the top; uphill; loop down, loop right, and up.]

Start a little below the top line; curve up right to the top line; slant down to the bottom line; retrace up, and make a hill to the right; retrace up; make another hill to the right, and swing up.
[Start below the top; make a cane, up over the hill, up over the hill again, and up.]

Start a little below the top line; curve up right to the top line; slant down to the bottom line; retrace up; make a hill to the right, and swing up.
[Start below the top; make a cane, up over the hill, and up.]

Start at the top line; curve down left to the bottom line; curve up right to the beginning, and close; loop right, swing up, and stop.
[Top start; around down, close up, loop right, through, and stop.]

Start at the top line; slant down to the bottom line; retrace up; curve down right to the middle line; curve left, and close.
[Top start; down, up, around halfway, and close.]

Start a little below the top line; curve up right to the top line; curve down right to the bottom line; loop right, and swing up.
[Start below the top; curve up, around, down, loop right, and up.]

Start at the top line; slant down to the bottom line; retrace up; curve down right to the middle line; curve left, and close; slant down right to the bottom line, and swing up.
[Top start; down, up, around halfway, close, slant down right, and up.]

Start at the bottom line; go uphill to the top line; loop left down to the middle line; curve down right to the bottom line; curve up left, across the uphill; sidestroke right, and stop.
[Bottom start; uphill high, loop through the middle, curve down, around, through the uphill, sidestroke, and stop.]

Start a little below the top line; slant down to the bottom line, and curve up left; sidestroke right. Make an overhill-underhill crossbar at the top line.
[Start below the top; down, around, up, and sidestroke. Wavy cross.]

Start a little below the top line; curve up right to the top line; slant down to the bottom line, and curve right; slant up to the top line; retrace down, and swing up.
[Start below the top; make a cane, around, up, down, and up.]

Start a little below the top line; curve up right to the top line; slant down to the bottom line, and curve right; slant up right to the top line; sidestroke right, and stop.
[Start below the top; make a cane, around, slant up right, sidestroke, and stop.]

Start a little below the top line; curve up right to the top line; slant down to the bottom line, and curve right; slant up to the top line; retrace down, and curve right; slant up to the top line; sidestroke right, and stop.
[Start below the top; make a cane, around, up, down, around, up again, sidestroke, and stop.]

Start a little below the top line; curve up right to the top line; slant down right to the bottom line, and swing up. Cross through the letter with a slant down left.
[Start below the top; curve up, slant down right, and up. Cross down left.]

Start a little below the top line; curve up right to the top line; slant down to the bottom line, and curve right; slant up to the top line; retrace down to halfway below the bottom line; loop up left, and through.
[Start below the top; make a cane, around, up, down under water, loop up left, and through.]

Start a little below the top line; curve up right to the top line; curve down right to the bottom line; curve down right again to halfway below the bottom line; loop up left, and through.
[Start below the top; curve up, around, down, around again, and down under water, loop up left, and through.]

Affixes

Prefixes

Prefix	Common Meaning	Example
(a-)	not, without	atypical
(anti-)	against	antipathy
(bene-)	well	beneficial
(bi-)	two	bicycle
(circum-)	around	circumference
(com-)	together	commit
(contra-)	against	contradiction
(counter-)	opposition	counterpoint
(dis-)	opposition, not	disappear, dishonest
(ex-)	former	ex-president
(extra-)	outside, beyond	extracurricular
(fore-)	before	foreground
(in-)	not	indirect
(inter-)	between	interstate
(intra-)	within	intramural
(mal-)	bad	malfunctioning
(micro-)	small	microscope
(mid-)	middle	midweek
(mis-)	wrong	miscount
(mono-)	one	monotone
(multi-)	many	multitude
(non-)	not	nonliving
(per-)	through	permeate
(poly-)	many	polysyllabic
(post-)	after	postscript
(pre-)	before	preview

Prefix	Common Meaning	Example
(pro-)	for	prochoice
(re-)	again	review
(semi-)	partly	semicircle
(sub-)	under	submarine
(super-)	above, beyond	superman
(syn-)	together, with	syndrome
(trans-)	across	transportation
(tri-)	three	triangle
(ultra-)	above, extremely	ultramodern
(un-)	not	unhappy
(uni-)	one	uniform
(vice-)	instead of	vice-president

Suffixes

Prefix	Common Meaning	Example
(-able, -ible)	capable of being	attainable
(-age)	state of	storage
(-al)	relating to	arrival
(-ance)	relating to	acceptance
(-ant, -ent)	one who	tenant
(-ary)	relating to	commentary
(-ate)	act	confiscate
(-ation)	action	complication
(-cle, -ule, -ling)	small	duckling
(-ence)	relating to	preference
(-er, -or)	one who	sailor
(-graph)	writing	autograph
(-ic)	pertaining to	poetic
(-ify)	to make	solidify
(-ious)	full of	spacious
(-ish)	state of being	foolish
(-ist)	one who	pianist
(-ity)	state or condition	civility
(-ize)	to make life	familiarize
(-less)	without	lifeless
(-like)	similar to	childlike

Prefix	Common Meaning	Example
(-ment)	result	development
(-ness)	state	happiness
(-ology)	a science	biology
(-ory)	place where	dormitory
(-ous)	full of	joyous
(-ship)	condition of	friendship
(-tude)	quality or quantity	certitude
(-ty)	quality or quantity	certainty
(-ure)	action, result	failure
(-ward)	spatial direction	forward

▼

Appendix D

1,000 Instant Words

These words make up 90 percent of all written language. Check off the words your child masters as you use this list to help your child develop reading and spelling skills.

_____	1. the	_____	31. but	_____	61. some
_____	2. of	_____	32. not	_____	62. her
_____	3. and	_____	33. what	_____	63. would
_____	4. a	_____	34. all	_____	64. make
_____	5. to	_____	35. were	_____	65. like
_____	6. in	_____	36. we	_____	66. him
_____	7. is	_____	37. when	_____	67. into
_____	8. you	_____	38. your	_____	68. time
_____	9. that	_____	39. can	_____	69. has
_____	10. it	_____	40. said	_____	70. look
_____	11. he	_____	41. there	_____	71. two
_____	12. was	_____	42. use	_____	72. more
_____	13. for	_____	43. an	_____	73. write
_____	14. on	_____	44. each	_____	74. go
_____	15. are	_____	45. which	_____	75. see
_____	16. as	_____	46. she	_____	76. number
_____	17. with	_____	47. do	_____	77. no
_____	18. his	_____	48. how	_____	78. way
_____	19. they	_____	49. their	_____	79. could
_____	20. I	_____	50. if	_____	80. people
_____	21. at	_____	51. will	_____	81. my
_____	22. be	_____	52. up	_____	82. than
_____	23. this	_____	53. other	_____	83. first
_____	24. have	_____	54. about	_____	84. water
_____	25. from	_____	55. out	_____	85. been
_____	26. or	_____	56. many	_____	86. called
_____	27. one	_____	57. then	_____	87. who
_____	28. had	_____	58. them	_____	88. oil
_____	29. by	_____	59. these	_____	89. its
_____	30. words	_____	60. so	_____	90. now

_____ 91. find	_____ 129. help	_____ 167. went
_____ 92. long	_____ 130. through	_____ 168. men
_____ 93. down	_____ 131. much	_____ 169. read
_____ 94. day	_____ 132. before	_____ 170. need
_____ 95. did	_____ 133. line	_____ 171. land
_____ 96. get	_____ 134. right	_____ 172. different
_____ 97. come	_____ 135. too	_____ 173. home
_____ 98. made	_____ 136. means	_____ 174. us
_____ 99. may	_____ 137. old	_____ 175. move
_____ 100. part	_____ 138. any	_____ 176. try
_____ 101. over	_____ 139. same	_____ 177. kind
_____ 102. new	_____ 140. tell	_____ 178. hand
_____ 103. sound	_____ 141. boy	_____ 179. picture
_____ 104. take	_____ 142. following	_____ 180. again
_____ 105. only	_____ 143. came	_____ 181. change
_____ 106. little	_____ 144. want	_____ 182. off
_____ 107. work	_____ 145. show	_____ 183. play
_____ 108. know	_____ 146. also	_____ 184. spell
_____ 109. place	_____ 147. around	_____ 185. air
_____ 110. years	_____ 148. form	_____ 186. away
_____ 111. live	_____ 149. three	_____ 187. animals
_____ 112. me	_____ 150. small	_____ 188. house
_____ 113. back	_____ 151. set	_____ 189. point
_____ 114. give	_____ 152. put	_____ 190. page
_____ 115. most	_____ 153. end	_____ 191. letters
_____ 116. very	_____ 154. does	_____ 192. mother
_____ 117. after	_____ 155. another	_____ 193. answer
_____ 118. things	_____ 156. well	_____ 194. found
_____ 119. our	_____ 157. large	_____ 195. study
_____ 120. just	_____ 158. must	_____ 196. still
_____ 121. name	_____ 159. big	_____ 197. learn
_____ 122. good	_____ 160. even	_____ 198. should
_____ 123. sentence	_____ 161. such	_____ 199. American
_____ 124. man	_____ 162. because	_____ 200. world
_____ 125. think	_____ 163. turned	_____ 201. high
_____ 126. say	_____ 164. here	_____ 202. every
_____ 127. great	_____ 165. why	_____ 203. near
_____ 128. where	_____ 166. asked	_____ 204. add

_____ 205. food	_____ 243. those	_____ 281. watch
_____ 206. between	_____ 244. both	_____ 282. far
_____ 207. own	_____ 245. paper	_____ 283. Indians
_____ 208. below	_____ 246. together	_____ 284. really
_____ 209. country	_____ 247. got	_____ 285. almost
_____ 210. plants	_____ 248. group	_____ 286. let
_____ 211. last	_____ 249. often	_____ 287. above
_____ 212. school	_____ 250. run	_____ 288. girl
_____ 213. father	_____ 251. important	_____ 289. sometimes
_____ 214. keep	_____ 252. until	_____ 290. mountains
_____ 215. trees	_____ 253. children	_____ 291. cut
_____ 216. never	_____ 254. side	_____ 292. young
_____ 217. started	_____ 255. feet	_____ 293. talk
_____ 218. city	_____ 256. car	_____ 294. soon
_____ 219. earth	_____ 257. miles	_____ 295. list
_____ 220. eyes	_____ 258. night	_____ 296. song
_____ 221. light	_____ 259. walked	_____ 297. being
_____ 222. thought	_____ 260. white	_____ 298. leave
_____ 223. head	_____ 261. sea	_____ 299. family
_____ 224. under	_____ 262. began	_____ 300. it's
_____ 225. story	_____ 263. grow	_____ 301. body
_____ 226. saw	_____ 264. took	_____ 302. music
_____ 227. left	_____ 265. river	_____ 303. color
_____ 228. don't	_____ 266. four	_____ 304. stand
_____ 229. few	_____ 267. carry	_____ 305. sun
_____ 230. while	_____ 268. state	_____ 306. questions
_____ 231. along	_____ 269. once	_____ 307. fish
_____ 232. might	_____ 270. book	_____ 308. area
_____ 233. close	_____ 271. hear	_____ 309. mark
_____ 234. something	_____ 272. stop	_____ 310. dog
_____ 235. seemed	_____ 273. without	_____ 311. horse
_____ 236. next	_____ 274. second	_____ 312. birds
_____ 237. hard	_____ 275. later	_____ 313. problem
_____ 238. open	_____ 276. miss	_____ 314. complete
_____ 239. example	_____ 277. idea	_____ 315. room
_____ 240. beginning	_____ 278. enough	_____ 316. knew
_____ 241. life	_____ 279. eat	_____ 317. since
_____ 242. always	_____ 280. face	_____ 318. ever

_____ 319. piece	_____ 357. several	_____ 395. certain
_____ 320. told	_____ 358. hold	_____ 396. field
_____ 321. usually	_____ 359. himself	_____ 397. travel
_____ 322. didn't	_____ 360. toward	_____ 398. wood
_____ 323. friends	_____ 361. five	_____ 399. fire
_____ 324. easy	_____ 362. step	_____ 400. upon
_____ 325. heard	_____ 363. morning	_____ 401. done
_____ 326. order	_____ 364. passed	_____ 402. English
_____ 327. red	_____ 365. vowel	_____ 403. road
_____ 328. door	_____ 366. true	_____ 404. half
_____ 329. sure	_____ 367. hundred	_____ 405. ten
_____ 330. become	_____ 368. against	_____ 406. fly
_____ 331. top	_____ 369. pattern	_____ 407. gave
_____ 332. ship	_____ 370. numeral	_____ 408. box
_____ 333. across	_____ 371. table	_____ 409. finally
_____ 334. today	_____ 372. north	_____ 410. wait
_____ 335. during	_____ 373. slowly	_____ 411. correct
_____ 336. short	_____ 374. money	_____ 412. oh
_____ 337. better	_____ 375. map	_____ 413. quickly
_____ 338. best	_____ 376. farm	_____ 414. person
_____ 339. however	_____ 377. pulled	_____ 415. became
_____ 340. low	_____ 378. draw	_____ 416. shown
_____ 341. hours	_____ 379. voice	_____ 417. minutes
_____ 342. black	_____ 380. seen	_____ 418. strong
_____ 343. products	_____ 381. cold	_____ 419. verb
_____ 344. happened	_____ 382. cried	_____ 420. stars
_____ 345. whole	_____ 383. plan	_____ 421. front
_____ 346. measure	_____ 384. notice	_____ 422. feel
_____ 347. remember	_____ 385. south	_____ 423. fact
_____ 348. early	_____ 386. sing	_____ 424. inches
_____ 349. waves	_____ 387. war	_____ 425. street
_____ 350. reached	_____ 388. ground	_____ 426. decided
_____ 351. listen	_____ 389. fall	_____ 427. contain
_____ 352. wind	_____ 390. kind	_____ 428. course
_____ 353. rock	_____ 391. town	_____ 429. surface
_____ 354. space	_____ 392. I'll	_____ 430. produce
_____ 355. covered	_____ 393. unit	_____ 431. building
_____ 356. fast	_____ 394. figure	_____ 432. ocean

_____	433. class	_____	471. yes	_____	509. test
_____	434. note	_____	472. clear	_____	510. direction
_____	435. nothing	_____	473. equation	_____	511. center
_____	436. rest	_____	474. yet	_____	512. farmers
_____	437. carefully	_____	475. government	_____	513. ready
_____	438. scientists	_____	476. filled	_____	514. anything
_____	439. inside	_____	477. heat	_____	515. divided
_____	440. wheels	_____	478. full	_____	516. general
_____	441. stay	_____	479. hot	_____	517. energy
_____	442. green	_____	480. check	_____	518. subject
_____	443. known	_____	481. object	_____	519. Europe
_____	444. island	_____	482. am	_____	520. moon
_____	445. week	_____	483. rule	_____	521. region
_____	446. less	_____	484. among	_____	522. return
_____	447. machine	_____	485. noun	_____	523. believe
_____	448. base	_____	486. power	_____	524. dance
_____	449. ago	_____	487. cannot	_____	525. members
_____	450. stood	_____	488. able	_____	526. picked
_____	451. plane	_____	489. six	_____	527. simple
_____	452. system	_____	490. size	_____	528. cells
_____	453. behind	_____	491. dark	_____	529. paint
_____	454. ran	_____	492. ball	_____	530. mind
_____	455. round	_____	493. material	_____	531. love
_____	456. boat	_____	494. special	_____	532. cause
_____	457. game	_____	495. heavy	_____	533. rain
_____	458. force	_____	496. fine	_____	534. exercise
_____	459. brought	_____	497. pair	_____	535. eggs
_____	460. understand	_____	498. circle	_____	536. train
_____	461. warm	_____	499. include	_____	537. blue
_____	462. common	_____	500. built	_____	538. wish
_____	463. bring	_____	501. can't	_____	539. drop
_____	464. explain	_____	502. matter	_____	540. developed
_____	465. dry	_____	503. square	_____	541. window
_____	466. though	_____	504. syllables	_____	542. difference
_____	467. language	_____	505. perhaps	_____	543. distance
_____	468. shape	_____	506. bill	_____	544. heart
_____	469. deep	_____	507. felt	_____	545. sit
_____	470. thousands	_____	508. suddenly	_____	546. sum

_____ 547. summer	_____ 585. instruments	_____ 623. outside
_____ 548. wall	_____ 586. meet	_____ 624. everything
_____ 549. forest	_____ 587. third	_____ 625. tall
_____ 550. probably	_____ 588. months	_____ 626. already
_____ 551. legs	_____ 589. paragraph	_____ 627. instead
_____ 552. sat	_____ 590. raise	_____ 628. phrase
_____ 553. main	_____ 591. represent	_____ 629. soil
_____ 554. winter	_____ 592. soft	_____ 630. bed
_____ 555. wide	_____ 593. whether	_____ 631. copy
_____ 556. written	_____ 594. clothes	_____ 632. free
_____ 557. length	_____ 595. flowers	_____ 633. hope
_____ 558. reason	_____ 596. shall	_____ 634. spring
_____ 559. kept	_____ 597. teacher	_____ 635. case
_____ 560. interest	_____ 598. held	_____ 636. laughed
_____ 561. arms	_____ 599. describe	_____ 637. nation
_____ 562. brother	_____ 600. drive	_____ 638. quite
_____ 563. race	_____ 601. cross	_____ 639. type
_____ 564. present	_____ 602. speak	_____ 640. themselves
_____ 565. beautiful	_____ 603. solve	_____ 641. temperature
_____ 566. store	_____ 604. appear	_____ 642. bright
_____ 567. job	_____ 605. metal	_____ 643. lead
_____ 568. edge	_____ 606. son	_____ 644. everyone
_____ 569. past	_____ 607. either	_____ 645. method
_____ 570. sign	_____ 608. ice	_____ 646. section
_____ 571. record	_____ 609. sleep	_____ 647. lake
_____ 572. finished	_____ 610. village	_____ 648. consonant
_____ 573. discovered	_____ 611. factors	_____ 649. within
_____ 574. wild	_____ 612. result	_____ 650. dictionary
_____ 575. happy	_____ 613. jumped	_____ 651. hair
_____ 576. beside	_____ 614. snow	_____ 652. age
_____ 577. gone	_____ 615. ride	_____ 653. amount
_____ 578. sky	_____ 616. care	_____ 654. scale
_____ 579. glass	_____ 617. floor	_____ 655. pounds
_____ 580. million	_____ 618. hill	_____ 656. although
_____ 581. west	_____ 619. pushed	_____ 657. per
_____ 582. lay	_____ 620. baby	_____ 658. broken
_____ 583. weather	_____ 621. buy	_____ 659. moment
_____ 584. root	_____ 622. century	_____ 660. tiny

_____ 661. possible

_____ 662. gold

_____ 663. mild

_____ 664. quiet

_____ 665. natural

_____ 666. lot

_____ 667. stone

_____ 668. act

_____ 669. build

_____ 670. middle

_____ 671. speed

_____ 672. count

_____ 673. cat

_____ 674. someone

_____ 675. sail

_____ 676. rolled

_____ 677. bear

_____ 678. wonder

_____ 679. smiled

_____ 680. angle

_____ 681. fraction

_____ 682. Africa

_____ 683. killed

_____ 684. melody

_____ 685. bottom

_____ 686. trip

_____ 687. hole

_____ 688. poor

_____ 689. let's

_____ 690. fight

_____ 691. surprise

_____ 692. French

_____ 693. died

_____ 694. beat

_____ 695. exactly

_____ 696. remain

_____ 697. dress

_____ 698. iron

_____ 699. couldn't

_____ 700. fingers

_____ 701. row

_____ 702. least

_____ 703. catch

_____ 704. climbed

_____ 705. wrote

_____ 706. shouted

_____ 707. continued

_____ 708. itself

_____ 709. else

_____ 710. plains

_____ 711. gas

_____ 712. England

_____ 713. burning

_____ 714. design

_____ 715. joined

_____ 716. foot

_____ 717. law

_____ 718. ears

_____ 719. grass

_____ 720. you're

_____ 721. grew

_____ 722. skin

_____ 723. valley

_____ 724. cents

_____ 725. key

_____ 726. president

_____ 727. brown

_____ 728. trouble

_____ 729. cool

_____ 730. cloud

_____ 731. lost

_____ 732. sent

_____ 733. symbols

_____ 734. wear

_____ 735. bad

_____ 736. save

_____ 737. experiment

_____ 738. engine

_____ 739. alone

_____ 740. drawing

_____ 741. east

_____ 742. pay

_____ 743. single

_____ 744. touch

_____ 745. information

_____ 746. express

_____ 747. mouth

_____ 748. yard

_____ 749. equal

_____ 750. decimal

_____ 751. yourself

_____ 752. control

_____ 753. practice

_____ 754. report

_____ 755. straight

_____ 756. rise

_____ 757. statement

_____ 758. stick

_____ 759. party

_____ 760. seeds

_____ 761. suppose

_____ 762. woman

_____ 763. coast

_____ 764. bank

_____ 765. period

_____ 766. wire

_____ 767. choose

_____ 768. clean

_____ 769. visit

_____ 770. bit

_____ 771. whose

_____ 772. received

_____ 773. garden

_____ 774. please

_____ 775. strange	_____ 813. cook	_____ 851. thick
_____ 776. caught	_____ 814. bones	_____ 852. blood
_____ 777. fell	_____ 815. tail	_____ 853. lie
_____ 778. team	_____ 816. board	_____ 854. spot
_____ 779. God	_____ 817. modern	_____ 855. bell
_____ 780. captain	_____ 818. compound	_____ 856. fun
_____ 781. direct	_____ 819. mine	_____ 857. loud
_____ 782. ring	_____ 820. wasn't	_____ 858. consider
_____ 783. serve	_____ 821. fit	_____ 859. suggested
_____ 784. child	_____ 822. addition	_____ 860. thin
_____ 785. desert	_____ 823. belong	_____ 861. thin
_____ 786. increase	_____ 824. safe	_____ 862. position
_____ 787. history	_____ 825. soldiers	_____ 863. fruit
_____ 788. cost	_____ 826. guess	_____ 864. tied
_____ 789. maybe	_____ 827. silent	_____ 865. rich
_____ 790. business	_____ 828. trade	_____ 866. dollars
_____ 791. separate	_____ 829. rather	_____ 867. send
_____ 792. break	_____ 830. compare	_____ 868. sight
_____ 793. uncle	_____ 831. crowd	_____ 869. chief
_____ 794. hunting	_____ 832. poem	_____ 870. Japanese
_____ 795. flow	_____ 833. enjoy	_____ 871. stream
_____ 796. lady	_____ 834. elements	_____ 872. planets
_____ 797. students	_____ 835. indicate	_____ 873. rhythm
_____ 798. human	_____ 836. except	_____ 874. eight
_____ 799. art	_____ 837. expect	_____ 875. science
_____ 800. feeling	_____ 838. flat	_____ 876. major
_____ 801. supply	_____ 839. seven	_____ 877. observe
_____ 802. corner	_____ 840. interesting	_____ 878. tube
_____ 803. electric	_____ 841. sense	_____ 879. necessary
_____ 804. insects	_____ 842. string	_____ 880. weight
_____ 805. crops	_____ 843. blow	_____ 881. meat
_____ 806. tone	_____ 844. famous	_____ 882. lifted
_____ 807. hit	_____ 845. value	_____ 883. process
_____ 808. sand	_____ 846. wings	_____ 884. army
_____ 809. doctor	_____ 847. movement	_____ 885. hat
_____ 810. provide	_____ 848. pole	_____ 886. property
_____ 811. thus	_____ 849. exciting	_____ 887. particular
_____ 812. won't	_____ 850. branches	_____ 888. swim

_____ 889. terms
_____ 890. current
_____ 891. park
_____ 892. sell
_____ 893. shoulder
_____ 894. industry
_____ 895. wash
_____ 896. block
_____ 897. spread
_____ 898. cattle
_____ 899. wife
_____ 900. sharp
_____ 901. company
_____ 902. radio
_____ 903. we'll
_____ 904. action
_____ 905. capital
_____ 906. factories
_____ 907. settled
_____ 908. yellow
_____ 909. isn't
_____ 910. southern
_____ 911. truck
_____ 912. fair
_____ 913. printed
_____ 914. wouldn't
_____ 915. ahead
_____ 916. chance
_____ 917. born
_____ 918. level
_____ 919. triangle
_____ 920. molecules
_____ 921. France
_____ 922. repeated
_____ 923. column
_____ 924. western
_____ 925. church
_____ 926. sister

_____ 927. oxygen
_____ 928. plural
_____ 929. various
_____ 930. agreed
_____ 931. opposite
_____ 932. wrong
_____ 933. chart
_____ 934. prepared
_____ 935. pretty
_____ 936. solution
_____ 937. fresh
_____ 938. shop
_____ 939. suffix
_____ 940. especially
_____ 941. shoes
_____ 942. actually
_____ 943. nose
_____ 944. afraid
_____ 945. dead
_____ 946. sugar
_____ 947. adjective
_____ 948. fig
_____ 949. office
_____ 950. huge
_____ 951. gun
_____ 952. similar
_____ 953. death
_____ 954. score
_____ 955. forward
_____ 956. stretched
_____ 957. experience
_____ 958. rose
_____ 959. allow
_____ 960. fear
_____ 961. workers
_____ 962. Washington
_____ 963. Greek
_____ 964. women

_____ 965. bought
_____ 966. led
_____ 967. march
_____ 968. northern
_____ 969. create
_____ 970. British
_____ 971. difficult
_____ 972. match
_____ 973. win
_____ 974. doesn't
_____ 975. steel
_____ 976. total
_____ 977. deal
_____ 978. determine
_____ 979. evening
_____ 980. nor
_____ 981. rope
_____ 982. cotton
_____ 983. apple
_____ 984. details
_____ 985. entire
_____ 986. corn
_____ 987. substances
_____ 988. smell
_____ 989. tools
_____ 990. conditions
_____ 991. cows
_____ 992. track
_____ 993. arrived
_____ 994. located
_____ 995. sir
_____ 996. seat
_____ 997. division
_____ 998. effect
_____ 999. underline
_____ 1000. view

Notes

Chapter 3

1. J. Werry, address, 7th Annual National Conference for Children and Adults with Attention Deficit Disorder, November 1995, Washington, DC.
2. R. Barkley, *Attention Deficit Hyperactivity Disorder in Children: A Handbook for Diagnosis and Treatment* (New York: Guilford Press, 1990).

Chapter 4

1. L. Clark, *S.O.S.: Help for Parents* (Bowling Green, KY: Parents Press, 1996).
2. T. Phelan, *1-2-3 Magic* (Glen Ellyn, IL: Child Management Press, 1985).
3. R. Lavoie, *Learning Disabilities and Disciplines: When the Chips are Down.* (1997). Produced by PBS Video, 1320 Braddock Place, Alexandria, VA. 22314-1698; 800-424-7963.
4. H. G. Parker, *The ADD Hyperactivity Workbook* (Plantation, FL: Impact Publications, 1988).
5. B. D. Ingersoll and S. Goldstein, (1995) (New York: Doubleday).

Chapter 5

1. R. B. Brooks, *The Self-Esteem Teacher* (Circle Pines, MN: American Guidance Service, 1991).
2. N. Braden, *How to Raise Your Self-Esteem* (New York: Bantam Books, 1987).
3. S. Coopersmith, *Developing Motivation in Young Children* (San Francisco: Albion Press, 1975).
4. M. Levine, *Keeping A Head in School* (Cambridge, MA: Educators Publishing Service, 1990).

303

5. J. Segal, "Teachers Have Enormous Power in Affecting a Child's Self-Esteem," *Child Behavior Development Newsletter, 4.1* (Providence, RI: Brown University, 1988).

6. Brooks, *The Self-Esteem Teacher.*

Chapter 6

1. J. W. Lerner, B. Lowenthal, and S. R. Lerner, *Attention Deficit Disorders: Assessment and Teaching* (Pacific Grove, CA: Brooks/Cole Publishing Co., 1995).

Chapter 7

1. D. N. Thurber, *D'Nealian Manuscript: A Continuous Stroke Approach* (Novato, CA: Academic Therapy Publications, 1984).

Chapter 8

1. P. M. Cunningham and D. P. Hall, *Making Words: Multilevel, Hands-On, Developmentally Appropriate Spelling and Phonics Activities* (Torrance, CA: Frank Schaffer, 1994). 800-334-4769.

2. P. M. Cunningham and D. P. Hall, *Making Big Words: Multilevel, Hands-On, Developmentally Appropriate Spelling and Phonics Activities* (Torrance, CA: Frank Schaffer, 1994). 800-334-4769.

3. G. G. Glass, *Glass Analysis for Decoding Only Teacher Guide* (Garden City, NY: Easier-to-Learn, 1976).

4. E. Fry, J. E. Kress, and D. L. Fontoukidis, *The Reading Teacher's Book of Lists, 3rd ed.* (Englewood Cliffs, NJ: Prentice-Hall, 1993), pp. 22–28. Reprinted by permission of Edward Fry. 800-920-0579.

5. G. Fernald, *Remedial Techniques in Basic School Subjects* (New York: McGraw-Hill. 1943).

6. R. P. Carver, Information adapted from *Reading Rate: A Review of Research and Theory* (San Diego: Academic Press, 1990).

7. R. G. Heckelman, "N.I.M. Revisited," *Academic Therapy, 21* (1986), 411–420.

8. S. J. Samuels, "The Method of Repeated Readings," *Reading Teacher, 32* (1979), 403–408.

Chapter 9

1. J. B. Schumaker, P. H. Denton, and D. D. Deshler, *The Paraphrasing Strategy* (Lawrence, KS: Learning Strategies Curriculum, 1984).

2. A. S. Palinscar and A. L. Brown, "Interactive Teaching to Promote Independent Learning from Text," *Reading Teacher, 39* (1986), 771–777.

3. R. Stauffer, *Directing the Reading–Thinking Process* (New York: Harper & Row, 1975).

4. D. M. Ogle, "K-W-L: A Teaching Model that Develops Active Reading of Expository Text," *Reading Teacher, 3* (1986), 564–570.

5. E. Carr and D. Ogle, "K-W-L Plus: A Strategy for Comprehension and Summarization," *Journal of Reading, 30* (1987), 626, 631.

6. M. A. Mastropieri, "Using the Keyboard [sic] Method," *Teaching Exceptional Children, 20 (2),* (1988), 4–8.

7. J. B. Schumaker, D. D. Deshler, S. Nolan, F. L. Clark, G. R. Alley, and M. M. Warner, "Error Monitoring: A Learning Strategy for Monitoring Academic Performance of Learning Disabled Adolescents," *Research Report No. 32* (Lawrence, KS: University of Kansas Institute for Research in Learning Disabilities, 1981).

8. M. R. Moreau and H. Fidrych-Puzzo (1994). *The Story Grammar Marker* Available from: Discourse Skills Productions, 10 Coed Drive, Easthampton, MA 01027; 800-484-7347 (Enter Code 4SGM).

9. M. Schlegel and C. S. Bos, "STORE the Story: Fiction and Fantasy Reading Comprehension and Writing Strategy," unpublished manuscript, University of Arizona, Department of Special Educational and Rehabilitation, Tucson.

10. C. S. Bos, "Process-oriented Writing: Instructional Implications for Mildly Handicapped Students," *Exceptional Children, 54* (1985), 521–527.

11. J. E. Spark, *Write for Power* (Los Angeles: Communication Associates, 1982).

12. C. S. Bos and P. C. Anders, "Interactive Teaching and Learning: Instructional Practices for Teaching Context and Strategic Knowledge," in B. Y. L. Wong and T. E. Scruggs (Eds.), *Interactive Research in Learning Disabilities* (New York: Springer Verlag, 1990), 166–185.

Chapter 10

1. S. P. Miller and C. D. Mercer, *Strategic Math Series: Addition* (Lawrence, KS: Edge Enterprises, 1991–1993).

2. C. A. Thornton and M. A. Toohey, *Matter of Facts: Addition; Matter of Facts: Subtraction; Matter of Facts: Multiplication; Matter of Facts: Division* (Oaklawn, IL: Creative Publications, 1984).

3. Rhyme Times, P.O. Box 1015NB, Niwot, CO 80544-1015; 303-652-2382.

4. White Birch Educational Tools, RR1, Box 692, Corinth, VT 05039; 802-439-5063.

5. J. Bullock, *TOUCH MATH,*™ *The Touchpoint Approach for Teaching Basic Math Computation, 4th ed.,* Innovative Learning Concepts, 6760 Corporate Drive, Colorado Springs, CO 80919-1999; 800-888-9191.

Chapter 11

1. National Research Council, "Everybody Counts: A Report to the Nation on the Future of Mathematics Education" (Washington, DC: National Academy Press, 1989).

2. Summary of *Curriculum and Evaluation Standards for School Mathematics,* National Council of Teachers of Mathematics, 1989.

3. J. F. Cawley, J. H. Miller, and B. A. School, "A Brief Inquiry of Arithmetic Word-Problem-Solving Among Learning Disabled Secondary Students," *Learning Disabilities Focus, 2* (2), (1987), 87–93.

4. W. P. Dunlap and A. H. Brennan, "Developing Mental Images of Mathematical Processes," *Learning Disabilities Quarterly 2* (2) (1979), 89–96.

5. J. E. Fleischner, M. B. Nuzum, and E. S. Marzola, "Devising an Instructional Program to Teach Arithmetic Problem-Solving Skills to Students with Learning Disabilities," *Journal of Learning Disabilities, 20* (1987), 214–217.

6. C. D. Mercer and S. P. Miller, *Strategic Math Series: Substraction* (Lawrence, KS: Edge Enterprises, 1991–1993).

7. M. Montague and C. S. Bos, "The Effect of Cognitive Strategic Training on Verbal Mathematical Problem-Solving Performance of Learning Disabled Adolescents," *Journal of Learning Disabilities, 19* (1986), 26–37.

8. J. Piaget, "How Children Form Mathematical Concepts," *Scientific American, 189 (5)* (1953), 74–79

Index